Findings

In Metaphysic, Path, and Lore

BY THE SAME AUTHOR

Doorkeeper of the Heart: Versions of Rabi'a

Hammering Hot Iron:
A Spiritual Critique of Robert Bly's Iron John

The System of Antichrist:
Truth and Falsehood in Postmodernism and the New Age

Cracks in the Great Wall:
The UFO Phenomenon and Traditional Metaphysics

Legends of the End:
Prophecies of the End Times, Antichrist,
Apocalypse, and Messiah from Eight Religious Traditions

The Virtues of the Prophet:
A Young Muslim's Guide to the Greater Jihad,
The War Against the Passions

Folk Metaphysics:
Mystical Meanings in Traditional Folk Songs and Spirituals

Who is the Earth?
How To See God in the Natural World

Reflections of Tasawwuf
Essays, Poems, and Narrative on Sufi Themes

Shadow of the Rose:
The Esoterism of the Romantic Tradition
(with Jennifer Doane Upton)

Knowings:
In the Arts of Metaphysics, Cosmology, and the Spiritual Path

The Wars of Love (in press)

Charles Upton

FINDINGS

In Metaphysic, Path, & Lore

*A Response to the
Traditionalist / Perennialist School*

SOPHIA PERENNIS

SAN RAFAEL, CA

First published in the USA
by Sophia Perennis
© Charles Upton 2009

Series editor: James R. Wetmore

For information, address:
Sophia Perennis, P.O. Box 151011
San Rafael, CA 94915
sophiaperennis.com

Library of Congress Cataloging-in-Publication Data

Upton, Charles, 1948–
Findings in metaphysics, path, and lore: a response to the
traditionalist/perennialist school / Charles Upton.

p. cm.
ISBN 978 1 59731 096 3 (pbk: alk. paper)
1. Religion—Philosophy. 2. Tradition (Philosophy). I. Title.
BL51.U69 2009
202—dc22   2009047926

CONTENTS

INTRODUCTORY NOTE

THE TRADITIONALIST/PERENNIALIST SCHOOL mentioned in the title of this book by now comprises three generations of writers on metaphysics, esoterism and "comparative religion"—the followers and colleagues of René Guénon, Ananda Coomaraswamy, Marco Pallis, Titus Burckhardt, Martin Lings, and Frithjof Schuon. For the past twenty years I have immersed myself in this school, during which time they provided me with the major elements of my intellectual outlook, doctrines and perspectives that I am sure will remain with me for the rest of my life. Having fully internalized their principles, at least up to the limits of my capacity, I now feel moved to respond to the Traditionalists on the basis of what they taught me. I am not entirely uncritical of their writings, but I am more deeply grateful to them that I can easily put into words. Having been filled by them to overflowing, it is now time to return the gift, and become empty again. As William Blake wrote in *The Marriage of Heaven and Hell*: "In Seed Time learn, in Harvest teach, in Winter enjoy."

CHARLES UPTON, September of 2009

i

PART ONE:
FROM, AND TO,
THE TRADITIONALSITS

One:

TRAILS GO NOWHERE

Frithjof Schuon's Six Stations of
Wisdom in Theory and Practice

PREFACE

FRITHJOF SCHUON, who passed away in 1998 at the age of 90, was the last true and plenary master of the Traditionalist School; the present essay was written in order to highlight, and expand upon, the practical essence of Frithjof Schuon's teaching for the spiritual life.

Schuon, in his many books, showed himself to be an esoterist, metaphysician, and comparative religionist without peer in his own time, and with few peers in any time. And unlike his predecessor René Guénon, he stepped beyond "pure" metaphysics by applying metaphysical principles to the actual practice of the spiritual life. Yet spiritual direction makes up only a small part of his published work—not surprisingly, since such guidance, by its nature, must mostly be a personal matter between the guide and the disciple. True spiritual guides are rare, however, which is why many of us must make do with the guidance we find in books—illuminated, God willing, by His Grace. According to Schuon, and in line with Hindu doctrine, as the human collective and the revealed religions degenerate in the latter days of the Kali-yuga, the Grace of God becomes all the more available to those who turn to Him— assuming they still understand the possibility and significance of such a turn.

When a shorter version of this essay appeared in *Parabola* magazine [Fall, 2009] one of Frithjof Schuon's closer disciples took me to task for casting Shaykh Isa's pearls before swine, so to speak, for dragging out into the public arena what should properly be reserved for those who have taken his spiritual method and influence seriously enough to have joined his *tariqa* and followed his more quintessential and personal teachings. He further expressed his worry that the article might give aid and comfort to those who apparently wish to falsely present Schuon in non-traditional guise as a universal teacher or popular guru, operating outside Tradition, rather than a Sufi Shaykh whose "plenary esoterism" nonetheless transcended exoteric Islam, and whose doctrines by their very nature could appeal only to those few *jñanis* or *arifin* capable of understanding them and profiting from them. In order to do what I can to obviate any possible misunderstandings on this score, let me quote from Shaykh Isa himself:

> orthodoxy is the principle of formal homogeneity proper to any authentically spiritual perspective; it is therefore an indispensable aspect of all genuine intellectuality....To be orthodox means to participate by way of a doctrine that can properly be called "traditional," in the immutability of the principles which govern the Universe and fashion our intelligence [from "Orthodoxy and Intellectuality" appearing in *Stations of Wisdom:* World Wisdom Books, 1995; p.1].

> a given religion in reality sums up all religions and ... all religion is to be found in a given religion, because Truth is one [from "To Refuse or to Accept Revelation" appearing in *From the Divine to the Human*: World Wisdom Books, 1982; p.138].

As for the danger of revealing Schuon's "inner teachings", I must emphasize that this essay simply represents my own personal response to Schuon's published writings, specifically *Stations of Wisdom*. Once one's ideas are made public so that anyone at all might read them (even if the number of readers is very small), there is no way of controlling — as there is, at least to a degree, in a tight-knit group — what people will draw from them, either in terms of serious distortions or of novel perspectives that may touch upon certain implications of the ideas in question that their original recipient either did not recognize, or simply wasn't interested in. Suffice it to say that this essay does not represent Schuon's ideas as he himself taught them, but merely my own personal "take" on those ideas, or rather on those aspects of them he was willing to express openly; I basically took from them what I myself needed. His own rendition of them in *Stations of Wisdom* is purely crystalline and "*brahmanic*", whereas mine introduces, as it were, a *kshatriya* element, where the quality of the "Greater *Jihad*" predominates. Schuon's presentation of the Stations is truly "quintessential"; mine has more to do with their multiple ramifications. Those who knew Frithjof Schuon personally and accepted him as their Shaykh must be painfully aware of how imperfect my rendering of those ideas is; yet even an outer reflection of a deep esoteric truth, providing that it does not actually subvert the meaning of that truth, may still stand as a distant sign-post pointing to the original Source.

I: PRELIMINARY ORIENTATION

If we are convinced that we are not as we should be, but have it on good authority that there *is* a way we should be, and also a way, or method, of attaining that condition—a state that is not only ideal, but also *normal*—then we can speak of a Path. And if we conceive this sort of "ideal normalcy" in terms of God, or Absolute Reality— our proper relationship with Him, or even our complete union with Him—then we are thinking in terms of the Spiritual Path.

Our aspiration, then, would seem to be that we move from "here", our present condition, to "There", our fully-realized state. God, however, is already everywhere, and therefore already *here*. This truism has led some non-traditional spiritual teachers—I'm thinking particularly of Alan Watts and Jeddu Krishnamurti—to concentrate on the paradoxical aspects of the Path. How can we move from illusion to Reality without first granting that illusion a certain reality of its own, thereby getting in our own way? And how can we conceive of Reality as *elsewhere* without casting a veil over Its presence—*here*?

The Zen practitioners have addressed this paradox by asserting that "in order to be Enlightened, first you have to be Enlightened" and "all beings are Enlightened from the beginning." But if there are still *complaints*—complaints on the order of "If I am already Enlightened, then why am I still immersed in suffering and delusion?"— then we may turn for further enlightenment to William Blake's proverb, "If the fool would persist in his folly, he would become wise." Here the Blake conceives the Spiritual Path not as the attainment of a distant Absolute, but the "wearing out" of those tendencies—passions, intellectual errors, distractions of all kinds— that prevent us from realizing our present, and eternal, identity with It; this is why the Sufis characterize the Path not as "travel *to* God" but as "travel *in* God". In the words of Dante Alighieri (as both author and character) from his *Purgatorio*: "To return to where I am/ I travel thus"—or, as Beat Generation poet Lew Welch once put it: "Trails go nowhere. They end exactly/ Where you stop."

Still, it appears that there is something to be done. God's part—to be Who He is, to give us the gift of His existence, and guidance, moment by moment—is His business. Our business is to follow that guidance, to *receive* that existence. The fact that we are all virtually, or in essence, one with God *now*, neither obviates the Path nor fulfills it. There are still things to be done. And these tasks—though they may be illusory in the *absolute* sense—are nonetheless necessary. The question is, whose responsibility are they? Who is the one walking the Spiritual Path? Who is the Doer?

The Tibetan Buddhists conceive of Enlightenment as the union of Wisdom, *prajña*, and Means, *upaya*. *Upaya* comprises the methods to be employed, the tasks we must accomplish in order to attain Enlightenment; *prajña* is the eternal presence of Enlightenment, without regard to any task we might perform or fail to perform. If we concentrate on the Means alone, we will never reach the Goal; the Way is infinite, and life is short. But if we concentrate only on Wisdom, then we are left with nothing but an abstraction, a truism: all beings may be Enlightened from the beginning, but if I am still suffering in the bonds of passion and illusion, then this "truth" won't do me a bit of good. The only Way is to simultaneously unveil Wisdom by the power of Means, and break our attachment to Means by the power of Wisdom. If Wisdom is not already *here*, we will never reach It; if we don't labor to reach It, It will never be *here*.

In theistic terms, the Path is the progressive realization that God, not "me", is the Doer, that no-one walks the Spiritual Path but He. As the Advaita Vedantins put it, "He is the One and Only Transmigrant." (In view of this, it may be useful to imagine that our spiritual practices are being performed by God, not by us; in the words of Buddhist teacher Chögyam Trungpa, "effort just comes to you.") Nonetheless, the responsibility to walk that Path is still ours—at least initially. According to Sufi master Javad Nurbakhsh, "At the beginning of the Path, if you claim that all your actions are really performed by God, then you are an unbeliever; at the end of the Path, if you claim that you are the author of any action whatsoever— you are an unbeliever." The upshot is that, except at its first beginning and its final end, the Spiritual Path is an ongoing dialogue between human effort and the Generosity and Grace of God.

In Sufism, the relationship between Grace and effort is expressed in terms of the various "States" and "Stations" through which the Sufi passes on his path to God—or, rather, his path *in* God. States are gifts of God which can be neither merited nor produced at will; "Stations" are spiritual achievements of the Sufi himself, based upon his ability to actualize the virtues—virtues like humility, zeal, trust in God, etc. States may announce stations; they may even be considered virtual Stations in themselves; but only the labor to assimilate the freely-bestowed Grace of a State can turn it into a Station. God may plant the grain, water it, harvest it, thresh it, winnow it, grind it, bake it into bread, slice and serve it; He may even place it in our mouths. But it is up to us, at the very least, to chew, swallow and digest it.

Different Sufi authors are known for their widely divergent portraits of the Stations of the Path, usually expressed in terms of various virtues—first conceived, then realized—ranging from a mere handful to a hundred or more, as in Ansari's famous *Sad Maidan* (*A Hundred Fields of Battle*). Certain Eastern Orthodox writers, such as St. John Climacus, have produced very similar *schemata*, and there is no question that the *Divine Comedy* of Dante is not only a catalogue of posthumous states, but also a detailed description of the Spiritual Path as it may be walked in this very life.

No scheme of the Stations of the Path, however, should be taken as absolutely or literally true; all are mere suggestions or simplified indications of the actual complexity and profundity of it—given that no two moments or states of consciousness are perfectly identical in the entire collective experience of the universe. They should be understood as broad outlines only. Nor should the very notion of a linear succession of Stations be absolutized. We may be called upon to retrace our steps so as to perfect a Station only imperfectly realized before—and if any Station is perfectly realized, it immediately opens into all of them. The Goal is not at the distant end of the Path, but directly beneath our walking feet.

II: THE SIX STATIONS OF WISDOM IN THEORY

So much for the general nature of the Spiritual Path. What follows is my understanding of a particular rendition of that Path produced by Frithjof Schuon—an inspired epitome of the spiritual life in its essential realities and requirements presented with great economy and simplicity, which came to him through a vision of the Virgin Mary. I have added the notion of the inversion and "re-edification" of the three primary faculties of the soul—*thought, feeling* and *will*—and the practice of recognizing the four fundamental feeling-tones of the fallen soul—*hurt, fear, anger* and *sadness*—as ultimately the products of direct and specific commands from God, but the basic scheme of this rendition is Schuon's alone, as it appears in his book *Stations of Wisdom.*

The spiritual method taught by Schuon is epitomized in six "Stations". These are the receptive and active aspects, respectively, of Will, (One and Two), Love (Three and Four), and Intelligence (Five and Six). They are: *Purity; Combat; Peace; Fervor; Discrimination between the Real and the unreal;* and *Identification with the Real.* Note, however, that the "generic" quality of this scheme, which allows it to illuminate different versions of the Path taken from different traditions, does not mean that it constitutes a Path in itself: the Spiritual Path can effectively be walked only within the matrix of a single revealed spiritual Way. Nor is my own practice of drawing doctrine and lore from more than one tradition intended to deny this truth. One religion may elucidate a particular aspect of the Path better than the others do (this being all that *spiritually* justifies "comparative religion"), yet each religion contains all that is needed, in terms of doctrine, method and Grace, to walk the Path to its End.

The human soul is made up of three primary faculties: the rational mind, the affections, and the will. It is also host to That which transcends it, the Spiritual Intellect. In the original, unfallen soul as God created it, the rational mind turns to the Intellect for its first principles; the will obeys the directives that the rational mind derives from those principles; and the affections empower the will to obey the rational mind both constantly and willingly.

In the fallen soul, however, the Spiritual Intellect is veiled, consequently this hierarchy is inverted. The affections are now attracted to inappropriate objects (as when Eve ate the apple) without regard for what the rational mind—in its unfallen state—directs; the will follows these wayward affections by intending and enacting what they have suggested (as Eve offered the apple to Adam, who also ate); and the rational mind (somewhat like the Serpent in the garden) is pressed into the service of the will, both to suggest to it various ways it might transgress, and to justify and *rationalize* those transgressions.

In its earlier stages, the purpose of the spiritual Path is to return the soul to its original nature as God made it, thus re-establishing its proper hierarchy, where the rational mind obeys the Intellect, the will obeys the rational mind, and the affections obey the will. This aspect of the Path makes up the lesser or *psychic* mysteries, which are covered by the first four of Schuon's Six Stations—One and Two being the conformation of the will to the rational mind (since in the war against the passions to protect the original virginity of the soul, the rational mind is the General), and Three and Four, the conformation of the affections to the will (since God only becomes the object of Fervor when the will is freed from the tyranny of the affections and fixed upon Him, thereby becoming the affections' master).

These four Stations represent the re-ordering of the soul in its *active* mode, the return of its ability to act in line with spiritual principles. The human soul is also capable, however, of operating in *receptive* mode—as in the case of memory, for example, as well as in the *objective imagination*, which is poles apart from subjective fantasy. When the affections are receptive they are capable of reflecting the Intellect directly, without the mediation of either the rational mind or the individual will, like a calm sea on a windless day reflecting the image of the Sun—an ability that defines the whole *imaginal* aspect of spiritual contemplation, as well as the contemplation of spiritual beauty in nature and art, and is related most directly to the Fourth Station, *Peace*.

The last two Stations of the Path comprise the greater or *pneumatic* mysteries. In the Fifth Station, the rational mind perfectly conforms itself to the Uncreated Intellect, thus positing God, not itself, as the Discriminator between Real and unreal; in the Sixth Station, the rational mind is completely swallowed up in the Contemplative Intellect, becoming little more than a tool by which that Intellect may outwardly express itself.

The first Station, *Purity*, is our original "adamic" nature—in Islamic terms, our *fitrah*. Purity fears to sully itself with the world and the passions, and firmly wills to remain in its original nature. It is intrinsic humility. [NOTE: Schuon sees *Purity* more in terms of repentance than as man's original nature to which repentance returns us, whereas, according to my perspective, repentance is centered more in *Combat*, given that, in practical terms, repentance makes it necessary for us to repel temptations, which we now clearly recognize for what they are; for the initial motion of repentance to remove all temptation at a single stroke is quite rare. And yet repentance can be virtually complete in its first dawning, given that our intention is pure; from this point of view, Schuon's rendition is more accurate than mine.]

In terms of its relation to the world, this *virginity* needs a Protector to defend it. The Second Station, then, is *Combat*—the war against whatever would adulterate that original purity of soul. Combat takes up arms against the passions with the weapon the "incensive faculty" of the Platonists (Greek *thymikon*, Arabic *ghadhab*), the Islamic "Greater *Jihad*", whereby all temptations to corruption are firmly repelled. In terms of the Spiritual Path, the incensive faculty is that which wills the destruction of all barriers to the soul's submission to God. And if the incensive faculty is the Warrior, the General in the Greater *Jihad* is the "rational faculty"

(Greek *logistikon*, Arabic *darraka*), capable of understanding the implications of divinely revealed or intellectually discerned moral laws, and applying them to particular situations, both individual and collective.

The Third Station, *Peace*, is victory in that war, making possible for the first time the clear and constant sense of God's presence, and firm trust in Him—because when the waves of self-will and concupiscence subside on the surface of the affective soul, the spiritual Intellect dawns, and it is the Intellect which sees God as if face-to-Face. It is gratitude, quiet joy; it is what allows us to contemplate the divine in Nature or sacred art; it is rest in the Beauty of God. In Eastern Orthodox terms, it is *apatheia*, spiritual impassivity. In Sufi terms, it is the full opening and stabilization of *al-Qalb*, the Heart, the true Center of the human being, where spiritual realities may be contemplated.

The Fourth Station, *Fervor*, is the full and intense desire to completely unite with the God whose presence, in Peace, has become the center of one's life and one's world. It is the purified form of Platonic "appetitive faculty" (Greek *epithymitikon*, Arabic *shahwa*) transferred from the relative, contingent and perishing world to the Eternal Creator—since when the Intellect reveals Truth, and the will is fixed on that Truth, the affections no longer oppose that will, but empower it. As expressed, for example, in the poems of Rumi, it is Love both consummated and unrequited, the Beloved both lost and attained—a paradoxical situation which ultimately results in the knowledge that what is intrinsically *not* (i.e., myself), except by God's gift of His Own Being, can never be literally united to what intrinsically *Is*, God Himself, Who is One without a second. Possible being can never unite with Necessary Being, because in Necessary Being all possibilities are already actualized, leaving mere potentiality without any Being of its own, or any possibility that Being might be actualized in terms of it: the unreal can never become the Real. But if this is so, then what is the meaning of Consummation, of Mystical Union, of the Divine Embrace? Rumi's answer, from the *Mathnavi* [A.J. Arberry translation], is as follows:

A certain man once came and knocked on the door of a friend.

"Who are you, faithful one?" his friend asked.

"I," he answered.

"Go away", the friend said. "It is not the proper time. There is no place for such a raw fellow at a table like mine." What shall cook the raw, but he fire of banishment and separation? What shall deliver him out of hypocrisy?

That wretched man departed and wandered abroad for a year, burned as with sparks of fire in separation from his friend. So, scorched, he was cooked; then he returned and once more circled about the house of his companion. Fearful a hundredfold, he gently knocked at the door, anxious lest any unmannerly word should escape his lips.

His friend called, "Who is that at the door?"

He answered, "You also are at the door, heart-ravisher!"

"Now," the friend cried, "since you are I, come in. O I! There is not room in the house for two I's."

Stations One and Two may be roughly placed under the heading of *karma-yoga*, the Way of Action (though in a radically sublimated and internal form), while Stations Three and Four make up *bhakti-yoga*, the Way of Devotion. But before we pass to Stations Five and Six, which together comprise *jñana-yoga*, the Way of Knowledge, we need to deal with the incipient *antinomianism* that has sometimes been falsely associated with this Way, the idea that those who aspire to *jñana* need not concern themselves with morality, much less with devotion to a Personal God. In *Language of the Self*, addressing those Western seekers who believe that they can follow the way of Ramana Maharshi—based on practicing the realization that "I am not the body, I am not the mind, in reality I am the Self (*Atma*)"— outside both morality and tradition, Frithjof Schuon says:

> As long as the mind exists—that is to say until death—it must worship the Divinity; without this attitude man would never really know that he is not the mind. A mind that worships does

not desire to be "I"; it is not acting at variance with the knowledge that "I am not the mind; I am *Atma*". But a mind that does
not bow down before the Godhead is an obstacle to
liberation. . . . In the same way . . . the mind which has not
been purified of the sicknesses of worldly man, which is not
free from pride, passion and ugliness of every kind, does not
allow the superimposition of the idea "I am the mind" to be
eliminated. The idea that "I am not the mind—or the body—
but *Atma*" only frees from the superimpositions on condition
that the objectivations—that is, the body, the soul, the
intelligence—realize *Atma* within the limits of their possibilities: the body by its purity, the soul by its devotion, and the
intelligence by its discernment, its logic. If the body is impure
through the tyranny of the passions, if the soul is impious by its
scorn of God, and if the intelligence is obscured by its preten-
tiousness and partiality, the idea that "I am neither this body,
nor this mind, but *Atma*" engenders the illusion—not the
consciousness—of being *Atma*; and this illusion may engulf
man in the torments of the *samsara*. . . . One may say: this
weakness is not myself; it is the mind. One cannot say: this
pride is not myself, it is the mind. Pride is always
"myself". . . . [*Language of the Self*: Madras: Ganesh & Co., 1959;
from the chapter "Self-Knowledge and the Western Seeker",
pp. 53–54. This chapter does not appear in some later editions.]

And so, to continue: The Fifth Station, *Discrimination between
the Real and the unreal*, is the noetic fruit of the love of God. What
never has and never could have existed—the world apart from God,
that is, including me myself—is now clearly seen as nothing, and is
consequently annihilated: this is the Sufi Station of *fana*, annihilation in God. *All is perishing except His Face* (Q. 28:88).

The Sixth Station, *Identification with the Real*, is what is left when
that-which-is-not disappears from the field. In the words of the
Vedanta, it is *tat twam asi*, "That Art Thou"—the equivalent of
which, in Christianity, is "it is not I who live, but Christ lives in me",
and in Islam, "he who knows himself knows his Lord." "That Art
Thou", however, does not mean "you (the subjective, psychic self)

are God"; it means "He (the Absolute Being) is your real Self", leaving no room in Itself for anything partial or psychic, anything that could call itself "me". The Absolute is not self-reflective; as the Total Subject, it is devoid of any limited and relative "subjectivity". It is not the union of two terms, the relative and the Absolute; it is not the identification of "me" with "God": The Absolute necessarily abides alone. *Truth hath come and falsehood hath vanished away. Lo! falsehood is ever bound to vanish* (Q. 17:18).

Nonetheless, as Schuon teaches, That which abides alone, as Absolute, is necessarily also Infinite, and the Infinite must infinitely radiate Itself, since no barriers can exist within It to prevent this radiation. It radiates Itself as the universe; it radiates Itself as me. But this "me" is no longer the devoted lover who longs to unite with the Beloved, nor the valiant knower who struggles to know the Real; it is no longer subjective; it is no longer self-identified. Before identification with the Real—as Schuon teaches—the lover and/or knower of God is "I" and the Beloved, the One Truth, is "He"; after identification with the Real, that One Truth, is "I", and that which was once the lover-and/or-knower, now no longer self-identified, now subsisting only as known and loved by that One Truth, is "he". This is the Sufi Station of *baqa*, subsistence in God. And since to realize *baqa* is essentially to return to the *fitrah*, to the Human Form as God made it and as it exists eternally in His contemplative regard, seeing that who God knows us to be is who we really are, Identification with the Real is also the realization of our original Purity on a higher level. And so the circle is complete.

II: THE SIX STATIONS OF WISDOM IN PRACTICE

In his writings, Frithjof Schuon presented his Six Stations of Wisdom as realities to be contemplated. He openly published very little, however, about how they are to be practiced and realized in the concrete.

In Buddhist terms, the three "active" stations, *Combat, Fervor* and *Discrimination,* are definite spiritual practices with their own requirements, methodologies and reality-checks; in Buddhist terms they constitute *upaya,* or Method. The three "passive" stations on the other hand—*Purity*, *Peace* and *Identification*—constitute *prajña*, or Wisdom. They are more the fruits of spiritual practice—or eternal realities underlying that practice—than practices in themselves. But while a clear and discriminating recognition of their particular qualities makes up most of what can be said about them, they nonetheless possess their own intrinsic requirements, and thus might be described, in a certain way, as practices in themselves—practices to be fulfilled, however, not by *doing*, but by *being*. And being, seen from one perspective, is the most *active* thing there is: great spiritual labor is required simply to receive, and assimilate, the freely-given grace of God. (NOTE: *Discrimination* is "active" because, in its initial stages at least, it is a thing to be done, while *Identification* "passive" because it simply is. But at a higher stage, *Discrimination*, insofar as it corresponds to the annihilation of the subjective ego, is passive; it is not something we perform but something we undergo—in view of the fact that the ego cannot annihilate itself. As Ramana Maharshi describes it, "the real Self is waiting to take you in. Then whatever is done is done by something else, and you have no hand in it." Likewise *Identification*, from a higher perspective, is not passive but active—supremely so, given that God is "Pure Act".)

Mercifully, masterpieces relating to spiritual combat, spiritual fervor, and discrimination between the Real and the unreal are readily available to us. Among the classics of *Combat* are large sections of the Eastern Orthodox *Philokalia* [in four volumes, published by Faber & Faber], as well as *Spiritual Combat* by the Roman Catholic priest Lorenzo Scupoli [Sophia Institute Press, 2002], represented in Eastern Orthodox terms by Theophan the Recluse and St. Nicodemus of the Holy Mountain as *Unseen Warfare* [St. Vladimir's Seminary Press, 1997], and al-Ghazzali's *Breaking the Two Desires*, from Sufi Islam [The Islamic Texts Society, 2007]. The classics of *Fervor* include the *Mathnavi* [6 volumes, translated by Reynold A. Nicholson Reynold A. Nicholson, Gibb Memorial Trust, 1990], the *Divan-i-Shams-i-Tabriz* [now available as *Jan-i jan: muntakhabati az Divan-i Shams hamrah ba tarjumah inglisi va tuzihat (Selected Poems from the Divan of Shams of Tabriz)*, translated by Reynold A. Nicholson: Nashre Namak, 2002], and the *Quatrains* of Jalalluddin Rumi, the full title of this last being *The*

Quatrains of Rumi (*Rubāʿiyāt-é Jalāluddīn Muhammad Balkhā-Rūmī* [Sophia Perennis, 2008]. And the classics of *Discrimination* include all the works, both writings and dialogues, of Sri Ramana Maharshi, as well as the Sufi classic relating to the development of this station, *The Mawāqif and Mukhātabāt* of Muhammad Ibn ʿAbdi ʿL-Jabbār Niffari [edited and translated by Arthur John Arberry, The Gibb Memorial Trust, 1987]. In these precious books (and more titles could be added) are to be found methods by which one may concretely and efficaciously practice Schuon's Six Stations of Wisdom—though certainly not in the full light of his own subtleties. And although *Purity, Peace* and *Union* are harder to speak of— the first two being profoundly "inner", and the last, totally without qualities—certain intimations of the nature of these stations also exist in the great treasury of world spiritual literature now available to us.

The practice of *Purity* is: to fear corruption by the world, and to maintain one's spiritual virginity in the face of it. Purity as *intellectual* as well as *passional* virginity is well expressed in the following passage from *The Golden Fountain* by Lilian Stavley [World Wisdom Books, 1982]:

> Fear curiosity. Fear it more than sin. Curiosity is the root, and sin the flower. This is one of the reasons why we should never seek God merely with the intelligence: to do so is to seek Him, in part at least, through curiosity. God will not be peeped upon by a curious humanity. The indulgence in curiosity would of itself explain the whole downfall, so called, of man ... curiosity is the mother of all infidelity, whether of the spirit or of the body [p.11].

It is this quality of fear, fear to be sullied by the world on the plane of either the intellect, the affections, or the will, which spiritual *Combat*, Purity's active complement, exists to preserve and defend. Purity is spiritual virginity, and virginity is intimately bound up with the fear of corruption, the virtue of *shame*. It's hard for us to see shame as a virtue nowadays; ultimately following Freud, we tend to think of it as a kind of illness, as something that prevents us from being one with ourselves—by which we mean one with our passions, which we consider to be "who we really are". But in reality, shame is perhaps the most fundamental virtue of all:

> When we say that something is shameful [we mean] that we would be ashamed to get involved with it; if we are not *shameless*, if we retain a healthy sense of shame, we will not do things that violate our own integrity or that of others. We will experience an inner check; we will feel "guilty before the fact". It ought to be clear that without this kind of shame, we will corrupt ourselves with every breath we breathe. [Charles Upton, *Hammering Hot Iron: A Spiritual Critique of Bly's Iron John*, Sophia Perennis, 2005].

Purity is also an essential quality of the Celestial Feminine, embodied in the Islamic world by the Prophet's daughter Fatima, and in both the Islamic and the Christian worlds by the Virgin Mary, both of whom exhibited what might be called "the rigor of innocence":

> The suppression of feminine spiritual innocence ... is a conspiracy which includes women as well as men. Men fear the celestial feminine because they fear the image of the torture they have inflicted upon their own feminine souls. But women also fear [her] because they identify her torment with their own potential vulnerability ... [what we really fear, however, is] her power, her moral authority, her immense ability to heal wounds and reconcile enemies, as well as her quality of unrelenting justice.... [Charles Upton, *Hammering Hot Iron: A Spiritual Critique of Bly's Iron John*].

Purity is the abstinence of the soul from all secondary determinations, so that it may rest in the *fitrah*, the original form in which God created it. Esoterically speaking, when the Prophet Muhammad, peace and blessings be upon him, is described as "unlettered", this means that he lived consciously from a stratum of his being previous to, and deeper than, the impressions of past experience, the "written word". Because he was pure of the *written* word, free from the traces of the past, he was able to hear, and obey, the *spoken* Word of God in this very moment. In the words of the Sufi master al-Shibli, "Abstinence is that you abstain from everything other than God Most High".

The practice of *Combat* is: to repel temptations immediately, the instant they appear, by the power of purified anger. As such it is much more than simply the striking of a martial pose in the face of all that is false and corrupt; it is not to be prematurely identified with spiritual victory, nor is it limited contemplative vigilance, though this is certainly one facet of its nature. Depending on how deeply the soul is sunk in the passions, it may dawn upon us as the spiritual equivalent of bloody, hand-to-hand combat, in all the terror and the *degradation* of war. (The quality of a traditional exorcism, its direct confrontation with the Powers of Darkness—which are also the Powers of Ugliness—may give some sense of the rigors of this *agon*). And if Combat is truly a Station of Wisdom, then spiritual suffering cannot be limited to voluntarily adopted ascetical practice. It is not something we simply "opt" for based on our predilections, something that *jñanis* or *gnostics* need not concern themselves with; the paramount *jñani* of modern times, Ramana Maharshi, himself endured great suffering as his spiritual destiny of "infused *jñana*" pressed in upon him. (The essence of the gnostic way is *disillusionment*—and what is more productive of purgatorial suffering than this?) Suffering is not a personal choice; whatever we may choose to embrace or reject, suffering will come. The question is, do we know how to put it to good use? According to *The Gospel of Thomas*, "If you knew how to suffer, you would know how not to suffer." And in the words of God as directed to St. Catherine of Sienna:

> I wish thee to know that all the sufferings which rational creatures endure depend on their will, because if their will were in accordance with Mine they would endure no suffering; not that they would have no labors on that account, but because labors cause no suffering to a will which gladly endures them, seeing that they are ordained by My will.

Those mercifully born without deep attachments to the passional ego, or who by the grace of God were wise enough in their younger days not to pay court to it, need not spend years in the trenches, in the war against the passional soul, the *nafs al-ammara*—but such people are rare. For many of the rest of us, the war against the passions is a bloody and seemingly interminable struggle, a struggle that only ends at the moment when, having come to the end of our own resources, God Himself takes the field—at which point the Enemy we found ourselves powerless to overcome is no longer anywhere to be seen: because God alone is.

The *practice* of Peace, in volitional terms, is *islam*: the constant and ongoing submission to the will of God, minute by minute, breath by breath (the Arabic words *islam*, "submission", and *salaam*, "peace", being from the same root). In intellective terms, it is to cultivate—painstakingly, constantly and deliberately—a subtle emotional sensitivity, and contemplate the Divine Beauty by means of it. Peace is the "introverted", receptive complement to Fervor. The station of Peace, considered not only as the fruit of victory in spiritual Combat but as something to be intentionally developed in its own terms, is expressed in the following way by Jennifer Doane Upton:

> Developed feeling is refined and subtle, and far from being merely sentimental or demonstrative, it often withholds its own demonstration when such a manifestation would destroy the context which allows it to appear. Feeling must be cultivated, both for the sake of the fullness of human life, and because it itself can be a perfect vehicle for union with God, not only due to the psychic energy it releases, but also because of the particular perceptions which only developed feeling can give. This is not "bhakti" as we usually think of it. There are certain avenues to the Transcendent Intellect which open only through feeling.

Peace is the station of Divine Beauty. The Beauty of God possesses an intrinsic rigor that casts all lesser beauties out of the soul, teaching us slowly but surely how to endure the Divine Mercy. According to Jennifer Doane Upton,

> Beauty is one of the paths to spiritual Truth. Nothing compares with Beauty—that Beauty which attaches itself to the True, the Real, that is, and not that other beauty which participates almost completely in the world, and demands that we

love this crass, habitual world, even if we have to swallow our truest feelings. That beauty breaks our hearts by putting up a wall between us and God, and finally tries to convince us that we can no longer reach God, and that God no longer wants us. How that beauty hates the other more beautiful Beauty, and does everything in its power to keep us from seeing it. It even puts out our eyes. But that other Beauty, the paradisiacal Beauty, still comes to us, and when we are blind it penetrates the pores of our skin, for nothing in this world can deny us the vision of Paradise.

It is important not to allow Peace to degenerate into spiritual complacency, or see it as a mere "rest after labors". In the words of Martin Lings, from *Symbol and Archetype* [Fons Vitae, 2006]:

> all those who pass through the gates of Heaven incur thereby a tremendous responsibility; it is henceforth the function of each to be, himself or herself, an integral feature of the celestial Garden, a source of felicity for all the other inmates, a vehicle of the Divine Presence [pp. 47–48].

The fruit of the pacification of the soul is expressed by St. Bernard in these terms:

> In prayer one drinks the wine that gladdens a man's heart, the intoxicating wine of the Spirit that drowns all memory of the pleasures of the flesh. It drenches anew the arid recesses of the conscience ... fills the faculties of the soul with a robust faith, a solid hope, a love that is living ... it enriches all the actions of our life.

And in the words of Dionysius the Areopagite:

> Now let us praise with reverent hymns of peace the Divine Peace which is the source of all mutual attraction. For [this] quality ... unites all things together and begets ... the harmony and agreement of all things ... all things long for It and It draws their manifold separate parts into the Unity of the Whole. ...

Peace, in volitional terms, is the station of *islam*, of perfect submission to God. When the will is pacified, the waves of the passions
subside; this is the station named by the Eastern Orthodox Christians *apatheia*. And when the passions are pacified, the spiritual
Intellect dawns.

Fervor as a practice is very easily misunderstood. Fervor is active;
it is the active aspect of the affections in the context of the spiritual
life. But this does not mean that we can call up feelings of fervor or
devotion to God by an act of will, nor should we try to. A large part
of the Station of Fervor comprises the science of how to deal with
the feelings that God produces in us, not all of which are pleasant,
exalted, or what we usually think of as "spiritual" (some, in fact, will
be excruciating). Our feelings often appear to us as aspects of the
passional ego alone, as all the "emotional baggage" we wish we
could get rid of; and when we discover that we cannot in fact get rid
of it (as we most certainly will discover), what else can we do but try
to repress it—in other words, lie to ourselves? The practice of Fervor, however, begins with the recognition that such feelings are ultimately being produced in us by God Himself, that they in fact
constitute a precise set of commands and prohibitions designed to
lead us to Him, and to which we are required to *actively* give our
assent; they are aspects of the passional ego in the process of being
"convicted of its sin" and deconstructed by God's Grace. For example, *anger* may be recognized as a command either to completely
renounce all action, or to perform one particular action, *immediately*, in the context of the knowledge that, in reality, only God is the
Doer. Likewise *fear* is a command that we allow ourselves to be
totally obliterated by the overwhelming power of God's Majesty.
Hurt commands us to let go of all those expectations that God is
continually frustrating in us, and place ourselves in His hands "like
a corpse in the hands of a washer of the dead". And *sadness,* the felt
absence of God in this world, commands us to indulge in "nostalgia
for Paradise", to long for Him in that other, distant world, until all
separation between the two worlds is overcome.

One of the most common errors at the Station of Fervor is to
identify the affections with the passions, and consequently identify
spiritual impassivity, *apatheia*, with emotional repression; however,

as Marty Glass teaches us (in his wonderful *Eastern Light in Western Eyes*, Sophia Perennis, 2003), passions are not feelings per se, but "feelings that we immediately identify with." If we falsely posit our feelings as passions (thus turning them all over to the Devil), we have thereby made the commitment to eliminate them as if they were all vices or temptations—a commitment that is both false in theory and impossible to fulfill in fact. But if we posit them as commands and prohibitions—and insights and unveilings—sent by God Himself, then we cannot repress them; we must follow them to their ultimate ends, until we determine exactly what God is requiring of us by means of them. And the ultimate End of all human feelings is the Love of God, which, though necessarily expressing itself through the deepest feelings the human soul is capable of, is essentially beyond feeling. Combat has to do with repelling temptations to sinful acts; Fervor, with freeing our feelings from the grip of the passional ego by recognizing them as commands of God, and ultimately as *acts* of God. And of this whole dimension of the spiritual life, Jalalluddin Rumi is the unrivalled Master. The following are seven of his Quatrains, in my "poetic" versions of the translations of Ibrahim W. Gamard and A.H. Rawan Farhadi [*The Quatrains of Rumi*, Sophia Perennis, 2008]:

> Since the day my eyes first beheld your face
> Their bloody tears of longing have never ceased.
> If I take a cup without you, let it be poison!
> If I am forced to live without you, let it be death!

> I saw you last night, O my beloved, in a passion of separation;
> With cruelty and rancor you were telling me, "Get out!"
> Today I wake to find I have been driven out of my own soul;
> I am washing my cheeks in the blood of that separation.

> "The pain of longing for You grows on me," I said.
> "Blessed is the soul who has arrived at such pain" He said.
> "My heart has become blood and pours from my eyes," I said.
> "What has flowed for you." He said, "has flowed for no other."

> "The time has come for you to accept my care", He said.
> "That's why I am transforming your soul into a house full of fire.

Beneath your soul's veil you are a mine packed with gold;
I am throwing you into that fire to purify you, like ore".

Your tyranny is far sweeter than another's faith;
Your obscurity, far better than another's clearness.
Your insult is sweeter than another's mouthful of praise;
Your taunt, than greeting another face to face.

O wounded heart, your balm has finally come;
Joyfully draw your breath, for in this very moment
A Beloved who can grant the wish of every lover
Has come into this world in human form.

When my heart's true Form returns to that heart
My lost and impoverished heart returns to its place.
Even if life has passed, even if only a single breath is left to me,
When He returns, *everything* returns.

To sum up: When our passional feelings are deconstructed
through obedience to the divine Commands hidden within them,
the affective substance of the soul is centered and unified in the fervent love of God.

The practice of *Discrimination* is a bit harder to talk about,
because it contains the essential question "who is the discriminator?" If *I* discriminate between the Real and the unreal, my discrimination stays on the mental level; it remains part of the self-reflexive
subjectivity that true Discrimination recognizes as unreal, and consequently dispels. Discrimination begins with an understanding of
the world as *Maya*, as insubstantial in itself apart from God, and
proceeds to the further understanding that all I hold myself to be is
an aspect of that *Maya*, including the part of me that believes that it
can practice Discrimination. The only true Discriminator is God,
Who, though He truly is "the Knower of Each Separate Thing" (one
of the "Ninety-Nine Names of God" in the Islamic tradition),
knows all things only as Himself. If I posit my limited subjective self
as the knower, the one capable of discriminating between the Real
and the unreal, then I am deluded by *Maya*; God Alone is the
Knower. In relation to Him, that subjective, psychological self is not
the Witness but the witnessed, not the Knower but the known; that

self truly exists not as it holds itself to be—which is all illusion—but only as God knows it to be—which is all Truth. In the words of Ramana Maharshi:

> It is the Self-luminous existence-consciousness which reveals to the seer the world of names and forms both inside and outside. The existence of this existence-consciousness can be inferred by the objects illuminated by it, [but] it does not [itself] become an object of consciousness [*The Collected Works of Ramana Maharshi*: Sophia Perennis, 2006; p.55].

Frithjof Schuon, in *Survey of Metaphysics and Esoterism* [World Wisdom Books, 1986], writes as follows about the passage from the Fourth to the Fifth Station, from *Fervor* to *Discrimination*:

> when the perception of the Object is so intense that the consciousness of subject vanishes, the Object becomes Subject, as is the case in the union of love; but then the word "subject" no longer has the meaning of a complement that is fragmentary by definition; it means on the contrary a totality which we conceive as subjective because it is conscious. When we place the emphasis on objective Reality—which then takes precedence in the relation between the subject and the object—the subject becomes object in the sense that, being determined entirely by the object, it forgets the element consciousness; in this case the subject, inasmuch as it is a fragment, is absorbed by the Object inasmuch as it is a totality, as the accident is reintegrated into the Substance. But the other manner of seeing things, which reduces everything to the Subject, takes precedence over the point of view that grants primacy to the Object: if we adore God, it is not for the simple reason that He presents Himself to us as an objective reality of a dizzying and crushing immensity—otherwise we would adore the stars and nebulae—but it is above all because this reality, a priori objective, is the greatest of subjects; because He is the absolute Subject of our contingent subjectivity; because He is at once all-powerful, omniscient and benefic Consciousness [pp.39–40].

As for how Discrimination is to be practiced as a spiritual way,

Ramana Maharshi's method of "self-enquiry", based on the question "Who Am I?", is perhaps the most lucid description we possess. In the process of self-enquiry, the practitioner realizes:

> The gross body which is composed of the seven humors (*dhatus*) I am not; the five cognitive sense organs, viz. the senses of hearing, touch, sight, taste, and smell, which apprehend their respective objects, viz. sound, touch, color, taste, and odor, I am not; the five conative sense organs, viz. the organs of speech, locomotion, grasping, excretion and procreation, which have as their respective functions, speaking, moving, excreting, grasping, and enjoying, I am not; the five vital airs, *prana*, etc., which perform respectively the five functions of in-breathing, etc., I am not; even the mind which thinks, I am not; the nescience too, which is endowed only with the residual impressions of objects, and in which there are no objects and no functionings, I am not.... After negating all the above mentioned as "not this", "not this", that Awareness which alone remains— that I am [*The Collected Works of Ramana Maharshi*, p. 33].

> However, To enquire "Who am I?" really means trying to find out the source of the ego or the "I"-thought. You are not to think of other thoughts, such as "I am not this body." Seeking the source of the "I" serves as a means of getting rid of all other thoughts. We should not give scope to other thoughts ... but must keep the attention fixed on finding out the source of the "I"-thought by asking, as each thought arises, to whom the thought arises. If the answer is "*I* have the thought", continue the enquiry by asking "who is this 'I' and what is its source?" [*Be As You Are: The Teachings of Sri Ramana Maharshi*, edited by David Godman: Arkana, 1985; p.73].

After the rise of the "I"-thought there is the false identification of the "I" with the body, the senses, the mind, etc. "I" is wrongly associated with them and the true "I" lost sight of. In order to sift the pure "I" from the contaminated "I", this discarding [of the "sheaths", the *koshas*—body, senses, mind, etc.] is mentioned. But it does not mean exactly discarding the non-Self, it

means the finding of the real Self. The real Self is the infinite "I".
That "I" is perfection. It is eternal. It has no origin and no end.
The other "I" is born and also dies. It is impermanent. See to
whom the clinging thoughts belong. They will be found to arise
after the "I"-thought. Hold the "I"-thought and they subside.
(Then) trace back the source of the "I"-thought. The Self alone
will remain [ibid., pp. 73–74].

According to the Maharshi, the Self is that which witnesses the
arising and disappearing of the "I"-though, a thought which—
though it is not exclusively a veil over the Self but also the sign of
the reality of the Self, according to Shankaracharya—in itself possesses only a virtual reality. It is only the false identification of the
Self with body, senses, mind, etc. that gives rise to the illusory "I"-
thought; consequently, as soon as the "I"-thought is clearly witnessed by the Self, it disappears; this is the Sufi *fana*. The Self abides
as *That Which Is*; simultaneously, the "I"-thought is known as *that
which is not*, and never could have been. The final fruit of this process of self-enquiry is a state in which:

> [Knowledge] is firm and effortless abidance in the Self, in
> which the mind which has become one with the Self does not
> subsequently emerge again at any time. That is, just as every-
> one usually and naturally has the idea "I am not a goat nor a
> cow nor any other animal, but a human" when he thinks of his
> body, so also when he has the idea "I am not the principles
> (*tattwas*) beginning with the body and ending with sound
> (*nada*), but the Self which is existence, consciousness and bliss,
> the innate self-consciousness (*atma prajña*)," he is said to have
> attained firm knowledge [*The Collected Works of Ramana
> Maharshi*, p.58].

And when such knowledge dawns as a stable realization, the Station of Discrimination is complete; only Union remains.

The practice of *Identification with the Real*—insofar as it may be
called a practice—is as we have already seen the "firm and effortless
abidance in the Self, in which the [individual] mind which has
become one with the Self does not subsequently emerge again at

any time". Ramana Maharshi further characterizes the Station of Identification in these terms:

> What exists in truth is the Self alone. The world, the individual soul and God are appearances in it, like silver in mother-of-pearl; these three appear at the same time and disappear at the same time. . . . The Self is that where there is absolutely no I-thought. That is called "Silence" [*The Collected Works of Ramana Maharshi*, p. 37].

The Maharshi could distinguish "himself" from others for the purpose of communication, but his identification—or rather, the Absolute Self's identification—with the body, speech and mind of the one known to others as "Ramana Maharshi" was totally extinguished. And lest we think that the idea of Identification with the Real is never encountered in the Abrahamic religions, this Identification is clearly is alluded to by Meister Eckhart in the following passage, which can stand as a perfect expression of the Sufi station of *baqa*:

> I pray God that He may quit me of God, for His Unconditioned Being is above God [along] with all distinctions. It was here [in Unconditioned Being] that I was myself and knew myself. . . . I am my own first cause, both of my eternal being and of my temporal being. . . . It is of the nature of the eternal birth that *I have been*, that *I am now*, and *shall be forever*.

This is the ladder of the Six Stations. From the perspective of the soul we may imagine ourselves climbing it rung-by-rung, but from the perspective of God—from the vantage point of Liberation already virtually realized—we can see that it is the grace of the Fifth and Sixth Stations, as Knowledge, that empowers us to pass through the Third and Fourth, and the grace of the Third and Fourth Stations, as Love, that empowers us to pass through the First and Second. And though the perspective on the Six Stations I have adopted shows them as hierarchicalized and successive, but this is not the only way of looking at them. From a different but equally valid point of view, the Six Stations radiate simultaneously, like the six directions of space, from a common Center. This Center may be imaginally identified with the Northern or Hyperborean Mary, whose epithet "Star of the Sea" identifies her with the Pole Star, and whose constellation is the *Septentrion*, the seven stars of the Little Bear. Like the Buddhist Prajñaparamita, the Virgin in this aspect represents the primal virginity of Space, the Matrix that allows all things to appear, beyond the world of attraction and repulsion, affirmation and denial, exactly as they are.

Two:

WHAT IS A "TRADITIONALIST"?

Some Clarifications

I HAVE BEEN ASKED by Ali Lakhani, editor of *Sacred Web*, to write a reply to Dr. Hajji Muhammad Legenhausen's article "Why I Am Not a Traditionalist." In order to do this, I suppose I must call myself a Traditionalist, and try to explain why I have chosen to follow the Traditionalist path. But it turns out that this apparently simple task is not as straightforward as it seems.

Dr. Legenhausen, while recognizing Traditionalism's critique of the modern world and its interest in metaphysics and sacred art as valuable and inspiring, objects to it on both theological and socio-logical grounds. He accuses the movement of basing itself on an "esoteric pluralism" which falsely claims the power and the right to evaluate all religious traditions from an "abstract" point beyond them, and of fostering dangerously reactionary political theories and movements. He claims that Traditionalists do not recognize the inevitability of modernism, and are consequently beset by impossible fantasies of returning to earlier more "traditional" social forms. And he claims that little separates the Traditionalist School from many Islamic groups and movements characterized (at least by western journalists) as "fundamentalist", outside of a general intellectual elitism and "elevation". To Dr. Legenhausen, Islamic Traditionalism is apparently little more than a kind of fundamentalism for the intelligentsia.

Dr. Legenhausen characterizes Traditionalism as "an ideology, in the general sense that it offers a system of ideas on the basis of which it recommends a social or political program." This description runs so directly counter to the writings of almost every major Traditionalist figure I have studied, and bears so little relationship to my own experience of twenty years of serious interest in, and interaction with, the Traditionalist School, that I am initially at a loss as to how to refute it. In terms of Traditionalism as I have known it, it is simply wrong. It's as if, by some powerful spell, the attention of the academic intelligentsia has been misdirected from the Moon to the finger pointing at it, after which that finger is discovered to be pointing not at the Moon at all, but rather toward a police station or auto repair shop. Nonetheless, I am not unaware that many groups with political ambitions, most often ultra-conservative if not actually Fascist or crypto-Nazi, have—largely under the influence of Fascist/Nazi fellow-traveler Baron Julius Evola—adopted the name "traditionalist," in some cases as early as the 1930s, and that some of these groups now claim to have drawn their inspiration in part from René Guénon—something they could only have done by ignoring the vast bulk of his writings, and by rejecting, or simply failing to understand, the very concept and purpose of metaphysics itself. My own Traditionalism, on the contrary, is largely defined by the works of Frithjof Schuon and his major followers, and their own particular "edition" of Traditionalist ideas—for example, their acceptance (as opposed to Guénon's position) of the traditional Catholic and Eastern Orthodox sacraments as at least virtually initiatory, their dismissal of Evola based on his placing of the *kshatriya* or warrior initiation (ultimately related to the Catholic idea of the "active" life) on a higher plane than the *brahmanic* or priestly initiation (the "contemplative" life), etc. Though I am not an initiate of Schuon's Maryamiyya Tariqa, it has been Frithjof Schuon more than anyone else who has defined my intellectual horizon (with René Guénon a close second); this fact, as well as the general cultural insularity of the United States, has made it inevitable (providentially, I would say) that I would see Fascist "traditionalism" as alien territory, as well as making it very difficult for me to view Guénon's Masonic writings as in any way fundamental to his role as reviver of Tradition for the Western world. This article, then, will be a defense of "Traditionalism" as I have known it. Since there is no board of review to which I can appeal to redress the misuse of language, I am almost inclined to allow those seriously misinformed individuals who wish to reduce Traditionalism to a political ideology with metaphysical trappings to take the word itself, as long as I am allowed to keep the substance. Such a development, however, would make it more difficult for Traditionalists as I have known them to communicate with each other, and with others who find themselves attracted in the core of their being to the religious, metaphysical and esoteric heritage of the human race; so I feel I must do what little I can to "rectify the names" and set the record straight.

The "founders" of the Traditionalist School, René Guénon and Ananda Coomaraswamy, did not talk about "Traditionalism," but about the religious, metaphysical and esoteric traditions of the world, in light of the One Truth from which they proceed, and to which they provide formally distinct but essentially equivalent paths of return (if by "equivalent" we do not mean "interchangeable", but rather "equally efficacious"; see *The Nature of Ontological Perspectives*, below). It was Guénon who first defined what most later Traditionalists have meant by Tradition: the transmission of a perennial wisdom, unanimous in essence, from the beginnings of the human race to this present moment, a transmission punctuated and channeled by Divine revelations and continually renewed by the "supernaturally natural" human capacity (the phrase is Frithjof Schuon's) for the intellectual intuition of spiritual Truth. This faculty of Intellection, veiled in the general run of humanity, unveiled (to varying degrees) in the case of prophets and saints and sages, is traditionally considered to be the essence and *raison d'être* of the human form itself, what Muslims call the *fitrah*.

Once Guénon and Coomaraswamy had become aware of each other, and had begun to attract the attention of other writers who understood their basic viewpoint, it was inevitable that something like a "Traditionalist School" should begin to define itself as such. This represented a real gain in the understanding and expression of Tradition for the twentieth century, but it also carried with it an inevitable loss, in the sense that it now became possible to speak of "Traditionalist doctrines" as well as Tradition per se. Every writer who deals with Tradition, no matter how self-effacing he may be, inevitably puts his or her individual stamp on the doctrines he transmits, since universal Truth can only travel in this world through the "minute particulars" of culture, time, place and person. To the degree that this casts a veil of idiosyncrasy over timeless doctrines it is unfortunate, but insofar as it allows these doctrines to be expressed in the language of a particular place and time, so as to relate them to concrete social and mass-psychological conditions, to their dominant intellectual errors and specific spiritual potentials, then it is only good.

Be that as it may, it has now become both possible and necessary to differentiate "Traditionalism" from Tradition, so as to determine just how well what is rightly or wrongly characterized as Traditionalism serves to transmit Tradition, and in so doing to evaluate the strengths and weaknesses of the individual stamp that such writers as René Guénon and Frithjof Schuon have placed upon it. Schuon himself, in *René Guénon: Some Observations* [Sophia Perennis, 2004] as well as Jean Borella in his *Guénonian Esoterism and Christian Mystery* [Sophia Perennis, 2005] have done this service for Guénon without in any way diminishing his true stature and use; perhaps in the future someone will undertake to do the same thing for Schuon.

But this differentiation of Traditionalism from Tradition has also become necessary for another reason: the adoption, in a small way, of Traditionalism as grist for the mills of academia, which tend to grind pretty rapidly, though rather coarsely for all that. This development was represented and to a degree initiated by Mark Sedgwick's *Against the Modern World* [Oxford University Press, 2004], which did us all a great service, both in mapping out the Traditionalist historical landscape for the first time, in all its major ramifications, and in showing just how far various groups identified with Traditionalism—often via an interest in Guénon as seen through the eyes Evola, and seemingly limited to an interest in him as author of *East and West* [Sophia Perennis, 2001] and *The Crisis of the Modern World* [Sophia Perennis, 2001]—have departed from Guénon's the central doctrines, as well as those of Ananda Coomaraswamy and Frithjof Schuon. (By the time Guénon published his prophetic magum opus *The Reign of Quantity and the Signs of the Times* [Sophia Perennis, 2001] in 1945, his hopes for a renewal of the West based on the influence of Eastern spiritual doctrines and various forms of Masonry or "esoteric Christianity" had been superseded by his mature *eschatological* vision of the approaching end of the present *manvantara*; those who still follow *East and West* and *Crisis* over *The Reign of Quantity* have failed to follow their master to his ultimate conclusions.) Professor Sedgwick's book was, however, destructive in two ways: first, by its tendency, apparently inspired by the ambiguities of research done partly on the internet, to identify as "Traditionalist" groups with little or no relationship with the Traditionalism of Guénon, Coomaraswamy and Schuon, or even to their various Fascist perversions—such as the all-girl fantasy-cult known as Aristasia, who officially deny the existence of the male sex and like to pretend they are living in the first half of the twentieth century, and secondly, by his definition of the *raison d'être* of the Traditionalist School as *opposition to the modern world* (which explains his otherwise inexplicable treatment of *East and West* and *Crisis of the Modern World* as Guénon's central works) rather than the re-discovery and timely re-expression of the perennial Truth. Such a deviation is perhaps inevitable in any socio-historical treatment of Traditionalism, which must meet contemporary standards of academic "objectivity" by *referring* to metaphysical ideas without in any way *entertaining* them; and by adopting this approach Prof. Sedgwick has certainly made the work of the less meticulous among his fellow academicians much easier, since they can now oppose, or rally in support of, an inaccurate catch-phrase rather than confronting the rather forbidding opus of the Traditionalists themselves, and the great works of Tradition from which they draw their doctrines. This body of material is perhaps more forbidding to many academicians than to certain others (I am thinking of people like Eddie, the self-taught Latino metaphysician who calls me from time to time, and who bought Sophia Perennis' complete works of René Guénon from my publisher in hardcover because they won't deteriorate so easily in his back-pack). The academies, belying their Platonic name, by and large no longer teach metaphysical discourse, one of the two verbal "languages" in which Traditional doctrines are written—the other being symbolic mythopoeia. And mythopoeia itself has been dragged down by Jung and others from the plane of metaphysics to that of psychology, and by modern mythographers and folklorists all the way down to the level of cultural history. (Such studies are of course valuable in themselves, but they should not be used to obscure the very level of reality from which they draw so much of their material.) Thus it has become possible for the first time to say, as a professor from Dartmouth said to me in an e-mail correspondence immediately after 9/11, "I follow René Guénon but I am not interested in metaphysics"—which is like saying "I like Johann Sebastian Bach but I am not really that interested in his music."

The near-disappearance of the discipline of metaphysics in academia, at least in its more traditional forms, coupled with a relentless relativism and historicism, made it next to certain that many in the academies would follow Sedgwick in defining Traditionalism mostly in socio-historical terms. Now sociology and historicism certainly have something of value to say about Traditionalism, just as a socio-economic treatment of Johann Sebastian Bach in terms of his search for patronage, his role as capellmeister, etc., would say something of limited though real value about the great musician. But any treatment of Bach that largely ignored the quality of his music, just as any treatment of Traditionalism that ignores metaphysics—the "music" of metaphysics itself, the actual practice of it, not simply various historical theories about it—would miss the main point entirely. And Mark Sedgwick did indeed miss the main point entirely, in his move to trim Traditionalism so as to fit contemporary academic assumptions. His truncated approach certainly made it easier for many academics to approach the Traditionalist corpus without being embarrassed and confounded by their own lack of metaphysical grounding. But it did little or nothing to define the elements necessary for the concrete practice of metaphysics— the musical score, the instruments, the musicians and their training, and (not least) the *maestro*—without which any attempt to understand the meaning of the Traditionalist School is a chase after the wind.

So, in response to Dr. Legenhausen's "Why I Am Not a Traditionalist," I might reply that I am not a Traditionalist either, according to his definition of the term. In order to call myself a Traditionalist I must define my position much more narrowly, as "a Traditionalist according to Schuon, Guénon, Ananda Coomaraswamy, Marco Pallis, Titus Burckhardt, Martin Lings, Charles LeGai Eaton (this list is certainly not exhaustive) and the editorial viewpoint of the original *Studies in Comparative Religion*". This body of material presents a Traditionalism that is sufficiently unified in outlook and multi-dimensional in expression—and sufficiently *traditional*—to provide a stable intellectual standpoint. Furthermore, I must also define myself as one who, first and foremost, has not adopted this mass of doctrine as *ideology*, but rather as a set of concrete intellectual supports for the spiritual Path, in the recognition that Traditionalism has little or nothing to do with changing the world—to believe so is both doctrinally unorthodox and historically naïve—and everything to do with saving souls. In my view, Traditionalism is almost alone in allowing those who have understood that orthodox doctrine, spiritual depth and realized sainthood are to be found in more than one religious tradition, to nonetheless pursue the *one* tradition to which God has called them, without dissipating their spiritual energy in anti-traditional universalism and its various utopian schemes. And though I do not see any of the above writers as being intrinsically above criticism, it is nonetheless upon their ground—the ground of a Perennial Tradition which they largely rediscovered, for the West and for our time—that I stand.

Though Dr. Legenhausen finds much that is good in Traditionalism, he also maintains that "traditionalism seems to be too reactionary and too nostalgic to offer a workable way to move through and beyond modernity." Traditionalism as I know it is, however, essentially sober and without nostalgia, unless it be the "nostalgia for eternity." Rather, it is a mass of doctrine adequate to orient us, in intellect, will and affections, toward what the *Tao Te Ching* calls the Always So. Orientation to the Always So, to Absolute Reality and all the consequences that flow from it, is always available—God willing, and ourselves (also) willing to pay the price. As such it has nothing intrinsically to do with "working through and beyond modernity." It is intrinsically a-historical, though always (of course) vehicled by historically-conditioned groups and institutions. It invites us to accept religion in its essence, and to do what religion has always allowed and required human beings to do: to transcend ourselves, to die as limited, ego-bound creatures and be reborn—or re-envisioned—as directly dependent upon, and as dimensionally-limited creations or reflections of, God Himself, in this very moment. If Tradition (in Guénon's sense) were in any way *evolutionary*, if humanity's ability to understand the essence of spiritual Truth were capable of a fundamental progressive development (whether or not seen as based on the success of "further research"), then earlier stages of its development could really be left behind, and any desire to return to them legitimately characterized as nostalgic, reactionary or atavistic. But since eternal Truth cannot be left behind, such characterizations are out of place. God is certainly the "Ancient of Days," but this in no way renders Him *passé*. The One who says "I am Jehovah: I have not changed" can also say, without contradiction, "Behold, I make all things new." When the Prophet Muhammad, peace and blessings be upon him, said, "before He created the universe, God was alone, without a partner," and Hazrat 'Ali replied "and He is even now as He was," this in no way contradicted the words of the Holy Qur'an [55:29] *every day doth some new work employ Him*. His Oneness, His Aloneness, His Changelessness are in fact the guarantee of His eternal Newness and Freshness; only the Changeless can impregnate each passing moment with its particular and eternal character without being swept away into the dustheap of things dead, gone and moribund. And insofar as Traditionalist doctrine draws from the eternal well of Revelation and Intellection, it too enshrines a core of Truth that cannot be corrupted by time. As for being reactionary, Traditionalism does indeed "react," as religion has always done, against the passions, against the system of passion-bound collective egotism known as This World, against all that veils or perverts the image of God within the human soul, all that makes us less than ourselves, while inflating our empty pretensions beyond all bounds. Truth does not change, nor do the fundamental passions and intellectual errors of the fallen soul. But the social, cultural and historical renditions of these passions and errors do change, which necessitates a continual updating of religion's critique of This World and a constant re-presentation, in contemporary terms and in response to contemporary conditions, of the perennial Truth.

Dr. Legenhausen characterizes the metaphysics and esoterism of Traditionalist doctrine in the following terms: "Its positive theses about perennial philosophy romanticize the occult aspects of the world's religious traditions and are backed by unsupported assumptions, tenuous comparisons based on a prejudiced selection of materials, and rather wild speculations." If so, its speculations are no more wild than those of the Prophet Muhammad, 'Ali ibn Abi-Talib, al-Ghazzali, Ibn al-'Arabi, Jalaluddin Rumi, Suharawardi, Mulla Sadra, Moses de Leon, Isaac Luria, Plato, Aristotle, Plotinus, Iamblichus, St. Paul, St. Augustine, St. Thomas Aquinas, Origen, Clement of Alexandria, Dionysius the Areopagite, Maximos the Confessor, Scotus Eriugena, Meister Eckhart, Dante Aligheri, Ramanuja, Shankaracharya, Ramakrishna, Ramana Maharshi, Swami Ram Das, the *I Ching*, Lao Tzu, Chuang Tzu, Confucius, Nagarjuna, Ashvagosha, Milarepa, Dōgen—a list which could be almost indefinitely extended. These figures, and hundreds like them, represent the highest, deepest and widest expressions, outside the revealed scriptures themselves, of the intellectual and spiritual heritage of the human race. And Traditionalist doctrine, insofar as it lives up to its name and has not become deviant, draws almost exclusively upon this heritage, as well as upon the word of scripture itself. The deeper doctrines of these sages are not essentially "occult," (certainly not in the sense of heterodox modern "occultism"), unless we denote by this word that which is effectively hidden from most people, though not from the saints and sages. And there is no saint or sage of any tradition who has not known— either intellectually or existentially—the essence of what Traditionalism teaches, and declares to be necessary for Salvation, Enlightenment, or Liberation. This is not because Traditionalist doctrines represent a kind of meta-religion superseding the revealed traditional paths, but because each of these paths does indeed, from its own unique perspective, touch upon Absolute Truth. And certainly the Bible, the Qur'an, the Upanishads may appear to some to be filled with romanticism and wild speculation, but only those whose minds are essentially closed to the mystical aspects of spiritual truth will see them like this. To reject Traditionalist doctrine (though certainly not to simply criticize it) is to implicitly reject almost the entire spiritual heritage of the human race—to put what in its place?

At this point I must address a "perennial" difficulty of discourse on spiritual matters—that of spiritual or intellectual pride. I have clearly implied here that Dr. Legenhausen's mind is closed to the mystical aspect of spiritual truth, though certainly not to its social and moral aspects, while my own mind is not thus closed. Here we encounter the great danger of the open public expression of esoteric truth such as so often takes place in our times, and even seems to be called for by the quality of these times. In earlier days, as well as in many places in today's world outside the modern west, such expressions might have resulted, and sometimes still do result, in the arrest and even the execution of the one offering them. In today's west the danger is more subtle, but possibly even more insidiously dangerous on a spiritual level. I am referring to the danger of *insolence*, of offering unmerited insult to those of sincerity, good character, wide education and solid mental intelligence. Places and times that repaid (or presently repay) the open expression of mystical truth with martyrdom, at least exhibit the virtue of taking spiritual things seriously. Today's west, on the other hand, is insufferably glib about mystical doctrines, so much so that many self-styled esoterics will often express open scorn for those "mere moralists" without whom this wonderful "open" society that allows them to speak and write without persecution would long since have fallen into total ruin. I sincerely hope that I have avoided this trap. However, I can only speak as I am given to speak, and so the reader must expect that from time to time I will speak on my own authority, on the theory that "because I see, I know"—to which Dr. Legenhausen has every right to reply, "I, however, do not see what you see, I see something else. Your 'seeing' cannot establish truth for me, nor (for that matter) for anyone else who does not see through your eyes." If this is indeed his position (I apologize for the audacity of putting these words in his mouth), then I entirely accept it, as I must. Nonetheless, I must also proceed to express myself in the only way I can, and if this results in there being no real point of concrete dialogue between us, since we are speaking on essentially different levels, then I see no way this problem can be avoided. In truth, it never could.

Dr. Legenhausen takes his most succinct definition of Traditionalism from Jaroslav Pelikan, to the effect that "*Tradition* is the living faith of the dead; *traditionalism* is the dead faith of the living. *Tradition* lives in conversation with the past, while remembering where we are and when we are and that it is we who have to decide. *Traditionalism* supposes that nothing should ever be done for the first time, so all that is needed to solve any problem is to arrive at the supposedly unanimous testimony of this homogenized tradition." In my opinion, however, it would be much more accurate to say that Tradition lives in conversation with Eternity. It is related to the past by virtue of the fact that what has already happened, and is thus temporally established, provides a more complete (though still limited) reflection of what is eternally established by God's timeless and present Act of Creation than the uncertain possibilities of future time. Tradition's special relationship with the past is not based on nostalgia for a better time so much as on the intrinsic relationship of God as Pure Act with what has already been temporally actualized—not to mention the more obvious fact that all "examples" or "exemplars" of any kind whatsoever must necessarily occupy the past or the present, not the future. On the other hand, Tradition is also a dialogue with the future. The Hebrew word *Kabbalah*, usually translated as "tradition," actually denotes an openness and readiness on the part of the "sons" to receive the wisdom of the "fathers." This wisdom may emanate from Eternity as represented by "the Ancient of Days," the Always So, but from the point of view of the "sons"—who comprise anyone in need of teaching, open to teaching, and actually in the presence of teaching—it arrives from the direction of their "future"; it is first potency, then act, first a longing for Wisdom, then (God willing) the actuality of Wisdom itself. Only those individuals or groups or cultures who think they can effectively possess the truths of their religious traditions without in fact actualizing them, in the present moment, in the living human soul, are "moribund." They have left the past *in* the past. They have not called it forward; they have not called it up; they have not made their own spiritual futures pregnant with it. Yes, there is such a thing as the "dead hand of tradition"; it is the hand of whoever is unwilling to grasp the plough and move forward on the spiritual path, whoever believes that he or she can somehow possess what they have never lifted their hand to take possession of. The metallurgist who leaves the ore in the ground in the belief that he that he thereby holds it in safekeeping has "buried his talent"—or rather, he has never smelted, hammered, cut and stamped it in the first place. That past he assumes is safely dead is in reality a living potential lying hidden in *his own* future—if he only knew. The ego, however—individual or collective—wants to possess spiritual truth, but it does not want to be changed by what it believes it holds title to. It thinks that it can possess God through identification alone, rather than by coming to realize, through death to all it has held itself to be, that it is in fact wholly possessed by Him. In the words of Frithjof Schuon, "Knowledge only saves us on condition that it enlists all that we are, only when it is a way and when it works and transforms and wounds our nature, even as the plough wounds the soil" (*Spiritual Perspectives and Human Facts*, pp.144–145). And the same can certainly be said of morality and religious law. Nor does Traditionalism as I have defined it believe that "nothing should be done for the first time"; rather, it knows that all things that are of God can *only* be done for the "first time", for the first time and never again—and also (speaking from a different perspective) *always* again, just like the first time. This is the principle of all canonical liturgy, like the Muslim *salat* or the Divine Liturgy of the Christians, which teaches us to recognize passing moments not as temporal sequence alone but also as unique instances of Eternity entering, by God's will, the temporal order: "Before Abraham came to be, I am." Their occasions may multiply, their reflections may perennially find their unique and chosen instances, but God's acts themselves, once spoken in His creative Eternity, remain what they are. They are the essences, the permanent archetypes, the Platonic Ideas. This is indeed the unanimous testimony of Tradition—not "homogenized" as Pelikan would have it, but rather refracting, by means of its multiple and unique facets, both spacial and temporal, the One Light.

Let us now proceed to answer various assertions of Dr. Legenhausen point-by-point, in his three categories of Pluralism, Modernism and Fundamentalism.

PLURALISM

[The italicized passages that follow in the rest of this chapter are quotations from the article by Dr. Legenhausen, "Why I am Not a Traditionalist", that appeared (and may still be posted) at http://www.religioscope.com/info/doc/esotrad/legenhausen.htm.]

The key ideas of the Traditionalists regarding the unity of religions [are]: (1) that all the major religions have a divine source; (2) that esoterically they are the same but exoterically different; and (3) that traces of the original perennial wisdom are to be found in the religions, are clearly stated by Madame Blavatsky in the introduction to The Secret Doctrine:

> The true philosopher, the student of the Esoteric Wisdom, entirely loses sight of personalities, dogmatic beliefs and special religions. Moreover, Esoteric philosophy reconciles all religions, strips every one of its outward, human garments, and shows the root of each to be identical with that of every other great religion [H. P. Blavatsky, *The Secret Doctrine*, vol. 1, p. 20, Theosophical University Press Online edition].

Frithjof Schuon, however, is explicitly opposed to "stripping the religions of their outward, human garments," which, while recognizing these as limitations, sees them as necessary and providential. And Blavatsky's "esoteric philosophy" does not reconcile the religions but simply denies them *en masse*. In *The Secret Doctrine* she limits to Judaism "phallicism and star-worship," calls Christ's cross a penis, asserts that "every 'sacrifice' or prayer to God is *no better than an act of black magic*," and says, "whatever the allegory [of the separation of the sexes in Genesis] may mean, even its exoteric meaning necessitates a *divine* Builder of man—a 'Progenitor.' Do we then believe in such 'supernatural' beings? We say, No. Occultism has never believed in anything, whether animate or inanimate, outside nature." A more total contradiction than the one between these lurid and materialistic assertions and the doctrines of Guénon, Schuon and the Traditionalist School is simply not imaginable.

The main differences between Blavatsky and the Traditionalists are:

(1) she rejects the concept of a personal God found in the monotheistic religions as exoterically interpreted in favour of a more pantheistic view; (2) she considers Christianity to have deviated from the original doctrine, especially after Constantine, and in general, she holds that the forms of religion now found in the world are all to a greater or lesser extent deviations from the original doctrine she claims to have uncovered.

It is true that both Blavatsky and Guénon asserted the reality of a Primordial Religion, but this does not mean that Guénon got it from Blavatsky; even though he might or might not first have heard of it through the Theosophical Society, this in no way indicates that he would ever have taken the Theosophical Society as his authority for it. In Hinduism, the existence of a Primordial Religion is embraced by the doctrine of the *Sanatana Dharma* (in Muslim terms, *al-Din al-Fitrah*; cf. Q.3:3). Both Blavatsky and Guénon drew on traditional sources; the difference between them was that Guénon was largely true to his sources, while Blavatsky perverted them, in almost every case, by taking them out of their traditional contexts.

Guénon came to the conclusion that Madame Blavatsky was a charlatan . . . [but] this is not the place to evaluate Blavatsky's credentials. . . .

Perhaps, however, we can cut to the chase on this issue by quoting Blavatsky herself: "What is one to do when, in order to rule men, you must deceive them, when, in order to catch them and make them pursue whatever it may be, it is necessary to promise and show them toys? Suppose my books and *The Theosophist* were a thousand times more interesting and serious, do you think that I would have anywhere to live and any degree of success unless behind all this there stood 'phenomena'? I should have achieved absolutely nothing, and would long ago have pegged out from hunger." [Quoted in *The Spiritualists* by Ruth Brandon: Alfred A. Knopf, 1983, p.13]

The . . . pluralism advocated by Blavatsky and the Traditionalists . . . depends on a rather questionable reading of the texts of the world's religions. It requires that one hold that certain similarities in doctrine, especially esoteric doctrine, constitute the core of the religions, and that differences be dismissed as deviations. Blavatsky supported this

interpretation with the dubious claim that she had discovered the orig-
inal secret teachings. The Traditionalists, on the other hand, claim that
through intellectual intuition they are able to discern the common
essence. The method used is implausible. It is assumed at the outset
that the religions have a common esoteric essence, and the texts are
interpreted so as to accord with this principle. This is question begging.

Here Dr. Legenhausen seems to forget that he has already attributed the kind of "pluralism" which sees all religious divergences as
"corruptions" to Blavatsky, not to Guénon and the Traditionalists.
Blavatsky did not so much advocate pluralism as devalue, and often
slanderously attack, the revealed religions in the name of a universal
esoterism that could be practiced *as a religion in itself.* This putative
universal esoteric religion ultimately took the form of an "esoteric
Buddhism" which was neither truly esoteric nor traditionally Buddhist, and to which various occult and spiritualistic practices and
beliefs adhered. And Traditionalism does not "dismiss" differences
as "deviations," but sees in them providential variations of a common primordial tradition, designed to make saving truth available
to those living in different cultures and historical periods, as well as
to different spiritual "types." And for those in whom Intellection is a
working faculty, the Truth apprehended by "the eye of the Heart" is
not derived from a synoptic reading of the mystical and scriptural
texts of the various religions, based on an assumption of their common essence, but is seen directly; it is this intellective vision, in fact,
which makes the synoptic reading of such texts both possible and
valid. The faculty of Intellection may be nurtured by scripture and
tradition—its development entirely outside such a context is in fact
extremely rare, and in any case would lack any language in which to
express itself—but such Intellection in turn is the seal and proof of
scripture and tradition, just as the actual experiment is the proof of
a given scientific theory. The idea that religions have a common
esoteric essence is not *assumed*; it is *perceived.* And essential to such
perception is the intuition of the Absolute. If the various religions,
all of whom in their unique spiritual dialects posit an Absolute,
were not in fact talking about an actual Reality—necessarily One,
since a plurality of absolutes is absurd—they would be worse than
useless, mere caricatures of the truth like the atheists assume they

are, various brands and grades of "the opium of the people." If religion has any validity at all, it must refer to an actual transcendent Reality. And if more than one revealed religion is valid, as the doctrine of the Transcendent Unity of Religions declares, then all valid religions must ultimately be referring to the same Truth. The alternatives are either a radical exclusivism of one tradition which damns all others, or a devaluating relativization of all the religions, reducing them to self-referential belief systems with no Objective Referent at all—in other words, no God.

. . . according to Traditionalism [the criterion for religious truth] is something to be abstracted by intellectual intuition through a comparative interpretation of the world's esoteric religious teachings.

Intellectual intuition does not abstract; it sees. And what it sees is not a lowest theological common denominator based on an academic comparison of doctrines from different traditions, but rather the Unity of God—Allah according to His name *al-Ahad*. From the standpoint of this Unity, the similarities in religious doctrines— particularly metaphysical or mystical doctrines—as they appear in the different religious traditions are understood as signs of God's Unity, just as the irreducible doctrinal differences between the various traditions are recognized as signs of God's Transcendence of all the forms through which He manifests, of Allah according to His names *al-Quddus* (the Holy), *al-Ali* (the Highest), and *al-Haqq* (the Truth).

Pluralists are forced to claim that [contradictions between religious doctrines] are either due to corruptions in the religious traditions, or . . . to inessential factors, such as culture. This sort of claim is not supported by an examination of the texts. . . .

Again, the Traditionalists claim that apparent contradictions between the religions are providential and necessary; while relative, they are certainly not inessential, since the Absolute Truth must of necessity express itself in terms of a plurality of relative forms. No given possibility is *absolutely* necessary, but the existence of a realm or level of possibility and relativity *is* necessary. The following quotations from Frithjof Schuon, Titus Burckhardt and René Guénon, encapsulate the Traditionalist doctrine of the providential necessity of a plurality of religious forms, and of the spiritual necessity of adherence to *one* of these forms, given that the *religio perennis* is not and cannot be a form in itself:

> What in reality one has to understand, is that the undeniable presence of the transcendent truth, of the sacred and supernatural, in religions other than that of our birth, ought to lead us, not in the least to doubt the Absolute character proper to our religion, but simply to acknowledge the inherence of the Absolute in other doctrinal and sacramental symbols which manifest It by definition, but which also by definition—since they belong to the formal order—are relative and limited, despite their quality of uniqueness. The latter quality is *necessary*, as we have said, inasmuch as it testifies to the Absolute, but it is merely indicative from the point of view of the Absolute in itself, which manifests itself necessarily by uniqueness, yet just as necessarily—by virtue of Its Infinitude—by the diversity of forms.... A given religion in reality sums up all religions... all religion is to be found in a given religion, because Truth is one [Frithjof Schuon, *From the Divine to the Human*: World Wisdom Books, 1982; pp.137–138, from the chapter "To Refuse or to Accept Revelation"; italics mine].

> Every religion by definition wants to be the best, and "must want" to be the best, as a whole and also as regards its constitutive elements; this is only natural, so to speak, or rather "supernaturally natural"... religious oppositions cannot but be, not only because forms exclude one another... but because, in the case of religions, each form vehicles an element of absoluteness that constitutes the justification for its existence; now the absolute does not tolerate otherness nor, with all the more reason, plurality.... To say form is to say exclusion of possibilities, whence the necessity for those excluded to become realized in other forms.... [Frithjof Schuon, from *Christianity/Islam: Essays in Esoteric Ecumenism*: World Wisdom Books, 1985; p.151]

There is no spiritual path outside the following traditions or religions: Judaism, Christianity, Islam, Buddhism, Hinduism and Taoism; but Hinduism is closed for those who have not been born into a Hindu caste, and Taoism is inaccessible. [Titus Burckhardt, *Mirror of the Intellect*: SUNY, 1987; p.25, from the chapter "A Letter on Spiritual Method"]

Adherence to an exoterism is a preliminary condition for coming to esoterism and furthermore one must not believe that this exoterism can be rejected once initiation has been obtained, any more than the foundation can be removed once the building has been constructed." [René Guénon, *Initiation and Spiritual Realization*: Sophia Perennis 2001, p. 43, from the chapter "The Necessity of Traditional Exoterism"]

There are theological grounds within Islamic teachings to reject the religious pluralism of the Traditionalists. The problem is not merely that Islam forbids idol worship, while idol worship is intrinsic to the non-monotheistic traditions. The problem is where the criterion for religious truth is to be found. According to Islam that criterion is given in God's final revelation to man. . . .

This assertion is based on a failure to discern the difference in level between an idol and a sacred image. And, given the place of sacred icons in Eastern Orthodox Christianity, it is just as incorrect to associate "idol worship" strictly with the non-monotheistic traditions as it is to call the veneration of sacred images "idol-worship". Icons are not idols, any more than are the sacred images employed in the Hindu and Buddhist traditions. An idol, in the strict religious sense, is an image, statue or fetish which is literally believed to be a god: a *source* of Divine power, not merely a channel for it. To worship such an image as literally divine would be the equivalent of worshipping the Qur'an as a separate goddess, or doing the same with the Ark of the Covenant. The Prophet Muhammad himself, peace and blessings be upon him, recognized the sacrosanct quality of sacred images when he protected the icon of the Virgin and Child on the inner wall of the Kaaba from being destroyed along with the pagan idols that had collected there over the generations. The prohibition of sacred imagery in Islam, especially in terms of pictorial representations of Allah or the Prophet—though certainly *not* in terms of architectural design and calligraphy—cannot be used to call into question the validity of sacred imagery in non-Islamic contexts. The Prophet also expressed great respect for Christian monasticism, while making it clear that there was to be no monasticism in Islam; in other words, he recognized that particular supports for the spiritual life may be valid and effective in certain traditional contexts but not in others.

[Islam] presents a relatively egalitarian social ideal...[however] Traditionalists such as Martin Lings continue to defend the Hindu caste system as being a part of authentic tradition [as a manifestation of the hierarchical nature of being], rather than condemning it on the basis of Islamic teachings...Traditionalists base their evaluations on the conceit that they can view all of the religions from some higher transcendent perspective.

But the Holy Qur'an itself views the religions known to the Arabs in the Prophet's time from this "higher transcendent perspective," in its doctrine that all "people of the book" possess true and divine revelations, however much some nominal believers in these revelations may have fallen away from them; in the Qur'an itself, God directs Muhammad to say *we make no distinction between any of His messengers* [2:285]. Islam is not a *sect*. Though in its outer form it necessarily possesses forms peculiar to itself, laws and practices designed to recall believers to sanctity, and designed to meet the specific spiritual needs of the people to which it is addressed, in its essence it is a return to *al-Din al-Fitrah*, the primordial religion of the human race. In the words of the Qur'an (3:3): *He hath revealed unto thee (Muhammad) the Scripture with truth, confirming that which was (revealed) before it, even as He revealed the Torah and the Gospel.*

The Traditionalists would certainly accept egalitarianism in Islam insofar as it is an essential element, but they would not ignore the fact that such egalitarianism has not been the rule in historical Islam, only the ideal—not to mention the fact that traditional Islamic egalitarianism is fundamentally different from the revolutionary egalitarianisms, bourgeois and proletarian, of the west. The doctrine of the perfect Imam within Shi'ism, the pre-eminence (though not political entitlement) of the seyyeds, the Caliphs of Baghdad who were dynastic kings in all but name, show an egalitarianism greatly curtailed by the realities of history. History, too, however, is an expression of God's will and providence, as well as of the inevitable sufferings and shortcomings of earthly life, insofar as the universe is not God.

Intellectual intuition, even if accepted as a valid way of obtaining knowledge, does not support esoteric pluralism.

Why not? Intellection is not simply the realization of the Formless Absolute, or of Allah in terms of the Names of the Essence alone, but also of the metaphysical necessity, in light of the One, of possibility and multiplicity—what Frithjof Schuon calls *Maya-in-divinis.*

Esoteric differences among the religious differences are proportionate to their exoteric differences. Common features among religious traditions may be found by abstracting and generalizing from their exoteric features no less than from their esoteric features.

This is not correct. The esoteric aspects of the world's religions are much closer to true unanimity than their exoteric aspects, though never strictly identical. For example, the prophetic *hadith* "he who knows himself knows his Lord" is closely analogous to Meister Eckhart's "my truest 'I' is God" and St. Paul's "it is not I who live, but Christ lives in me", as both are to the Vedantic concept of the Indwelling Absolute Witness, the *atman.* On a more exoteric level, however, the doctrine of Jesus Christ as the only-begotten Son of God is contradicted by the *surah At-Tauhid* of the Qur'an where it is said of Allah *he neither begets not is begotten,* and also by the Hindu Puranas, where the major divine incarnations, the avatars of Vishnu, are not one in number but ten.

Pluralism conflicts with Islamic teaching, because Islam presents itself as the final and definitive religion for mankind and not as culture bound, while pluralism sees the differences between Islam and other traditions to be due to cultural accidents.

Islam does not deny the other revelations but confirms them. It declares itself definitive and "quasi-absolute" only insofar as it denies the possibility of a newer revelation before the coming of the Hour, and makes itself quasi-absolutely incumbent upon all who follow Muhammad, the last Prophet. And who could possibly say that the shari'ah, after 1400 years of interpretation, carries no cultural conditioning? The only aspect of Islam that is not (now) culture-bound is the essence of *al-Din*: submission to God. And submission to God is possible, and necessary, within every religion; as Jesus prayed in Gethsemane, "not my will but Thine be done." Even non-theistic Theravada Buddhism, in its practice of vipassana, requires that we witness the ongoing changes of bodily sensations, feelings, mind-set and mind-contents—including all the events of the world, precisely as experienced—with no editorializing or inter-ference. Such practice is strictly equivalent to submission to the Will of God, since whatever happens is in fact God's Will, given that He is *Lord of the worlds*, and that He shows us His signs both *in our souls* and *on the horizons*. The Transcendent Unity of Religions sees the differences between religions not as mere cultural accidents—not to mention the fact that the cultures initiated or modified by God's revelations are providential too, consequently there is nothing "mere" about them—but either as providential receptacles "wait-ing" for God's revelations, or as subsequent elaborations and echoes of those very revelations.

Traditionalists use tradition and the intellectual intuition of the principles of sophia perennis as their criteria of evaluation instead of the principles of Islam.

This should not surprise us, since one need not be a Muslim to be a Traditionalist—as Dr. Legenhausen elsewhere admits—and given that there is nothing essential in the *sophia perennis* which cannot be found, in its own unique rendition, in the religion of Islam. The question of whether various traditionalist writers speak in the lan-guage of "comparative religion," or that of a particular religion such as Islam, or Christianity (as do Philip Sherrard, James Cutsinger, Rama Coomaraswamy, and, insofar as he may be called a Tradition-alist, Jean Borella) depends largely upon their intended audience.

MODERNISM

Modernization is a fact of life. Traditionalists make some valid points about its failings, but on the whole, people do not have a choice as to whether they would like to live in a traditional or modern way. . . . Consider computerization. Dr. Nasr condemns this as modern and untraditional [cf. *Traditional Islam and the Modern World*, p.24, n.8]. *No doubt there is much about computer use that clashes with Islamic aims and values. To a large extent, however, it is unavoidable. On the other hand, there is much in computer use that serves Islamic aims. . . .*

Though I have composed this article on a computer, much faster and more easily than I could have on a typewriter, and though I use the internet almost daily for research purposes, I agree with Dr. Nasr (and Dr. Legenhausen) about the destructive quality of the medium, which has created, in "cyberspace," a reality at once less real and more rarefied than the natural world, a mode of perception which robs our sense experience of its substance, and consequently of our ability to recognize it as ensemble of "signs" of its Creator. Furthermore, cyberspace by its electronic rarefaction counterfeits the higher planes of Being, obscuring them more completely than even "industrial" materialism was able to do, and directly opening the door to René Guénon's "invasion of the infra-psychic." But I also agree with Dr. Legenhausen that modernization, and cyberspace, are facts of life. To imagine doing without them, outside (perhaps) of a monastic context, is a foolish fantasy; the real need is not to be *impressed* by them. The electronic media, and modernism as a whole, represent degradations of the entire cosmic environment and insidious violations of the human form—degradations and violations that, however, are predicted in the eschatological lore of every tradition as inescapable conditions of the "latter days", and which are thus, in the larger sense, entirely lawful according to God's will: not His *wish* for us, as expressed in the spiritual norms He has laid down for us, but His sovereign right to respond to transgression and imbalance with the rigor of divine Justice. The Holy Qur'an, in the *surah The Calamity,* speaks of *a day wherein mankind will be as thickly-scattered moths / And the mountains will become as carded wool*: which is to say that when the human psyche becomes unstable and "flighty", the world itself loses stability and substance. To engage in degradations which can be avoided is sinful; to accept and use degradations which cannot be avoided is simple realism. And if understood correctly, it may also be an approach to humility.

The critical historical attitude [in religious studies], once estab-
lished, can never be banished. There can be no restoration of meta-
physics to its former authority. This is felt nowhere so keenly as in
theology. The error of modernism is to believe that historical study
makes metaphysics otiose, merely another item for historical inquiry
itself. The error of traditionalism is to hope for a reassertion of meta-
physical principles in a victory over historical criticism.

Correct. Metaphysics is certainly not destined to triumph over
historical criticism on a collective level, though it may still be able to
set up for itself certain cultural refuges. But every human being
who, within the sanctuary of his or her own heart, is able to attain
true certainty as to the reality of metaphysics, and thus the reality of
God as an Absolute and Eternal Reality, transcending history while
acting freely within it—and in no way subject to historical influences, as certain heretics within various religions now so foolishly
and destructively assert—such a man or woman has a chance for
spiritual illumination in this world and Paradise in the next. As for
those who sacrilegiously attempt to make Allah, *Lord of the Worlds,*
Owner of the Day of Judgment the abject slave of history, theirs—in
the words of the Holy Qur'an—will be a painful doom, the nature
of which will be to inherit the precise quality and consequences of
their own shrunken and barren conception.

Theology . . . has been shaped by modern scientific, rational, and
historical assumptions. We participate in the age of which we are a part.

Certainly this is true. But it is equally true that insofar as modern
scientific, rational and historical assumptions deny God—and it is
clear that they largely do—then whatever has fallen under their
influence, rather than learning to respond critically and creatively
to such influence from its own eternal standpoint, is no longer *the-*
ology in any sense of the word. Historicism has forgotten eternity; it
has not abolished it. Anyone who remembers eternity, therefore,
will be free of historicism—not ignorant of it, certainly, but rather
fully equipped to understand it, criticize it, respond to it, and possibly even use it. But such a person will never pay court to it, since to
take what denies God as one's "spiritual guide" is purely and simply
to deny God Himself, and inherit the tremendous consequences of
such denial. God is indeed "above the historical flow of things,"

therefore theology, as the study of God, must embrace an a-historical element. Theology is better compared to the science of crystal-
lography than to that of historical criticism; the hardness,
translucence and octahedral crystal structure of the diamond are
not affected by human history, though they are certainly not
beyond the bounds of scientific analysis. As James Joyce said, "history is a nightmare from which I am trying to awake." May we all
awake from that nightmare, not into some fantasy of an idealized
past, but into the concrete knowledge that *all is perishing except His
face* (Q. 28:88).

*The challenge for Muslims and Christians is to find a way through
the process in which faith is maintained despite the evils of modernization. The hope for Muslim societies is that they may move beyond
modernization without suffering all the injuries this has brought in the
West, in shā'Allah.*

I could not agree more fully with this statement. And one of the
greatest of these evils, perhaps even the root of them, is the eclipse
of the metaphysical worldview, as well as its theological expression,
by the critical-historical one. The tools and procedures of critical
historicism certainly have their place, but to the degree that they
have come to dominate theology, they represent nothing less than
the death of religion, the empty shell of which may still retain that
name, while being devoid of the substance heretofore indicated by
it. Dr. Legenhausen makes it clear that nostalgia for an idealized
past, reactionary politics, and an unwillingness to understand the
nature and inevitability of modernism, are wrongheaded, barren
responses to the modern world; in this I fully agree with him. The
true function of religion is not to fight modernism blow for blow,
but to resist being destroyed by it, so that it may continue to point
to a Reality which lies beyond it—in the next world mysteriously
present in the Heart of this one—where are *gardens beneath which
rivers flow.* If this vision of the eternity of the Divine order and the
eschatological (*not* historical) inevitability of its triumph is maintained, then at least a remnant from Islam, as well as from the other
religions, will find their way beyond the evils of modernism. If this
vision is not maintained, if it is betrayed and abandoned, then truly
we will be *among the losers.*

Coomaraswamy and Guénon did not invent dissatisfaction with modernity. . . . Among the voices of dissent may be found Romantic poets, like Blake and Wordsworth, Catholic ultramontanists, philosophers from Nietzsche to Heidegger, and, not surprisingly, Blavatsky and Olcott. . . . For the Catholics, modern woes are due to neglect of the teachings of the Church. For the Romantics, the neglected truth is one that can only be grasped through the heart, or some sort of feeling or experience. For Heidegger, the problems of modern society are the result of a long progressive neglect of the question of Being stretching back to antiquity. For Blavatsky, Olcott, Guénon and Coomaraswamy, the problems of modernity arise from neglect of the perennial wisdom found in the esoteric teachings of the great religions. . . .

Certainly the Traditionalists are not alone in condemning modernity, nor is their critique the only valid one. All the "missing" elements in the collective human soul lamented by the above figures are, as it were, fragments of what an integral human being would be. All these critiques are right to a degree; none are exclusively right; and some are much more right than others—which is to say that these various critiques of modernity form a hierarchy. One of the things which distinguishes the Traditionalists from the other groups and individuals mentioned is their "universal eschatology," perhaps best expressed in Martin Ling's *The Eleventh Hour* [Archetype, 2002], or my *The System of Antichrist* [Sophia Perennis, 2001]. Their essentially entropic view of history, intrinsically opposed to progressivism and evolutionism, discerns a common doctrine in the Hindu *manvantara* or *mahayuga*, in the cyclical theories of the Greco-Romans, the Lakota and the Hopis, and clear reflections of this doctrine in the apocalyptic eschatologies of the Abrahamic religions. According to the prophetic *hadith*, "no generation will come upon you that is not followed by a worse"; in the words of the Holy Qur'an, *By the declining day, Lo! Mankind is in a state of loss.* (Q. 103)

In all of these groups there is a common implausible causal claim, that the neglect of some truths is what causes the problems associated with modernity. As far as I know, none of the members of any of the groups mentioned does anything to substantiate this claim. It is taken to be obvious that since moderns have neglected the Truth and have various social problems, the neglect is the cause of the social problems.

Consider the following statement by Dr. Seyyed Hossein Nasr:

> But the opposition of tradition to modernism, which is total and complete as far as principles are concerned, does not derive from the observation of facts and phenomena or the diagnosis of the symptoms of the malady. It is based upon a study of the causes which have brought about the illness. Tradition is opposed to modernism because it considers the premises upon which modernism is based to be wrong and false in principle [*Knowledge and the Sacred*, p. 84].

This is a gross oversimplification. The relation between modern thought and the characteristics of modern societies is a complex one in which social changes influence thought and vice versa. In order to understand the problems of modernity, more observation of facts and phenomena is needed than metaphysics. European modernization took place as European societies became increasingly industrialized. The changes wrought by industrialization led to shifts in political power and authority, and these shifts are reflected in modern political philosophies, including Marxism, liberalism and the various forms of traditionalism, for the reactions against the changes that accompanied industrialization are no less modern than the positivistic euphoria assailed by Guénon and Lings.

Dr. Legenhausen is right that Dr. Nasr's statement is oversimplified: in reality, the opposition of tradition to modernism is based on a close observation and analysis of the facts *in light of* metaphysics. But insofar as modernism denies the existence of God, the validity of religious revelations (including Islam), the existence of levels of Being higher and more inclusive than the material and/or socio-historical, and the reality of Divine Providence, it is indeed diametrically opposed to Traditional values. To the degree that it tolerates these things it is not entirely unfriendly to Tradition, but its denial is obviously much more fundamental than its "tolerance."

Dr. Legenhausen quotes René Guénon:

> What we call normal civilization is a civilization which is based on principles, in the true sense of the term, and where everything is ordained and hierarchically arranged in conformity

with these principles, so that everything there is seen as the application and extension of a doctrine purely intellectual or metaphysical in its essence; this is what we mean also when we speak of a "traditional" civilization. [Guénon, *Orient et Occident* (Paris: Payot, 1924, p. 236), cited in Quinn, p. 179]

Legenhausen comments:
The evils of feudalism are to be excused because feudalism is seen as an institution that was produced by a society dominated by Traditional beliefs and values and in turn the system protected those beliefs and values. The social pressures that made the feudal system intolerable and led to its overthrow are ignored, and the shift is glossed as having been brought about by a neglect of the perennial wisdom on which feudal society was based!

Social evils are inevitable. It is only when the *raison d'être* of a given social order becomes implausible to the mass of the people—when the payoff in terms of *meaning* is no longer felt to be worth the price in terms of suffering—that these evils gradually (and sometimes suddenly) become insupportable. It was the loss of the traditional worldview (a loss which made possible Cervantes' satirical treatment of chivalry in his *Don Quixote*) that rendered the undeniable evils of the feudal order ultimately intolerable.

In place of the modernist faith in unlimited progress in which technology and "enlightened" thinking are supposed to lead to a continual improvement in the human condition, Traditionalists posit that modernization is a process of unmitigated decline, explained by Guénon in terms of the grand cycles of Hindu cosmology.

Mitigated decline, I would rather call it. Traditionalist doctrine leaves rooms for periodic "redresses" interrupting the downward course of the cycle; a *hadith* is often quoted to the effect that "at the head of every hundred years, Allah will send one who will renew the religion." Each successive historical age represents a more-or-less effective struggle to rise from the pit of the decadence left by the demise of age before it, and to re-establish human life on a new level, one that is spiritually lower than the prime of the preceding age, but certainly higher and better than the chaos that characterized its end. A relatively secular analogy would be High Middle Ages in France, the later decline of the feudal order into absolute monarchy, the decadence of Versailles, the Revolution and the Reign of Terror, and then the relative stability—on an undeniably lower spiritual level than that of the medieval period—ultimately imposed by Napoleon.

While modernists seem blind to the spiritual crisis of modern man, the rape of the environment, the evils of colonialism and neo-colonialism, the weakening of the family, etc., Traditionalists seem blind to the benefits brought by modernization, the vast increase in literacy and availability of education, public health and sanitation, more humane treatment of prisoners and the insane, etc. The benefits of modernization cannot be ignored any more than its failings, even when judged not by the standards of modernity itself, but in accordance with traditional values. It is pointless to attempt any overall evaluation by which to justify the claim that modernity is better than what preceded it or worse. In some respects it is better, and in other respects worse.

It is undoubtedly true that Traditionalists are sometimes blind to, and thus take for granted, the achievements of modernity—one of which is the very democratic "freedom of speech and religion" which allows them to practice their religions and publish their doctrines. An overall evaluation of modernity, however, is only possible if the eternal destiny of the human soul is recognized as the highest value, thus making it possible—though certainly not easy—to judge *any* society *definitively* in terms of whether it openly supports, passively tolerates, or actively opposes the recognition and pursuit of this highest value. To the degree that societies are considered only in terms of how well they serve worldly well-being, such definitive judgments cannot be made.

According to Catholic traditionalists, the traditions of the Church are sacred because the Holy Spirit guides the Church through history. This doctrine means that practices and beliefs that have no other justification than that they have been around as long as anyone can remember are given an aura of holiness.

On the contrary, they are justified by their effective theurgic power, which must be based on traditional sacramental forms—or at least forms that have not been so fundamentally altered that they no longer recognize the essential Cause or the intended effect of the sacrament in question—as well as on an unbroken apostolic succession through which the "initiatory" power of the sacrament is transmitted. To take an analogy from genetics, if an individual is adopted rather than begotten in only one generation of a family tree, the entire original genetic heritage is lost. This analogy is imperfect in that it leaves out of the question the operation of that Grace which "bloweth where it listeth," but it does give a clear picture of one undeniably necessary, though not sufficient, dimension of Tradition—the one called in Sufism the *silsilah* or chain of transmission, and in Christianity "the apostolic succession".

[*Both*] *Catholic and Guénonian traditionalists see traditions as sacred because they are in some way manifestations or elaborations of divine revelation. Revelation becomes manifest in tradition. This sort of veneration of tradition results in a very extreme sort of conservatism, one that is open to moral criticism according to the very tenets and values of the traditions the Traditionalist pretends to defend.*

Does Dr. Legenhausen deny that what we know today as the religion of Islam is in fact a manifestation and elaboration of a specific divine revelation, the Holy Qur'an? And if not, then what is left of Islam as a religion? In places he seems to condemn secularization, but this *is* secularization, precisely.

Traditionalism is . . . an ideology in the sense that it: (1) *contains a more or less comprehensive theory about the world and the place of man in it;* (2) *sets out a general program of social and political direction;* (3) *it foresees itself as surviving through onslaughts against it;* (4) *it seeks not merely to persuade but to recruit loyal adherents, demanding what is sometimes called commitment;* (5) *it addresses a wide public but tends to confer some special role of leadership on intellectuals.*

This might or might not be a valid definition of an ideology, but is it not also quite close (with a few possible exceptions) to the general definition of the exoteric or socio-historical aspects of a religion—*any* religion, including Islam?

As for the political program of Traditionalism, it is perhaps most clearly stated by Dr. Nasr:

In the political domain, the traditional perspective always insists upon realism based upon Islamic norms. In the Sunni

world, it accepts the classical caliphate and, in its absence, the
other political institutions, such as the sultanate, which developed over the centuries in the light of the teachings of the
Sharī'ah and the needs of the community. Under no condition,
however, does it seek to destroy what remains of traditional
Islamic political institutions.... As for the Shi'ite world, the
traditional perspective continues to insist that final authority
belongs to the Twelfth Imam, in whose absence no form of
government can be perfect. In both worlds, the traditional perspective remains always aware of the fall of the community
from its original perfection, the danger of destroying traditional Islamic institutions and substituting those of modern,
Western, origin.... [Seyyed Hossein Nasr, *Traditional Islam in
the Modern World*, p.17]

*Traditionalists... laud governments based on the sovereignty of
sultans and so-called caliphs as traditional, while playing down the
corruptions and excesses of such governments as imperfections that
should be tolerated to prevent the danger that some Western model of
government might come to power. This is reactionary politics at its
worst.*

If Dr. Nasr is indeed proposing the restoration of the caliphate, or
some equivalent of the Ottoman sultanate, or some other form of
"imposed Tradition", as inseparable from Traditionalism, I cannot
follow him in this hope. But I don't believe this is what he is saying.
Insofar as Dr. Nasr refers to an attempt to preserve what remains of
traditional Islamic political institutions, such an attempt is indeed
Traditional, at least insofar as it can be successful without the establishment of reactionary "fundamentalist" governments which may
claim this as one of their goals, while in effect destroying what
might have remained of such institutions in their truly Traditional
form. In the early stages of the Iranian Revolution, certain Sufis, or
people sympathetic to Sufism, saw in the Ayatollah Khomeini the
possibility of a restoration of a true Traditional culture on the
socio-political plane—perhaps influenced by the "Sufi" pretensions
of Khomeini himself! Included among these idealists were certain
individuals who had been attached, as Dr. Nasr was, to the Imperial

Iranian Academy of Philosophy, which flourished under the patronage of the Shah's wife, the Shahbanou Farah Pahlavi. The reality, unfortunately, was other than they had expected: the widespread oppression of Sufism in Iran [see Leonard Lewisohn, *Bulletin of the School of Oriental and African Studies* of the University of London, volume 61, Part 3: Oxford University Press, 1998].

Furthermore, Dr. Legenhausen's characterization of "Traditionalist politics" according to Seyyed Hossein Nasr is directly contradicted by a half-sentence that Dr. Legenhausen conveniently deleted from the above quotation, its place now occupied by an ellipsis. The sentence in question actually reads: "Under no condition, however, does [the traditional perspective] destroy what remains of traditional Islamic political institutions, *which are controlled by traditional restraints, in the hope of installing another Abu Bakr or 'Umar but meanwhile settling for some form of dictatorship.*" [italics mine]. Dr. Legenhausen implies that Dr. Nasr's traditionalism, "reactionary politics at its worst," might even support a modern-day attempt to restore the caliphate; in so doing, he falsely characterizes Dr. Nasr's position and completely inverts his meaning. In reality Nasr criticizes both the foolishly reactionary tendency of fundamentalists to believe that the era of the "rightly-guided caliphs" can be restored at this late date, and their parallel tendency to adopt what is worst in western political organization.

Insofar as monarchical governments, however corrupt, preserve the collective sense of the reality and sovereignty of God—and I am not saying that the caliphate, the Ottoman sultanate, or other forms of monarchism necessarily did this in every case, or if restored would necessarily do so today—they serve Tradition as I understand it. The question, which must be answered on a case-by-case basis, is whether the corruption exhibited by such forms of government, or the secularization and democratization, according to the western model, which have often arisen in reaction to this corruption, have cast a deeper shadow on religion in the mind of the masses—a difficult question to answer, since the corruption of ancient regimes and the revolutionary democratization which such corruption has often called up may be seen as aspects or phases of the same cultural and spiritual degeneration. As a Sufi, I can state that no amount of patronage of Sufism can ever erase the crimes of the late Shah of Iran, just as no amount of progressivism and democratization can justify Ataturk's massacre of Sufis and other traditional Muslims. And I must also point out that the political triumph of Iranian Sufism in the Safavid Dynasty made "Sufi" a dirty word for generations; that major figures of the Nimatullahi Sufi Order in Iran supported the constitutionalist movement in the early twentieth century; and that the present Shi'ite regime in Iran has been extremely oppressive to Iranian Sufis, even though certain Sufis or Sufi-influenced individuals saw in it, at least in its earlier stages, the triumph of Traditional principles. So from the point of view of my own path, no form of government appears to be either necessarily good for or necessarily destructive to traditional spirituality. The real question is: does a given society as a whole believe in God, and does it embrace elements which support a sense of the sacred and an intuition of higher realities? The two most religious societies in the world, outside the Muslim world, are probably now India and the United States. Does this mean that, as opposed to the view of most Traditionalists, democracy is necessarily the best form of government when it comes to support for Tradition, and that democracy imposed on an ancient traditional caste system which is still partly in force is even better? Not necessarily. It simply means that the factors which most profoundly affect the state of religion and Tradition are not always political in nature. The French Revolution which ultimately established a bourgeois democracy was violently anti-clerical in its early stages, but ultimately came to terms with the churches; the American Revolution established religious freedom; the Russian Revolution made religious piety a social crime, while preserving, by its very oppressiveness, a deep core of Russian Orthodox spirituality. What most deeply undermines religion and Tradition are certain collective attitudes, such as distrust for traditional religious authority, the devaluation of metaphysics, the replacement of religion by psychology, and the reign of scientism— attitudes which, though they may be unleashed in part (directly or indirectly) by wars and revolutions, often pursue future courses that do not necessarily parallel the political histories such wars or revolutions initiate.

The question that remains unanswered by Traditionalists is how to apply such [metaphysical] principles in the present circumstances of modernization. [William W.] Quinn [author of The Only Tradition, SUNY, 1997] suggests, on the basis of his readings of Coomaraswamy and Guénon, that this intellectual elite might serve a function similar to that of the Hindu Brahmans as a priestly caste to reestablish Tradition after the passing away of the modern age.

Theosophist William Quinn's fantasies of a restored hierarchical, traditional culture ruled by "scientist/metaphysicists" in the latter days of the present cycle are entirely un-traditional, and precisely correspond to Guénon's description, in *The Reign of Quantity*, of a regime of "counter-initiation" in the end times, characterized by "inverted hierarchy" and identified with the rule of antichrist. [See the chapter "Vigilance at the Eleventh Hour: A Refutation of *The Only Tradition* by William W. Quinn" in my *The System of Antichrist: Truth and Falsehood in Postmodernism and the New Age*: Sophia Perennis, 2001.] According to Traditionalist doctrine as I have known it, metaphysical principles *cannot* be collectively applied, at least to any great degree, in these latter days.

Dr. Legenhausen summarizes, in eight points, his disagreements with Traditionalism's critique of modernity:

First, there is the dubious idea that explicit or implicit belief in various principles causes a society to have the characteristics it exhibits, so that the ills of modernity are simplistically attributed to deviations in beliefs.

Certainly the most basic conceptions held by a given society have great influence upon its character, since they control both what is believed to be possible and what is considered as desirable. No doubt there is a two-way influence in any society of belief upon conditions and conditions upon belief, as well as a type of belief or ideology which, as Marx showed, is merely a "mystification" of, or "superstructure" built upon, the foundation of material conditions. But in a deeper sense, the material conditions and inherent beliefs of a given society are united in a single *ethos*, and the emergence of such *ethoi* is a function of God's will operating in conditions. In the words of the Qur'an (41:53), *We shall show them Our signs on the horizons*—in conditions—*and in themselves*—their conceptions—

until it is clear to them that it is the Truth. Suffices it not as to thy Lord, that He is Witness over everything?—over both conditions and conceptions? For example, according to Frithjof Schuon, it was Julius Caesar who created the socio-political framework that was destined to receive the Christian revelation, just as Alexander the Great established the culture-area destined to be occupied by Islam. God willed to prepare historical vessels capable of receiving the immense, civilization-creating "conceptions" which were the great revealed religions. Both were needed for the traditional civilizations in question to emerge; nonetheless, the vessels remained a passive *material* ready to be shaped by the life-giving *form* of God's revealed Word.

Second, Traditionalists contrast the evils of modernity with a romanticized picture of traditional societies.

Poisoned and jaded by modernism, by the endless wars and barbarisms and vulgarities of modern history, we no longer believe that any societies ever *were* romantic, that to first see the gleaming walls of the Potala after a long Himalayan trek could ever have been a truly visionary experience, only a cheaply "romanticized" one. (And if not Lhasa, what about Jerusalem? And if not Jerusalem, what about Mecca? Or Samarkand?) To deny the real abuses of traditional societies is dishonest; to deny the possibility of a romantic society, of a society which is *felt* to be romantic by its own citizens, is unrealistic, and historically quite ignorant. In Schuon's words, from *Understanding Islam*, p.37, "'romantic' worlds are precisely those in which God is still probable"—and if we do not see the value of a cultural environment which makes it easier to believe in God, even though we may realize that such environments are now largely a thing of the past, how can we say that we take God seriously?

Third, the Traditionalist analysis of pre-modern societies fails to do justice to the essential differences among them because it is motivated by the a priori assumption that they are all based on shared principles.

Traditionalism, at least as Schuon presents it, does not deny the differences between traditional societies, and has much to say about them (cf. his *Light on the Ancient Worlds*)—it simply does not concentrate upon them as of the first importance, since its goal is to establish the equally true and spiritually much more effective understanding that there really is a "unanimous tradition" underlying them, which a metaphysically informed reading of traditional texts and appreciation of traditional arts will readily discern.

Fourth, Traditionalists view modernization as unmitigated decline because they take adherence to Tradition as their evaluative standard rather than the standards inherent to the traditions themselves. This criticism may be presented as a logical one, revealing a contradiction inherent in the Traditionalist position, or as a theological criticism, that Traditionalism exalts Tradition in a manner not sanctioned by Islamic teachings.

But according to Islamic teachings (from the prophetic *ahadith*), "No generation will come upon you that is not followed by a worse", and "the Hour will not come until men dress in women's clothes and buildings are built that reach to heaven." And many of the later surahs of the Holy Qur'an also speak of the inevitable decline of the latter days: *By the declining day, Lo! Mankind is in a state of loss.* (Q. 103)

Fifth, the Traditionalist critique of modernity is based on intuitions about the deviant principles that dominate modern society rather than on historical analysis.

Is an understanding that the essential, determining worldviews of various societies change over time, and that these changes travel in a particular, dominant "direction"—that of decline—not a part of historical analysis? Why not? This is the essence of the Traditionalist critique of modernity; it may not represent the same conclusions Dr. Legenhausen has reached, nor the methods he employs, but it is certainly historical analysis and nothing else.

Sixth, deviation from Tradition is condemned without regard to any evaluation of whether change could be merited, because change is seen as opposition to the sacred as it has become manifest in tradition. While it presents itself as inheritor of the sapiential legacy of the traditional cultures of the world, in fact it impedes the exercise of wisdom to critically examine the conditions of what are considered to be authentic traditional societies.

This may be true to a certain extent, but only to insofar as Tradition is identified with social forms rather than metaphysical principles—with the relative historical expression of Absolute Truth, that is, rather than Absolute Truth itself. Furthermore, it is more to the point to critically examine the conditions of modern societies in terms of the barriers they erect against a collective sense of the reality of God, as well as the unique spiritual opportunities they may offer in spite of this. And far from seeing all change as opposition to the sacred, Martin Lings (for one) names three modern developments which provide spiritual opportunities unique to our time, these being encyclopedic knowledge; an "infused" detachment, based on "the sight of one's world in chaotic ruins," such as in earlier ages could only be attained by fierce asceticism; and the wisdom of old age—the old age of the cycle—resulting in a spiritual transparency, akin (in some ways) to an eternal youth.

Seventh, while Traditionalists condemn ideology as a modern phenomenon, what they offer is itself an ideology.

I disagree. They offer metaphysical doctrine, not ideology. Metaphysical doctrine exists to support contemplation and provide an intellectual context for the spiritual path; the criterion of value it applies to statements is the *truth* of those statements. Ideology, on the other hand, subordinates truth to worldly utilitarianism and the ability to motivate groups to act in certain ways. It is true that religious law also exists to motivate groups to act in certain ways, but with a view to the salvation of their souls, and to the creation and maintenance of a religiously-based society only as a way of furthering this primary goal. Religious law and even metaphysics are capable of falling from the level of moral and intellectual doctrine (respectively) to the level of ideology, but this is only a perversion of their original intent, as today's religious terrorists have made abundantly clear.

Eighth, Traditionalism is politically reactionary.

Traditionalism as I have known it, though it is always in danger of descending into the kind of concretization and literalism reactionary politics represent, and tends to be generally conservative, is essentially a-political. It is *not* a political ideology, reactionary or otherwise. And in point of fact, to advocate a return to earlier forms of political organization of the kind that were in force when societies were organized on more Traditional principles—or at least to view such a return as intrinsic to Tradition and under all circumstances unambiguously in service to it—is not in fact Traditional; I must agree with Dr. Legenhausen on both the undesirability and the impossibility, in many cases, of such a development. Plato, in his *Republic*, analyzed the inevitable descent of the cycle of manifestation in political terms. Rule by the aristocrats would give way to rule by the timocrats, followed by that of the oligarchs or plutocrats, and then by the democrats, after which the cycle would end in tyranny. Transposed into Hindu terms (which is legitimate up to a point, since the Platonic doctrines are in fact a kind of western outpost of the great Indo-European lore-hoard), this would indicate that rule by the *brahmin* caste (as represented by the archaic hieratic civilizations) would be succeeded by rule by the *kshatriyas* (feudalism, perhaps), then the *vaishyas* (the bourgeoisie), then the *sudras* (the working class), and finally the *pariahs* (possibly the lumpen proletariat—a development perhaps heralded in the United States by California governor Arnold Schwartzenegger, and former Minnesota governor Jesse Ventura). Be that as it may, the fact remains that the descent of political organization from forms open to the transcendent Intellect to forms largely closed to it—in other words, the descent from order into chaos, or in Guénonian terms (in *The Reign of Quantity*) from the Essential to the Substantial pole, is an entirely traditional doctrine. The attempt to retain a higher form when descent into a lower form threatens is understandable and justifiable up to a point; a higher social good—and there is no higher social good than a collective orientation to the Divine—should not be given up when there is any possibility that it might be retained. But when this possibility is exhausted, then the attempt to retain it will inevitably transform it into a negative caricature of itself, the self-contradiction and corruption of which will only hasten its end. In one of the great ironies of history, Plato himself tried to establish his Republic ruled by contemplative intellectuals—one of whose qualifications was to be their *lack of political ambition*—through seeking patronage from a political strong-man, the Tyrant of Syracuse, who (predictably) simply held him for ransom until his friends bailed him out. A similar story is told by Chuang Tzu of a failed attempt by Confucius to educate and reform the warlord Robber Chih. Traditionalist doctrine (as for example, that of Martin Lings in *The Eleventh Hour*) accepts that we are now living at the tail-end of the Kali-yuga—thus to expect a worldly restoration of Traditional culture at this late date flies directly in the face of Traditional doctrines (as, for example, the Hindu doctrine that "one of the signs of the Kali-yuga is the appearance of enlightened saints in the lower castes"), and may be one of the factors which will bring about the final counterfeit of true spirituality, the reign of *al-dajjal* or antichrist.

The life of Abraham, the history of Judaism through Exodus, and to a degree the early history of Islam, all have to do with God's actions, by means of His prophets, to liberate His people from the oppressiveness of archaic hieratic civilizations that had fallen into decay. By God's command, Abraham emigrated from Chaldean Ur; Joseph was imprisoned in Egypt (though he ultimately rose to a high position); Moses freed the Hebrews from Egyptian domination; Muhammad initiated a revelation which empowered the Arabs to conquer much of the known world, including what were, at least to some degree, the last echoes of the ancient hieratic civilizations of the Near and Middle East, in the form of the Byzantine and Persian empires. When the Muslims entered Persia as conquerors, they declared: "We have come to teach you to worship God rather than men."

In earlier world-ages, when the human collectivity was more permeable to the light of God than it is today, hieratic civilizations, such as the system of the Hindu *varnas*, undoubtedly worked to present the collective in question with an effective image of *ontological* hierarchy in the guise of *social* hierarchy. The god-king was the visible image of God, the priestly caste the outer manifestation of the angelic orders, etc. (In order to understand how this could be, let the reader try to conceive of what the life of a faithful Buddhist must have been like in the last surviving hieratic civilization, that of Lamaist Tibet.) But in the Kali-yuga—and everything we know as *history* today, we must remember, is embraced by this Yuga— hieratic civilizations tend to become transformed from *hierophanies* into *idols*. If Egypt had not retained some of its sacred character, the prophet and patriarch Joseph could never have been a high official in the government of the Pharaoh. But if it had not essentially lost this character later on, becoming transformed from an earthly expression of the celestial order into an idolatrous counterfeit of it, God would never have raised up Moses.

So the question arises: What is the function of the Traditionalist appreciation for ancient spiritual civilizations, or medieval ones, given that such civilizations cannot and *should* not be resurrected? Can this be anything more than a useless, paralyzing nostalgia? The answer is: that whatever spiritual potentials can no longer be realized externally, in the *zahir*, thereby become transformed into *esoteric* truths which can now be realized internally, in the *batin*. Take, for example, the traditional caste structure, of which India presents the most complete and intact image, though this too is fast decaying. According to traditional Hindu doctrine (I have Dr. Rama Coomaraswamy to thank for this piece of information), the role or *dharma* of the warrior caste, the *kshatriyas*, was to protect the *brahmins*, the priestly caste, thus freeing them to fulfill their ritual and contemplative duties for the good of the entire collective. Guénon, in *Traditional Forms and Cosmic Cycles* [Sophia Perennis, 2003] saw in the Old Testament figure of Nimrod, who built the Tower of Babel, the story of an ancient revolt of the *kshatriyas* against the *brahmins*. But when the priests no longer in fact rule society, this role having been taken over by the warriors, what is the value in exalting the idea of a hieratic ("priest-ruled") civilization? The value, again, is esoteric, given that the traditional exaltation of the *brahmins* over the *kshatriyas* is the outer image of an inner spiritual truth, an *eternal* truth, occupying the plane of esoteric anthropology: the exaltation of the Intellect over the will in the human soul. The direct perception of spiritual Truth, not the will, is the crown and center of the human form. If the will serves the Intellect, it will order the life of the soul—and insofar as is possible, the outer life of the man—so as to protect the Intellectual center, both from disturbing social influences and from the possibility of rebelliousness on the part of the will itself. In such a condition the human form is correctly hierarchialized or *edified* ("built up," in the sense that the human soul is the *edifice* or *temple* of the Spirit); the several faculties of the soul all occupy their proper places; consequently the individual in question is an "upright man" (in Hebrew, a *tzaddik*). But if the will rebels against the Intellect and attempts to occupy its place, the result is a luciferian fall, a loss of the full stature of the human form, and consequently the degeneration of the entire cosmic environment, of which the human form, esoterically speaking, is the Seed and the Center; in the words of the Holy Qur'an (33:72), *We offered the Trust to the heavens and the earth and the hills, but they shrank from bearing it and were afraid of it. And man assumed it. Lo! He hath proved a tyrant and a fool.* Power can only act meaningfully in service to knowledge; if it attempts to serve itself, it loses its entire use and rationale, and becomes a "mad dog." So here, in terms of the hierarchical relationship between the Intellect and the will, we can see precisely how the truths once *socially* manifest in earlier ages can now become *esoterically realized.* This is the whole reason for the appreciation of earlier more traditional cultures, and the precise method to be followed in protecting and saving their spiritual essence. To believe that such cultures can be resurrected in the *zahir* is indeed either barren nostalgia or dangerous reaction, as Dr. Legenhausen has pointed out; to realize them in the *batin,* however, is the furthest thing from nostalgia. Rather, it is a way of nurturing and developing the soul by feeding it on spiritual qualities that were once expressed in social forms, but are now on a journey back to their eternal archetypes—their passage through human souls receptive to them being an essential stage of that journey. This is emphatically *not* to say that dead religions, such as that of Egypt, can be revived so as to function as viable spiritual paths in the present day. As René Guénon made crystal clear (whether or not he actually failed to apply his own principles in this regard when it came to his interest in Freemasonry), the spiritual Path requires an unbroken *silsilah* or chain-of-spiritual-transmission, stretching from one's present spiritual Master to the original Founder of the tradition in question, while any attempt to resurrect older traditions in the absence of such unbroken transmission is to potentially call up those dangerous "psychic residues" that haunt the tombs of religions dead and gone. (Schuon would apply Guénon's criteria to the priestly and sacramental order within traditional Christianity as a whole, not simply to whatever esoteric orders may have once existed within it, the equivalent of the Sufi *silsilah* in this case being the "apostolic succession".)

In terms of Islam, when the time of the four rightly-guided caliphs had passed, the institution of the Sufi *shaykh* or *murshid* grew up, to provide the Islamic collective with the kind of visible image of the Divine and the celestial order (though in an appropriately inner sense, not in any outer or literal sense) which the caliphs could no longer embody. The same function was fulfilled in Shi'ism by the Twelve Imams. But when the Twelfth Imam was occulted, he then could be realized only esoterically, only in the *batin*; the same holds true for the Sufi disciple whose veneration for his Master, via "projection," has led on to the direct and stable intuition of God, into Whom all projections are ultimately withdrawn: *la illaha ila 'Llah.*

Perhaps our best example of this spiritual internalization of social forms appears in the life of one of the greatest Christian esoterics, Dante Alighieri. The first part of his life was consumed by political action. As a "white" Guelph, his goal was the establishment of a Holy Roman Emperor strong enough to allow the Pope to fulfill his spiritual function without being forced to meddle in politics, but respectful enough of the Pope's spiritual prerogatives not to trespass upon them. In other words, he was working to restore the European equivalents of the *kshatriya* caste and the *brahmin* caste to their correct and traditional hierarchical order. He utterly failed in this, was exiled from Florence—and then wrote *The Divine Comedy*, in which all things were restored to their proper hierarchical order in the *batin*, the inner world, first on the Intermediary or Imaginal plane, the plane best rendered by mythopoeia, and lastly in the Unseen, where the spiritual path so magnificently laid out by Dante reaches its final End. Who among us wishes that he had stayed in politics and "won," rather than composing his *magnum opus*? Whatever he might have won would not have lasted, but the *Commedia* is for all time, and for eternity as well.

FUNDAMENTALISM

Traditionalists might well be considered fundamentalists, according to the way Western journalists and too many academics use this term.

I disagree. Any school of thought that maintains that each of the world religions possesses all that is required for salvation (in the individual order) and Liberation (in the transpersonal one) can in no way be called "fundamentalist"—however imperfect this term may be—since such fundamentalism is inseparable from an inflexible religious exclusivism; most academicians and journalists ought to be able to understand and accept this as fairly obvious.

. . . traditionalism is paraded as a more total rejection of modernity than that found in other Islamic groups. Fundamentalist governments are condemned for pursuing Western science and technology.

The problem is not science, but scientism—which, as Traditionalist writer and scientist Wolfgang Smith points out, is in effect inseparable from science as it is actually practiced under modernity—or as I would say, separable only for those whose intellectual attainments or deep piety reveal to them scientism's falsity. Traditionalists must and do accept, and use, modern technology; what they reject are the mystifying ideologies, the foolish and dangerous idealisms that surround it.

Dr. Nasr continues to distinguish traditionalism from fundamentalism in art and politics. In art, everything traditional is supposed to be beautiful, while the fundamentalists are tasteless. In general, those who are involved in what are called fundamentalist movements in Islam tend to be from the lowest strata of society, while traditionalists tend to be a very small group of highly educated people, some of whom, from Coomaraswamy to Dr. Nasr, have made important contributions to art criticism and aesthetics. The difference in attitudes toward the arts seems to have much more to do with education than ideology . . . the main differences Dr. Nasr elaborates between fundamentalism and traditionalism is that traditionalism is more absolute in its rejection of everything modern and Western. On this account, fundamentalism seems to be downright moderate! . . . he repeatedly emphasizes is that fundamentalism is crude and rude, but this seems to reveal more about social background than any defining difference in the essence of Traditionalism.

This argument, as it stands, is not valid, because most highly educated people, in both Muslim nations and the West, are not traditionalists, given that contemporary academia, whether "liberal" or "conservative," is not traditional. If Traditionalism were indeed a political ideology, then it might be true to say, within an Islamic context at least, that little separates Traditionalism from "fundamentalist" ideology outside the fact that Traditionalism is refined and sophisticated, thus limited to an intellectual elite, while fundamentalism is a "crude and rude" belief-system better suited to the uneducated masses. But since Traditionalism is not an ideology, Dr. Legenhausen's comparison of it to fundamentalist belief, and his characterization of it as even more "radically" anti-modern that of the militant Islamicists, are in no way valid. Traditionalism may see more deeply into the errors of modernism than the Islamic fundamentalists do, but it also recognizes that these errors, while certainly not to be complacently accepted, are an inescapable aspect of the tenor of the times, the latter days of the present cycle. Individual Traditionalist figures are, of course, free to pursue their own political ambitions according to their lights, but this in no way allows us to define Traditionalism in socio-political terms. Furthermore, to imply that refinement and sophistication are to be distinguished from "rudeness and crudeness" only by class position or level of education is not accurate. The sort of refinement Dr. Legenhausen apparently attributes to Traditionalists, based in an outward sense on an understanding of metaphysics and in an inward one (*insha'Allah*) on the actual practice of it, has no intrinsic relationship whatever to academic learning. The academies, by and large, no longer teach metaphysics, and there have always been *jñanis* or *arifs* in all traditions who, though entirely illiterate, have attained to perfect metaphysical knowledge via Intellection alone. The Prophet Muhammad himself, peace and blessings be upon him, was illiterate, yet there has been no greater sage within Islam than Muhammad. Civilizations based on Divine revelations, in which a traditional ambience remains intact, are capable of producing, if not "sophistication" in the present worldly sense of the term, certainly a high degree of spiritual and cultural refinement in people of all classes, educated or unschooled, literate or illiterate, rich or poor. In traditional societies, the people are the "folk" or the "faithful"; they are not the "masses." And if the terrorists of al-Qaeda are fundamentalists, then fundamentalists are in no way traditional, being diametrically opposed to Qur'an and *ahadith* on several major points, notably the prohibition of suicide and the traditional protection extended to women, children and non-combatants in time of war. If such mercy and basic humanity are to be damned with faint praise by being labeled refined and sophisticated rather than crude and rude, then so be it; refinement and sophistication are better than barbarism.

In the political realm, Dr. Nasr criticizes fundamentalists for accepting Western political institutions and ideas, including "revolution, republicanism, ideology and even class struggle in the name of a supposedly pure Islam" [Seyyed Hossein Nasr, *Traditional Islam in the Modern World*, p. 21]. *Among extremist fundamentalists, it is not difficult to find people who reject all of these Western innovations that Dr. Nasr condemns.*

The point is that many fundamentalists accept these things without realizing it. Vocal in their condemnation of the west, they unthinkingly adopt the very attitudes that they claim to reject. It is this unconscious self-contradiction, more than their practically necessary acceptance of modern conditions and technology, which distinguished them from Traditionalists. And are there really extremist fundamentalists who reject revolution?

In another essay, the differences are portrayed by Dr. Nasr in another way. He claims that fundamentalists usually share:

> opposition or indifference to all the inward aspects of Islam and the civilization and culture which it created, aspects such as Sufism, Islamic philosophy, Islamic art, etc. They are all outwardly oriented in the sense that they wish to reconstruct Islamic society through the re-establishment of external legal and social norms rather than by means of the revival of Islam through inner purification or by removing the philosophical and intellectual impediments which have been obstacles on the path of many contemporary Muslims. These movements, therefore, have rarely dealt in detail with the intellectual challenges posed by Western science and philosophy, although this trait is not by any means the same among all of them, some being of a more intellectual nature than others [Seyyed Hossein Nasr, *Traditional Islam in the Modern World*, p. 84].

However ... there are [traditional] Muslim groups that have been anti-intellectualist, anti-philosophical and rather outwardly oriented throughout the history of Islamic civilization ... [and] revolutionary Muslims who have been philosophers and mystics. ...

Though there have been revolutionary mystics in the history of Islam, such as Hasan ibn Sabah, and plenty of anti-intellectual traditionalists among the exoteric *'ulama*, I certainly accept as valid Dr. Nasr's criteria for distinguishing between fundamentalism and Traditionalism. In an Islamic context, Traditionalism is inseparable from Sufism, though not to be strictly identified with it, while most fundamentalists, particularly the Wahhabi fundamentalists who gave rise to al-Qaeda, consider *tasawwuf* to be intrinsically heterodox.

To summarize: It is true that René Guénon enunciated certain social principles that have been interpreted ideologically. Consequently the Traditionalists, often in spite of themselves, have apparently had a degree of influence on certain reactionary groups and ideologies. Furthermore, certain strands of Traditionalism now seem to be feeding in to Islamic and/or non-Islamic forms of globalism as well, primarily through the interfaith movement—a clearly anti-Traditional preoccupation, and one which continues to receive funds from various globalist figures and institutions (see *False Dawn: The United Religions Initiative, Globalism and the Quest for a One World Religion* by Lee Penn: Sophia Perennis, 2005)—as well as through at least a peripheral involvement with various emerging forms of western-influenced, universalist, hardly-Islamic Sufism, such as that purveyed by the Rumi Forum of Fethullah Gülen, one of whose agendas is the re-establishment of the caliphate. But it is clear that by the end of his life Guénon's sense of the eschatological denouement of the west, and the world as a whole, took him far beyond the ideological realm. And the fate of those who did attempt to formulate political ideologies on the basis of Guénon's doctrines—the sublimated Fascism of Julius Evola, the state "Fascist Bolshevism" of the Russian "Guénoniste" ideologue Alexander Dugin—have only demonstrated the wisdom of Guénon's ultimate aloofness from political activism of any kind. In my opinion, the value of Traditionalism does not lie in its supposed ability to formulate viable political ideologies in opposition to modernism, but in its power to strengthen and prepare the world's wisdom traditions, by means of both a critique of the modern world and a contemporary re-statement of their essential doctrines, to survive *in spite of* modernism—which, as Dr. Legenhausen correctly points out, must be dealt with as a given.

CONCLUSION

In the words of Charles Pegúy, "everything begins in mysticism and ends in politics." Traditionalism is not a political ideology and cannot be transformed into one without losing its essential character, and so arriving at its end. An understanding of traditional doctrines and values may suggest which side to take on a given issue, and certainly any political stance that protects the right of the traditional religions to retain their own beliefs and practices, or allows traditional metaphysical ideas to be freely expressed, is in service to Tradition. But what may in fact be a largely unconscious drift of the whole world toward the politicizing of everything, where what last year was "of course" metaphysical and a-political, this year is "of course" political and ideological, without any clear perception (or at least any clear acknowledgement) that a change has in fact occurred—such a drift must be resisted at all cost if Traditionalism is to survive.

The renewed expression of traditional doctrines by the major writers of the Traditionalist School is not designed to suggest or bolster any sort of political action, but to support and inform the inner life. Traditional doctrines certainly do not *forbid* certain forms of political activity, but they place such activity in a much wider context than that of individual ambition, or group interest, or the establishment of social justice, or even "saving the world" in worldly terms. The doctrine of *karma-yoga* from the *Bhagavad-Gita* is probably the clearest and most complete expression of this wider context, where even *dharma*, or sacred duty, must give way to *moksha*, liberation from the realm of becoming through realization of the Absolute.

No matter how worldly Christians may become, still, the sense that "My Kingdom is not of this world" is difficult to entirely lose sight of. Christianity spent its first 300 years in the catacombs, and after Constantine made possible the worldly establishment of the Christian church, a certain sense of self-betrayal haunted the faithful, a feeling which was given concrete expression in the flight of pneumatics and contemplatives to the deserts of Egypt and Syria. The kingdom of these Christian monks was certainly not of *that* world, the world of imperial Roman power—and in the face of worldly corruption and decay, the option of return to a catacomb church remains a living option for the Christian "remnant." The case of Islam, however, was very different. The Prophet Muhammad, peace and blessings be upon him, was commanded and empowered by God to fulfill a political as well as a purely spiritual ministry, and the unprecedented speed with which Islam conquered half the known world soon after his death has left Muslims with a sense—sometimes obscure, sometimes ideologically explicit—that Islam cannot properly be itself without some form of *dar al-Islam.* The formation of a Muslim Empire was a more-or-less direct overflow from the power of the Islamic revelation; this, as opposed to the Christian experience of the catacombs, is the history which inspires and haunts so many Muslims today. Yet Islam also had its pneumatics and ascetic contemplatives who turned their backs on worldly Islam, especially after the days of the first four "rightly-guided" caliphs were past. These were the Sufis, the first generations of whom were fierce ascetics and witnesses against an Islamic worldliness they felt had betrayed the more spiritual content of the Prophet's teaching and the inner message of the Noble Qur'an. And although early Sufism was not without its hermits, the Sufis never embraced a strictly cloistered form of monasticism, in line with the Prophet's teachings that "marriage is half the religion" and "there is no monasticism in Islam." They were always *of* the greater Muslim community, and to a large extent *in* it. Nonetheless, in a certain way they remained in "hidden exile." Instead of removing themselves en masse from the Muslim community, they developed a practice known as "solitude in company"; their spiritual inwardness was such that physical exile was by and large not necessary for the fulfillment of their function.

What if a time were to come when political activity within the

Muslim world could no longer be essentially Muslim in character, when the struggle to re-establish a "Muslim" empire, or a number of smaller political entities, could only be carried on by betraying the central principles of the Prophetic traditions and the Holy Qur'an? Would not such a time necessarily call up the idea a Muslim "remnant" analogous to the Jewish or Christian one? And who might function as the "seed" of such a remnant? Who but the traditional Sufis—those who are influenced neither by Islamicist ideology nor by the sanitized Sufism of the West? Certainly the Sufis as a whole have never shirked the call to the "lesser jihad" to protect the Muslim community from invasion and conquest. But what if a time were to come so corrupt that, at least under certain circumstances, the "greater jihad" remained the only honorable, the only spiritually possible course?

A seed, however, needs a ground in which to grow; a spiritual potential, if it is to take root in this world, needs a tradition within which to operate. Does Islam in fact possess such a tradition? Did Islam ever occupy catacombs of its own? Indeed it did. Before the *hijra* of the Prophet and his followers from Mecca to Medina, their position vis-à-vis the pagan Quraysh who ruled Mecca was in many ways analogous to the situation of the first Christians under the Jewish and Roman authorities. They were an oppressed minority, who were directed by the Prophet and the Qur'an to endure and hold their peace. Later, God sent surahs which commanded the Muslims to actively resist their oppressors, but before these surahs were received, the Muslims were truly in exile. In Mecca they were oppressed and shunned, and in the face of this oppression a party of them left Arabia, crossing the Red Sea and finding protection under the Negus, the ruler of a Christian kingdom (undoubtedly Ethiopia) on the African coast. It is said that when later surahs of the Qur'an contradict the commands given in earlier ones, the earlier ones are abrogated. Yet the abrogated surahs were never deleted; they remained part of the direct and spoken word of God that came to Muhammad. And while I am certainly not a student if *fiqh* (Islamic jurisprudence), I will hazard a speculation: that any *surah* or passage of the Qur'an that is abrogated is abrogated by *conditions*. The commands of God to a small, marginalized Islamic community in

Mecca were necessarily different from those addressed to an established Muslim political entity in Medina. God did not "change His mind"; a change in conditions simply placed the Muslims in relation to a different Name of God than had formerly been in force. Any word spoken by God is spoken in eternity; in that world it cannot be abrogated; as an act of Allah it is part of the eternal nature of things. In this world, however, the times—like the times set aside for the daily prayer or the fast in Ramadan—determine which aspects of God's eternal Word apply to present conditions, which are active and which latent, and which interpretation of a given Qur'anic text should be given precedence in relation to present conditions. So it is possible to imagine (and God knows best) that a time may come when conditions—conditions which are as much an expression of God's will as the verses of the Qur'an—may dictate that the commands of God to the fledgling Muslim community become active again, at least under certain circumstances. This possibility was in fact foretold by the *hadith* of Muhammad, quoted by Shaykh Abu Bakr Siraj al-Din (Martin Lings) in his book *The Eleventh Hour*, "Islam began in exile and will end in exile—blessed are those who are in exile!"

Among the closest of the Prophet's companions were those known as "the People of the Bench", whom Charles LeGai Eaton, in his *Islam and the Destiny of Man* [SUNY/Islamic Texts Society, 1985] characterizes as follows:

> enterprise was encouraged, but there were also those of a more contemplative temperament who had neither the skills nor the inclination to earn their own living, and they—as though to prove that the Muslim does not have to be an "activist"—were given an honoured place in the community. A space was found for them to sleep in the covered section of the new mosque and they came to be known as "the People of the Bench." They were fed with food from the Prophet's own table, when there was any to spare, and with roasted barley from the community chest; and of all these the most famous was Abu Huraira, which means "father of the little cat", who followed Muhammad everywhere—just as his little cat followed him—and to whose

prodigious powers of memory we owe a great number of recorded *hadiths*. Perhaps he might be regarded as the first of those of whom Muhammad was to say: 'The ink of the scholars is more valuable than the blood of the martyrs.' [pp. 116–117]

Here, even before the Sufi reaction to the degeneration of Muslim spirituality under the later caliphs, we have the seed of a Muslim "remnant" such as may be called for once again by the deepening corruption of the latter days (see *The Riddle of the Cave*, below). Islam will always have a place for vigorous action in the world in response to God's command, and the right of Muslim nations and communities to defend themselves by force of arms is not only guaranteed by the *shari'ah*, but universally recognized as a basic human right. But Islam must also retain a clear sense of the need for contemplative withdrawal from the field of action—for those commanded by God to take this course—and of contemplation as more essentially *active*, in its one-pointed concentration upon the reality of Allah, than the endless series of compromises, excesses and betrayals that make up war and politics. If it loses this sense of the value of inwardness, such as the Prophet exhibited during his retreats on Mt. Hira, and which made up the prelude to the advent of the Holy Qur'an, it will cease to be a *religion* in the full sense of that word.

And inseparable from the need for at least periodic withdrawal from the activity of the world is the sense of this world's ephemerality; the temporal aspect of detachment from the world is eschatology. The Prophet himself compared this world to a tree under the shade of which a rider rests for an hour, then rises and departs. And never have conditions more insistently demanded the attainment of an eschatological outlook as an inevitable part of spiritual and material realism. *By the declining day, Lo! Mankind is a state of loss.* (Q. 103:1) But as the world draws ever nearer to its end, it seems to project, and more powerfully every day, the temptation to deny this ephemerality, to take shelter under that flimsiest of roofs, *material conditions*, from the approaching dissolution of matter itself; this may in fact be part of what Jesus meant when he said that in the end times "they will pray for the mountains to fall and cover them." In times when the cosmic environment was more stable it was easier to imagine and accept its end, because the light of worlds higher than the material was not so deeply veiled. And it also may be true that the continuous multiplication of means and scenarios for the end of all life on earth is fueling our collective denial by reminding us that the Hour is indeed "too close for comfort." However, there is another reason why religious people of intelligence and good will tend to shy away from the eschatological dimension of things—that being the exploitation of eschatology by those forces, terrorist or otherwise, Muslim or otherwise, "fundamentalist" or otherwise, who seem to think that the most desirable thing would be to bring about the end of the world by launching Armageddon—as if it were possible to force God's hand, and as if they somehow believed He might appreciate their attempt to do so! Such people are without any sense of God's omnipotence, which is inseparable from His sovereign right to exercise it; they are lacking in even the rudiments of normal religious piety. It is Allah who is *Owner of the Day of Judgment*, not them! Such exploitation of apocalyptic fears works powerfully even on those who oppose it, by making them less willing to admit the true apocalyptic nature of our times, for fear of giving aid and comfort to these apocalyptic mad dogs. Yet simple realism—part of which is to admit the actual existence of the mad dogs in question—will lead any honest believer of any religion to understand and accept that these are indeed the latter days of the present cycle of manifestation, even though hundreds of years (or maybe the twinkling of an eye) may still lie before us. If such realism is denied, detachment from worldliness becomes impossible under present conditions. Everything becomes politicized, and all political initiatives start to take on the character of absolute imperatives. If we do not know God as *Lord of the Worlds*, we will think that saving or destroying or transforming the world is up to us alone, in our titanic and puny human arrogance; if we come to believe this, then all is lost. And one of the most potent antidotes to this collective disease, for those able to assimilate it, is the body of writings produced by the Traditionalist School.

I will end this essay by quoting those of Dr. Legenhausen's assertions with which I entirely and heartily agree:

Moderation requires an understanding of the current conditions of Muslim societies today and of the elements shaping them: from global market forces to popular religious beliefs and practices. How our societies are shaped and changed is largely out of our hands. Where we do have an opportunity to effect change or to modify its direction in some way, we need the humility to admit that the results of our interference in social, political and other cultural affairs are often other than we would predict. This, however, should not be cause for timidity, but for submission to Allah in obedience to His commands, knowing that in the ordinance of His prescriptions, He knows better. The violation of the moral precepts given by human conscience and confirmed by divine revelation to His prophets, peace be with Muhammad and his progeny and with all of them, can never be excused as a means to obtain otherwise desirable social or political goals. . . .

The challenge that faces Muslims today, is how to minimize the injuries, how to ride out modernization so that it does not take the same form among Muslims as it has in Christian society, how to preserve the sacred norms and values prescribed for us by Islam in these rapidly changing times. There are no simple solutions, no easy answers. An insistence on fundamental principles is not enough. The problem for Muslims is exactly how the fundamental principles of Islam are to be applied in the situations in which we find ourselves. Compromise is necessary because the traditional institutions and cultural forms are not sufficiently flexible to accommodate the changes with which contemporary Muslim societies are faced. Moreover, there is much in the traditional institutions that is not worth preserving. . . .

Today, we have to find ways to live in accordance with Islam that are appropriate to the exceedingly different circumstances in which we live. Social changes are being driven by rapid changes in technology that give no one time to adjust. This gives modern society an ugly mismatched quality. While certain measures can be taken to try to preserve some sort of proportionality, [social?] integrity becomes more of a utopian ideal than a realistic aim. In this effort, we can only rely on Allah and His aid as we seek to sort through the social, political, cultural and theological problems that face us.

I would only add that Traditionalist doctrine, insofar as it avoids the temptation to transform itself into a political ideology, as well as also the barren, reactionary nostalgia for which Dr. Legenhausen faults it, can provide the very "benchmark" by which Muslim societies, and religious societies and institutions the world over, can confront the challenge of modernity without betraying their eternal essence.

Three:

NECESSARY INFORMATION

The Value and Danger of the Interfaith Movement in a Globalist World

When has religion ever been one? It has always been two or three, and war has always raged among coreligionists. How are you going to unify religion? On the Day of Resurrection it will be unified, but here in this world that is impossible because everybody has a different desire and want. Unification is not possible here. At the Resurrection, however, when all will be united, everyone will look to one thing, everyone will hear and speak one thing. [Jalalluddin Rumi, *Signs of the Unseen (Fihi ma-Fihi)*: Threshold Books, 1994, p.29].

I

TODAY'S INTERFAITH MOVEMENT, insofar as its goal is the development of understanding and tolerance between the world's religions, is a good and necessary addition to any just and equitable society. It is open to serious doubt, however, whether simple interfaith dialogue can actually produce such understanding and tolerance on the geopolitical level, where interreligious violence is initiated and/or exploited by socio-economic forces and political power blocs whose ultimate intent is in no way religious. Nor is interfaith conflict the only thing in the religious domain subject to manipulation and co-optation. The Interfaith Movement itself must be on its guard against co-optation by forces that, under the banner of globalization and in reaction to the barbaric "religious"

80

terrorism now infecting our world, want to put all the world religions *in their place*: that is, under the political control of essentially non-religious authorities.

My perspective is essentially that of the Traditionalist or Perennialist school: René Guénon, Ananda Coomaraswamy, Titus Burckhardt, Martin Lings, Marco Pallis, Frithjof Schuon, Huston Smith, Seyyed Hossein Nasr, Whitall Perry, Mark Perry, Rama Coomaraswamy, William Stoddart, Joseph Epes Brown, Lord Northbourne, Elemire Zolla, Tage Lindbom, Rodney Blackhirst, Harry Oldmeadow, Jennifer Doane Upton, James Cutsinger, William Chittick, Sachiko Murata, Jean-Baptiste Aymard, Patrick Laude, Reza Shahkazemi, and many others. It goes without saying that these writers (living and dead) are not always of one mind; nonetheless the burden of their works represents a sophisticated perspective and a comprehensive body of doctrine that, almost alone in the modern world, allows us to understand both that all true religions ultimately emanate from, and exist as paths back to, the One Truth, *and* that a plurality of revelations of that Truth in this world is not simply a historical or geographical or cultural accident, but is in fact metaphysically necessary. The specific doctrine in which this truth is expressed is the famous "transcendent unity of religions", which teaches that the *unity* of religions is precisely *transcendent*; it is "not of this world".

To the degree that the Interfaith Movement becomes centered on the idea of "Inter" more than the idea of "Faith", it will serve neither the religions of the world nor the fundamental goal of religion itself: faith in God, the salvation of the soul, and ultimate spiritual Liberation, which (allowing for the diversity of religious languages) constitute the only reason for the existence of *any* religion. A few years ago I heard someone lament that a large percentage of students entering the schools of the Graduate Theological Union—a consortium of Catholic and Protestant seminaries situated in Berkeley, near the University of California—do not want to become Lutheran pastors or Presbyterian ministers or Catholic nuns or Episcopal or Catholic priests, but rather "Interfaith Ministers." But if all the ministers are now "Interfaith", what becomes of the very *faiths* between which they hope to bring greater understanding? Here we can see exactly how the Interfaith Movement, simply by default, could in fact weaken the religions it sincerely hopes to serve.

To situate one's "center" at the border between different religious universes taken as "belief-systems", rather than at the Center of one of them (which, ultimately, is also the One Center of all) is to deconstruct religion as a spiritually effective *vertical* relationship between humanity and the Absolute Source of both human life and the universe around us, and re-define it in primarily *horizontal* terms: as a cultural entity at war with or tolerant of, isolated from or in alliance with, ignorant of or well-informed about, other such entities. And once religion is defined in these terms, all the inter-religious tolerance in the world will not be able to re-awaken the lost sense of the Absolute, and of our responsibilities to It, without which religion has no legitimate reason to exist. A "tolerance" that makes all religions equal as socio-political "sectors" but shies away from the very sense of the Absolute that is every religion's *raison d'être*—for fear that the notion of God as Absolute Reality must always translate into this or that fanatical "absolutism"—is to subtly undermine *all* the religions in the name of making peace between them.

As in the world of interpersonal relations, peace can only be established and maintained between religions when the borders between them are respected. And yet if these borders become absolute—as, for example, if the preaching of the doctrine of one religion in an area where another religion dominates were to be strictly prohibited, not in the name of the dominant religion's claim or exclusive truth, but according to a view that defines *all* missionary activity as imperialistic—then religious *freedom* has been sacrificed in the name of religious *tolerance*. And to the degree that the work of mediating between the religions is given over to essentially non-religious bodies and forces—the United Nations, let us say, or the European Union— then all the religions are in danger of losing their traditional independence, *even in doctrinal terms*. (For example, Muslim nations that want to join the European Union must officially repudiate those verses of the Qur'an where homosexuality is strictly prohibited; and why should we expect the domination of religious doctrine by secular ideology to stop there?) If the Interfaith Movement is to fulfill its stated aim of establishing peace, tolerance and understanding between religions, it must be equally dedicated to maintaining the *freedom* and *independence* of the religions, since to place the traditional world religions under an increasing pressure of cultural, political and legal restriction in the name of moderating their excesses is to store up immense conflict for the future—possibly the fairly near future.

The rest of this essay is in the form of a book review: of *False Dawn: The United Religions Initiative, Globalism and the Quest for a One-World Religion* by Lee Penn [Sophia Perennis, 2005]. This book is a masterful critique of the excesses of the Interfaith Movement (of which the Movement as a whole can certainly not be held guilty), and also an exercise of "interfaith tolerance" in itself, since its author is a committed Christian (a Byzantine Catholic) and its editor (myself) a committed Muslim, who was also at pains, in the many footnotes the author graciously allowed me, to correct various misconceptions of the doctrines of the world religions, including Hinduism, expressed by some of the spokespersons of the United Religions Initiative. This review (which was published in slightly different form the journal *Sacred Web* 15, in the summer of 2005) is based on the doctrines of the Traditionalist School, and also (in part) directed to them, in view of the fact that they are no more immune to incursions of "anti-traditional" and "counter-traditional" forces (to use the terminology of the founder of the School, René Guénon) than are the world religions themselves in the chaos of the modern era. So while this review is certainly not "esoteric" in either the initiatory or the colloquial sense of that word, being entirely accessible to the general reader, it also offers a few glimpses into the "in house" dialectic going on within the Traditionalist School itself—a School whose influence continues to grow both in the Interfaith arena and within the religion of Islam.

THE REVIEW

The United Religions Initiative, founded in 1995 by William E. Swing, Episcopal Bishop of California, is the most ambitious interfaith organization presently operating in the world, the most "ecumenical" in outlook, and the one which seems to have the closest ties to various "globalist" figures and organizations. In *False Dawn: The United Religions Initiative, Globalism and the Quest for a One World Religion*, Lee Penn provides us with a detailed history of the movement, its predecessors, its ideological confederates, its allied organizations both religious and secular, its stated goals and its implicit agendas. He has taken a penetrating look at the dynamics of globalization through the lens of contemporary religion—both the established, organized religions and the new religious movements—and the picture he presents to us is both rarely illuminating and deeply chilling.

Religious universalism is not what it used to be. When René Guénon, Ananda Coomaraswamy and Frithjof Schuon were making their profound contributions to the doctrine which has come to be known (in Schuon's phrase) as the Transcendent Unity of Religions, the idea that all world religions were the providentially various dialects of a single language of Truth was fairly novel, shocking to many, and easily dismissed. Today it is a cliché. This is not to say that the religions are not still vigorously defending their boundaries. As globalization and a fast-shrinking world throw them into ever more violent confrontation, suspicion of universalists on the part of various religious "fundamentalists" is growing. On the other hand, religious universalism is a much more established doctrine, in worldly terms, than it was when Guénon, Coomaraswamy and Schuon were doing their ground-breaking work. And as inter-religious violence increases, it is swiftly becoming the "obvious" alternative to such violence in the minds of many, just as the dream of a One World Government is being increasingly identified with such ideals as "universal peace" and "global unity"—ideals which are uncritically accepted as both entirely possible and "quasi-absolutely" desirable by all too many well-intentioned but poorly-informed idealists. In *False Dawn*, Lee Penn demonstrates, with an irresistible tide of documentation, how religious universalism is being co-opted as the "spiritual ideology" of a globalism which is both fundamentally secular (Guénon's "anti-tradition") and busy inventing a One World Religion with pretensions to "mysticism" and "esoterism" (Guénon's "counter-tradition"). In *Theosophy, the History of a Pseudo-Religion* [Sophia Perennis, 2003], *The Spiritist*

Fallacy [Sophia Perennis, 2004], and *The Reign of Quantity and the Signs of the Times* (his prophetic masterpiece) [Sophia Perennis, 2001], René Guénon spoke cryptically of the counter-tradition and counter-initiation he saw brewing in various socially marginal but nonetheless highly influential sects and secret societies, foremost among them being the Theosophical Society, whose founders (H. P. Blavatsky and Annie Besant) openly declared their intent to destroy Christianity and "chase God from the skies". Now, at the beginning of the 21st century, Lee Penn has drawn aside the veil covering the activities of such groups, and revealed their growing interaction with the organized globalist elites. And though it has certainly changed over the years, the Theosophical Society, as an intellectual influence if not an organizing cadre, is still there. With entire justification, *False Dawn* could have been sub-titled "The Counter-Initiation Documented."

The author of *False Dawn* has produced an astounding exposé of the United Religions Initiative which explodes more pre-conceived assumptions than any book I have ever read. The URI numbers among its supporters Ted Turner, George Soros, George W. Bush and Sun Myung Moon; in light of this, I defy anyone limited to a left-wing or right-wing ideology to see it as it actually is. The author presents ample evidence that the New Age movement has become what I like to call it a "contingency ideology" of many among the globalist elites, who have adopted and *established* New Age beliefs just when the movement seems to be waning on a popular level. And it gives a clear picture of how some of the globalists would like to federate all the world's religions under a single authority, as a way of pacifying the religious "tribes" (religious fundamentalists, oppressed ethnic groups, nationalists) in the name of global unity and the New World Order. This is "McWorld" in the religious field—a "McWorld" that is busy preparing a "Jihad" of its own (this in allusion to the important book *Jihad vs. McWorld: How Globalism and Tribalism are Reshaping the World*, by Benjamin Barber, Ballantine Books, 1996).

Lee Penn's work is so much more sophisticated, comprehensive and well-documented (over 3000 footnotes!) than the usual conservative Catholic or Evangelical anti-New Age screed that there is simply no comparison. His conservative Catholic friends were in ecstasy over it—until they read his *Postscript*, where he warns us against some of the authoritarian, right-wing movements within Catholicism, such as Opus Dei, Tradition, Family and Property, and the Legionaries of Christ. His "authorities" include C.S. Lewis, George Orwell, G.K. Chesterton, Nietzsche (who so clearly declared and celebrated what the "dark side" was up to), Malcolm Muggeridge, the Popes Pius X and Pius XI, J.R.R. Tolkien, and René Guénon. He has presented us with a clearly Fascist-leaning Teilhard de Chardin—Chardin the darling of the liberal Catholics!—with a rabid New Age anti-Semitism among highly influential writers both living and dead, with a psychopathic Sun Myung Moon courted (literally!) by members of the U.S. House of Representatives, with a United Religions Initiative spoken highly of by both the Dalai Lama and the Chinese Communist state-run church, funded by both liberal foundations and those with close ties to the U.S. State Department, and which includes one convicted rapist and apparently al-Qaeda-connected Muslim, the most ultra-liberal Christians imaginable, anti-Communist Moonies, Anglicans, Wiccans, Neo-Pagans etc.—an "umbrella organization" with a vengeance. The author has been able to articulate this uncommon vision because he has spent a number of years looking in a direction that few others even recognize as existing—the reason for such incomprehension being (as I like to say) that the Devil now largely defines the sides we are asked to take and the ideologies we are required to choose from. Reading his book, it's as if we have suddenly discovered that our house has windows not only to the east and west, but to the north as well—and that the view through that north window is every bit as detailed, unified and articulate as our more familiar perspectives. It is not some hermetically-sealed world of the imagination, but a novel and indeed tremendously shocking view of the common world we inhabit—a world whose fate we share.

False Dawn is far more than an exhaustively documented history and critique of the United Religions Initiative, though it certainly is that. And it is more than just a history of the Interfaith Movement. It is, in fact, an analysis of *ideology of globalism* with special reference to the religious sphere. Taking the United Religions Initiative as a point of orientation, the author analyses not only the explicitly religious ideologies relating to globalization, their major patrons and spokespersons, and the organizations which exist to disseminate such ideas, but also investigates the membership and apparent agendas of highly influential secular organizations whose leaders— such as Mikhail Gorbachev and Maurice Strong (Chairman of the World Bank and close friend of George W. Bush)—have spoken well of the URI, organizations which share a similar ideological outlook. These groups include the State of the World Forum, the Earth Charter Initiative, Green Cross International, the Gorbachev Foundation, the World Future Society, the World Economic Forum, the U.N. Environmental Program, UNESCO, and the United Nations Population Fund. The author clearly demonstrates how a religious universalism with political backing, a universalism seeking political clout on a global scale, is inseparable from the push for a One World Government.

Lee Penn also demonstrates how globalization has given certain New Age teachers a worldwide pulpit, including Robert Muller (former Assistant Secretary General of the U.N.), Barbara Marx Hubbard (whose name was placed in nomination for the vice-presidency of the United States at the 1984 Democratic Convention, and who is presently a director of the World Future Society along with former U.S. Secretary of State Robert McNamara, Maurice Strong, and scholars from Georgetown University, the George Washington University and the University of Maryland), Avon Mattison, Corrine McLaughlin, Gordon Davidson, and probably the best-selling New Age teacher as of this writing, Neale Donald Walsch, author of the absurd and highly popular *Conversations with God* and its sequels. The reader will no doubt be interested to learn that, according to Walsch, Hitler went to heaven (because he didn't really hurt anyone; he just sent all those Jews to a better place, seeing that death is better than life), and that Barbara Marx Hubbard's "spirit guide" (who claims to be Jesus Christ) has called for the extermination of one-third to one-half of the earth's population. And Lee Penn exhaustively traces the history of the New Age movement to H.P. Blavatsky, founder of the Theosophical Society, and more directly to mid-20th century Theosophist Alice A. Bailey, founder of the Lucis Trust, who is spoken highly of by many of the New Age teachers listed above—and who herself (along with Barbara Marx Hubbard) celebrated the atomic bombing of Hiroshima and Nagasaki as a "spiritual initiation" for the earth! He also demonstrates the seminal influence of heterodox Catholic priest, author and paleontologist Teilhard de Chardin on the same sinister constellation of ideas.

For the most part, *False Dawn* reveals the core beliefs and shared agendas of the globalist wing of the Interfaith Movement in the words of its own spokespersons and publications. The massive amount of data the author has brought together may seem daunting at first to some readers, but it ultimately carries the day by its own weight, its outrageous audacity, and its ominous consistency. It is precisely this relentless documentation which finally *convinces.*

II

Given that secular ideologies, whether of the Left or the Right, have lost a great deal of the cultural force they possessed for most of the 20th century—postmodernity being notoriously suspicious of "overarching paradigms"—part of the burden of providing us with "the big picture" has fallen, or fallen *back*, on the organized religions, as well as on the myths and aspirations of various new religious movements. And even though religion, in essence, is better able to offer an all-encompassing worldview worth living by than any secular ideology, the partial collapse of secular ideologies in favor of this or that religious perspective has in effect "ideologized" the religions, narrowing their scope, shrinking their ontological vision, and dragging theology and morality (not to mention metaphysics) in the direction of propaganda and social action. (Renegade Traditionalist and Fascist fellow-traveler Baron Julius Evola heralded this degeneration when he falsely claimed that the *kshatriya* [warrior] initiation is higher than the *brahmanic* [priestly or sacerdotal] one—in other words, that action is higher than the contemplation.) For this reason, no social analysis that fails to take religious myth and dogma as seriously as it does any secular ideology will be capable of making sense out of the contemporary scene. And for those who understand that religion is not political or historical in essence, that it is a door to higher realities, a way of perfecting the human form and fulfilling the human trust, a clear understanding of the contemporary corruption and co-optation of the religious traditions is of vital importance, since without it they may be led to confuse the eternal form of the revelation they are struggling to live by with its own degenerate caricature. Both secular social analysts working to define the influence of religion on contemporary events, and religious believers trying to understand what is happening to their traditions, will find in *False Dawn* an indispensable aid—one that has arrived not a day too soon.

Furthermore, I believe that this book has something to say to the Traditionalist School in particular. It is my impression that "Traditionalist social analysis" desperately needs to be updated, now that Ortega y Gasset's "revolt of the masses" is largely a thing of the past, having been replaced—in the west at least—by Christopher Lasch's "revolt of the elites," the title of his final book, in which Lasch shows how it is now the masses who are relatively traditional, while the elites tend to be anti-traditional and progressive—notwithstanding the skill of people like George W. Bush in playing the role of "traditional conservative" and "American patriot" when it suits their purposes. We don't really have to be warned, again, against socialism, the "leveling" vulgarity of democracy and the tyranny of the machine, so much as we need to understand how traditional metaphysics and esoterism themselves could be perverted and co-opted by the coming globalist regime. Those identified with Traditionalism are familiar with worldly incomprehension and ridicule; they are used to being ignored. But in view of recent developments, one wonders how ready they are to deal with worldly *acceptance*, enthusiastic incomprehension, and the danger of ultimate co-optation, given that certain key globalist leaders are presently on the lookout for articulate religious universalists; they are *Now Hiring*. To be validated, to be accepted, to be *heard* by the world of men and affairs, after so long an exile, could prove for some a formidable temptation. This is not to say that the Traditionalist worldview, comprising the Perennial Wisdom plus a critique of the post-modern world in light of this Wisdom, is of no relevance in these times. Indeed, taken in its widest definition, it is possibly the one worldview which allows us to make entire sense of them. But according to its own principles, it cannot be of use to collectively organized humanity in these latter days, at least in uncorrupted form. Its use is and will be to give individuals a conceptual and, God willing, a spiritually practical way out of the Babylon of these latter days: "Come out of her, my people, that ye be not partakers of her sins, that ye receive not of her plagues" [*Apocalypse* 18:4]. Thus it can never be a mass movement while maintaining its true nature—God help us if it ever becomes one! It would be better characterized as an "underground railroad," a network of guides and safe houses designed to lead "freedmen" out of The World and into a quality of both earthly and transcendent human life which is no longer identified with that World. Whether or not those few who are attracted to the Traditionalist worldview constitute a spiritual "elite," it is at least certain that, given their spiritual and intellectual constitution, they cannot be saved without it.

There are, however, forms of religious or "spiritual" universalism that have always had a worldly goal in mind: the supplanting of the revealed religious traditions with a universal, syncretistic religion which will be the basis of a new "highly evolved" spiritual culture; this culture will be global in reach, and form the basis of a New Age for humanity. Dreams of a spiritual New Age were foreshadowed in the teachings of such figures as Joachim da Fiore [c. 1135–1202] with his idea of the Age of the Holy Spirit which is to follow the Age of the Father (the Old Testament) and the Age of the Son (the New Testament), as well as in certain worldly interpretations of the Ismaili Shi'ite doctrine that the Great Resurrection has already taken place, thus abrogating the Muslim *shari'ah*. Similar dreams re-surfaced during the Protestant Reformation, when even Jacob Boehme felt that he was living in a new spiritual age for humanity. Lee Penn traces the modern resurgence of such ideas to the Parliament of World Religions in 1893, where Swami Vivekananda preached his own version of religious universalism to a dazzled audience, and shows how they have always been central to the doctrines and aspirations of the Theosophical Society, whose influence on many contemporary New Age teachers he abundantly documents. The Traditionalist School has always taken great care (until recently) to distinguish itself from the kind of anti-traditional universalism preached by Madam Blavatsky, or Aldous Huxley, or Alan Watts. The speed of globalization, however, as well as the difficulty in defining its exact outlines and ideology, have led some writers who are at least sympathetic to the Traditionalist outlook, such as Enes Cariç, to treat it as if it promised to be a "new age" of inter-religious amity and dialogue, like Hellenistic Alexandria or Muslim Andalusia, in which the Traditionalist enterprise could well play a leading part. *False Dawn* demonstrates just how wrong this belief is. Globalization has already been fully infiltrated by the anti-traditional universalists, one of whose apparent agendas is to limit or actually *prohibit* religious proselytization, under some future global federation of religions, as a means to prevent inter-religious violence, looking on proselytization as the religious equivalent of one nation violating the borders of another. In such an atmosphere, the Traditionalists are much more likely to be co-opted than understood. URI founder Bishop William Swing, in his book *The Coming United Religions* [Co-Nexus Press, 1998], has even quoted from Huston Smith's introduction to Schuon's *The Transcendent Unity of Religions*, drawing from it the "lesson" that those who see all religions as various expression of the One Truth are the "esoterists," while those who hold to the exclusive truth of one religion are the "exoterists." According to him, the whole mass of anti-traditional, New Age, neo-Pagan, or ultra-liberal religious syncretists, subscribers to the popular cliché version of religious universalism, are "esoterists" in Schuon's sense of the word! He is unaware that Schuon balanced his universalism by teaching that the revealed religions are providential in their uniqueness and variety. Schuon says:

> Every religion by definition wants to be the best, and "must want" to be the best, as a whole and also as regards its constitutive elements; this is only natural, so to speak, or rather "supernaturally natural" . . . religious oppositions cannot but be, not only because forms exclude one another . . . but because, in the case of religions, each form vehicles an element of absoluteness that constitutes the justification for its existence; now the

absolute does not tolerate otherness nor, with all the more reason, plurality. . . . To say form is to say exclusion of possibilities, whence the necessity for those excluded to become realized in other forms. . . . [*Christianity/Islam: Essays in Esoteric Ecumenism*: World Wisdom Books, 1985; p. 151]

False Dawn should alert the Traditionalist School not to be unwittingly led astray by their own cosmopolitanism into making common cause with the agents, no longer clandestine but now publicly visible and active, of Guénon's "counter-initiation." It is much too late in the day for the Traditionalists to imagine they might one day have the power to influence the course of history. Their true role is to *save souls*, to define precisely how those who have seen beyond religious exclusivism can walk the Spiritual Path without betraying Tradition, either by attempting to travel the Path as self-determined freelances, or by falling in with the anti-traditional universalists.

Traditionalist School taught me (or perhaps it would be better to say "the lesson I drew from Traditionalism") was to preach the Transcendent Unity of Religions to militant religious exclusivists—not that they are likely to listen—and the need for commitment to a single religious tradition to promiscuous spiritual ecumenists—not that *they* are likely to listen, either. But I, at least, will be listening. God willing, I will heed the warning not to make an idol either out of my own religious tradition (Islam) or out of the kind of universal "generic" metaphysics some have drawn from the writings of the Traditionalist masters. If God is no more than "the God of the Christians" or "the God of the Muslims" then He has been degraded from the Absolute Reality to a simple tribal deity. Christianity and Islam and Judaism and Hinduism are true not because the God they worship is the God of Christianity or of Islam or of Judaism or of Hinduism, but because He is the Living God, the Reality Who transcends all of these, His Self-manifestations. But this realization in itself does not constitute an effective spiritual Path. The entire use of the doctrine of the Transcendent Unity of Religions is to help us understand God as transcending all forms, both cultural and natural, while manifesting Himself (in Mercy or in Wrath) by means of them, thus preventing us from worshipping the forms of our chosen religion in the place of God. Any effective spiritual Path, however, must be supported by these very religious forms, seen in their "metaphysical transparency". Though all true and revealed religions spring from the same divine Root, the nourishing fruit of this tree grows on the branches, not the trunk.

In the days of Schuon, Guénon and Coomaraswamy, the times required a concentration on the first of the above two "sermons." But our own time is very different. Only now can we say that the threat of a spurious religious universalism with real social power behind it has begun to equal that of the various militant religious exclusivisms. Alongside the ego of the religious fanatic, we must now place the ego of the religious universalist, who takes the Transcendent Unity of Religions, whether or not he calls it by that name, in an entirely horizontal manner, as if it meant no more than "since all religions are expressions of the same Truth, one religion is just as good as another—and an amalgam of the religions is even better, because each religion has *part* of the truth; when they are all united, then we will have the *whole* truth." As Seyyed Hossein Nasr has written:

> people search in these ecumenical movements for a common denominator which, in certain instances, sacrifices divinely ordained qualitative differences for the sake of a purely human and often quantitative egalitarianism. In such cases the so-called "ecumenical" forces in question are no more than a concealed form of the secularism and humanism which gripped the West at the time of the Renaissance and which in their own turn caused religious divisions within Christianity. This type of ecumenism, whose hidden motive is much more worldly than religious, goes hand in hand with the kind of charity that is willing to forego the love of God for the love of the neighbor and in fact insists upon the love of the neighbor in spite of a total lack of love for God and the Transcendent. The mentality which advocates this kind of "charity" affords one more example of the loss of the transcendent dimension and the reduction of all things to the purely worldly. It is yet another

manifestation of the secular character of modernism which in this case has penetrated into the supreme Christian virtue of charity and, to the extent that it has been successful, has deprived this virtue of any spiritual significance.... It would be less harmful to oppose other religions, as has been done by so many religious authorities throughout history, than to be willing to destroy essential aspects of one's own religion in order to reach a common denominator with another group of men who are asked to undergo the same losses. To say the least, a league of religions could not guarantee religious peace, any more than the League of Nations guaranteed political peace. [Seyyed Hossein Nasr, preface to *Shi'ite Islam* by 'Allamah Sayyid Muhammad Husayn Tabataba'i: SUNY, 1977; pp. 5–6]

Closely allied to this kind of false "exoteric" universalist who espouses a worldly ecumenism is the false "esoteric" universalist who believes that metaphysics can be a spiritual Path in itself, independent of any commitment to a traditional religious way, and whose non-traditional metaphysics (which may have been *abstracted* from the revealed religions, but are no longer effectively connected with any of them) are a great source of pride to him. He sees these generic metaphysics as transcending and superseding the religious traditions themselves, which he views as "good enough for simple believers" or "good enough for mere *bhaktas*," but in no way good enough for metaphysically sophisticated *jñanis* such as himself. He forgets both that true *jñana* is as far beyond the mental understanding of metaphysical principles as it is beyond religious sentimentality, and that the Transcendent Unity of Religions, once grasped, is actually a fairly elementary concept, for all the difficulty it presents to religious literalists; it in no way constitutes the final or even the penultimate content of *jñanic* realization. [NOTE: *Jñana*, in Hinduism, is the path to God through spiritual knowledge, just as *bhakti* is the path to Him through love. *Jñana* is roughly synonymous, in Islamic Sufism, with the Arabic *ma'rifa*, and, in Eastern Orthodox Christianity, with the Greek *gnosis* or *theoria*.]

III

The author of *False Dawn* was a serious Marxist in the 70's, and is now a conservative Catholic following the Byzantine rite. Like many ex-Marxists, he embraced a basically right-wing ideology for a while, after seeing the evils and shortcomings of his former world-view, and he continues to be essentially conservative. Over the past few years, however, he seems to have come to the conclusion that to see the world in terms of either left-wing or right-wing ideology—or *any* ideology—is to seriously hamper one's vision. The Left has certain evils on its radar-screen, and the sort of theory that can clearly analyze them and warn us against them. The same goes for the Right. Both, however, have their ideological blind-spots, and both—insofar as they are ignorant of metaphysics—tend to espouse what can only be called clear violations of the human form. Though the author has certainly been critical of the Left, sees the "ultimate evil" as more likely coming from a right-wing direction. A colleague of the author who wishes to be known as Miguel de Portugal, a Catholic follower of the Virgin of Fatima, a mystic who converted to Eastern Orthodoxy in the face of the apostasy of the Novus Ordo Catholic Church, has come to the conclusion that the era in which tradition is weakened and destroyed by left-wing (or populist) ide-ologies is giving way to one in which a right-wing (or elitist/author-itarian) reaction against the formless promiscuity of religious liberalism will succeed in setting up a counterfeit "tradition" to replace the real one, just as Hitler profited from the moral degener-acy of the Weimar Republic to establish his religion of blood, soil and the *führerprinzip*. This is Lee Penn's prediction as well. What is striking is that both reached substantially the same conclusion as René Guénon in *The Reign of Quantity*—and before having read him. In Guénon's words, which Lee Penn quotes (Lee discovered him in the course of writing *False Dawn*):

> The reign of the "counter-tradition" is in fact precisely what is known as "the reign of Antichrist". . . . His time will certainly no longer be the "reign of quantity," which was itself only the end-point of the "anti-tradition"; it will on the contrary be

marked, under the pretext of a false "spiritual restoration", by a sort of reintroduction of quality in all things, but of quality inverted with respect to its normal and legitimate significance. After the "egalitarianism" of our times there will again be a visibly established hierarchy, but an inverted hierarchy, indeed a real "counter-hierarchy", the summit of which will be occupied by the being who will in reality be situated nearer than any other being to the bottom of the "pit of Hell" [pp. 270–271].

It is to such developments as these that Traditionalist social criticism now needs to address itself. Basing his analysis on the changeless principles of traditional metaphysics, Guénon was able to see much further than most into the "dialectic" of the End Times. And due to the decline of secular ideologies, traditional metaphysics may in fact be the only vantage point from which the chaos and contradiction of the End Times may be clearly discerned. The internal contradiction of Marxism—and, in fact, of any "progressivist" ideology—is that it claims to provide an objective vantage point from which historical change can be viewed, while itself being subject to historical change; the yardstick by which we are to measure how high the water has risen is unreliable, since it itself is growing and/or shrinking at the same time. Those who have begun to understand how relative standards cannot objectively measure relative situations will be pushed either toward post-modernist nihilism, with its absolutization of the relative, or toward acceptance of objective standards which do not and cannot change, standards which can only be theological, and ultimately metaphysical. Yet the very need to embrace changeless standards in a world of immense and chaotic change can itself lead to great dangers, particularly the danger of falsely situating the Absolute in the embrace of the conditional—the root source of all fanaticism. The proper use of metaphysical principles in social criticism is emphatically *not* as a way of establishing a changeless kingdom of Truth on the shifting sands of conditional, worldly life. Its purpose is rather to discern that Truth beyond the veils of this conditional life, as a "kingdom not of This World." This created universe is both a veil over the Face of Truth and a tapestry of signs (the *ayat*) emanating from that Truth, and also leading back to It. This World, on the other hand, is God's creation seen through the veil of the ego; it is a veil pure and simple; there is no truth in it. The ever-changing forms in which This World clothes the same basic set of temptations must be constantly tracked—not in order to *control* This World, but in order—God willing—to become and remain *free* of it. Those who fail to understand this may be shocked to find themselves branded as agents of the "counter-initiation" when the final judgment arrives—like certain groups today who claim to be following Guénon, but who in reality are no more than right-wing political extremists with no understanding of metaphysics and little real interest in it. The falsehood of the month must be investigated and analyzed, until it is precisely revealed as a novel incarnation of the same perennial falsehood; only the liberated soul, the *jivanmukhta*, is free from this duty. If we are unwilling to undertake this kind of critical work, we may be tricked into the service of the very worldly masters we believe we have firmly repudiated, simply because they have presented themselves to us with unfamiliar faces and names. Freedom's price, as the saying goes, is eternal vigilance; *False Dawn* powerfully serves the kind of vigilance without which no true freedom is possible.

When my wife and I first met him, Lee was writing almost exclusively for a conservative Christian audience, in the kind of language they would readily accept. But as we shared with him our Traditionalist perspective over a period of years, it's as if we heard him breathe an almost audible sigh of relief. It's my impression that our presentation of Traditionalist ideas supported him in consciously accepting and expressing what he already essentially knew, and helped free him from the limitations of his conservative ideology, just as that ideology had freed him from his earlier leftist worldview—and all this without his "becoming a Traditionalist." He remains firmly within his traditional Christian worldview and sees no need to adopt another. But certain ideological (*not* theological) constrictions accidental to that worldview now seem to have dropped away. I submit that this is a service the ideas of Coomaraswamy, Guénon and Schuon can perform for a certain class of intellectual in these times. Not everyone is a metaphysician, or should be, but the *breath* of metaphysics may still quicken and liberate the mind of a scientist, or a social critic, or an investigative reporter. Metaphysical principles may transcend "mere facts," but facts are still the concrete *presence* of metaphysical principles in earthly life; anyone who disparages facts can in no way remain faithful to principles. The work of establishing facts, like the work of discerning principles, is in service to the One Truth.

In his *Speculative Postscript*, Lee Penn comes closer to producing a plausible socio-political scenario for the Apocalypse—which clearly must have an historical, socio-political aspect to it, even though, in essence, it is the definitive breakthrough of Eternity into time—than any writer I know; in this concluding section he brings prophesy and social criticism together in a way that is probably only possible in extremely late times. He is wise enough, however, to understand that this scenario is entirely speculative, and that the reality of the end of the age will transcend all our images and expectations. He writes:

> I now begin to look over the horizon, and to speculate about the implications and sequelae of the current push for a political, social and religious New World Order.
>
> It is not my intent to say, as a certainty, that the Apocalypse is upon is *now*. Still less do I intend the absurd exercise of setting the date for the Second Coming of Christ. Rather, I am arguing that if a New World Order is established (and various powerful forces are attempting to do this), the outcome will be far more complicated—with unexpected political and spiritual perils for the unwary—than most present-day traditionalists and conservative activists, commentators, visionaries, and novelists now expect.
>
> Let's begin by stipulating that we are in abnormal times, and have been since at least 1914. In normal times, Anglican bishops [William Swing] would uphold the doctrine and discipline of their church, and would not raise their hands during a Wiccan-led invocation of Hekate and Hermes. In normal times, billionaires [Ted Turner] would not declare themselves to be "socialists at heart," and would not fund movements that

undermine the society within which they prospered. In normal times, the ravings of Helena Blavatsky, Alice Bailey and their New Age followers would be of interest only to the physicians and ministers involved in healing the psyches and souls of these deluded people.

These are not normal times. Therefore, it is possible that, on the heels of a social, economic, or military disaster, the proponents of the New World Order—the URI and its interfaith associates, the globalist movements, and the devotees of Theosophy and the New Age movement—will have an opportunity to rebuild a shattered, disoriented world. Since some of our present-day political and spiritual leaders see themselves as midwives of radical change, we may be very close to such a forced-draft, global version of the Cultural Revolution. Abnormal times, indeed.

If there ever was a book capable of throwing light on some of the central developments of our time in both religion and politics, developments which our inadequate ideologies, as well as our simple factual ignorance, do not let most of us see, it is *False Dawn*. In this indispensable book Lee Penn has taken investigative journalism and social critique to the threshold of prophesy. In the words of Miguel de Portugal, "Once God has *False Dawn* out, whether one individual or a billion read it, it will not matter. He will not be able to be accused that such [a] soul destructive trap was not aptly covered, exposed and wisely published in a manner that would be available to one and all." Never has there been a clearer exposition of how both worldly and religious idealism can lead to the most horrendous unintended consequences, and how the false dream of *total unification* on the plane of earthly life is nothing but a misapprehension and misapplication of the Unity of God, and thus the most dangerous idol ever conceived by the mind of man—the one called *al-Dajjal* in Islam, and in Christianity, *Antichrist*. Nearly eight hundred years ago Jalaluddin Rumi, as we have seen above, already well understood the futility of it.

Four:

ON "NEO-PERENNIALISM"

A Misapplication of the
Transcendent Unity of Religions

IT SEEMS THAT some people are beginning to claim that Islam has a certain precedence over the other religions because it is "more universalist" than they are. But isn't this a contradiction in terms? I'm reminded of a joke I used to tell when I was a leftist activist. The Left, of course, has been notorious for its factionalism; my joke, or parody, went like this: "We're not the factionalists—*they're* the factionalists!" This joke was routinely met with blank stares; what was humorous to me was sober fact to my comrades. No matter that it was a contradiction, demonstrating how a denial of factionalism can in itself be an act of factionalism; they just didn't get it. It is much the same when one religion is claimed to be "more universalist" than the others; in this case, the denial of religious exclusivism is in itself an act of exclusivism.

Each religious revelation is unique and, in its deepest essence, incomparable. Moses may have struck the rock twice, but God never repeats Himself. Certainly He is the Universal, but He is also the Unique. And the expression of God's Uniqueness in this world must necessarily be in terms of the uniqueness of each divine revelation, each animal species, each human individual, each form occupying space and each particular moment of time. If I were to say to another person, "I am more universal than you are since I *include* you, while you clearly do not include me," would this not be a violation of courtesy? And would we not class the person making such a statement as a narcissist, if not a solipsist? Furthermore, would not the statement itself be a contradiction in terms, since there is nothing more *exclusive* than solipsism? To deny the world of relations-to-the-other by claiming that this world can exist inside oneself, or to expand one's identity so as to embrace all others *as oneself*, are the essential acts of human egotism in its introverted and extraverted modes. And the ego is nothing if not an exclusivist.

Our uniqueness lies in our relationship with God, and nowhere else. In relation to others, we must necessarily deal with what is common to us, but our relationship to God, like our relationship to our human beloved, is unique and incomparable. If Abraham, the friend of God, had not chosen this unique relationship, and also been chosen by it, if he had not rejected all affinity with, as well as all opposition to, the religious worlds around him, there would never have been a Judaism, a Christianity, an Islam.

If I am only able to relate to you on the basis of what (in the realm of form) we have in common, this is the same thing as saying that all I can see in you is myself. The root of relationship, which is also the essence of courtesy, is to relate to another from the standpoint of one's own uniqueness, which alone makes it possible for one to witness and protect and salute the uniqueness of another. Certainly this depth and intensity of relatedness could not be maintained without some sense of the things common to both parties; to always stand consciously in one's eternal archetype is formidable, beyond most people's capacity. Yet the fact remains that it is our "common uniqueness" which is the ultimate basis of that relatedness, not any set of definable similarities on the relative plane itself.

Each divine revelation contains all that is necessary for salvation: morality, metaphysics, ontology, epistemology, spiritual anthropology, spiritual method and the Grace to attain the End posited by that method. Therefore all revelations, in terms of the vertical dimension, the relationship of the soul or the community of believers to God, are "equally universal", at least in their essential cores. It is true that the Qur'an is more explicit about the universality of God's revelations to man, more accepting of other "peoples of the Book," than are the scriptures of Judaism and Christianity, though certainly not more so than Hinduism with its doctrine of the *Sanatana Dharma*. But if this greater acceptance were to become the basis for a claim of precedence—among Perennialists, that is, who claim to accept the doctrine named by Frithjof Schuon "the transcendent unity of religions", not among believers who do not, and whose religion consequently *must be the best* to them, according to Schuon in *Christianity/Islam: Essays in Esoteric Ecumenism* [World Wisdom Books, 1985], p. 151— then it would defeat its own purpose.

I am among those who hold to the transcendent unity of religions. According to Schuon, each of God's revelations to man is a unique rendition of the single and primordial Truth. And yet the diversity of such revelations is equally providential, each of them being, in Schuon's terms, "quasi-absolute," and thus mutually exclusive on the plane of form. The transcendent unity of religions, though it requires a certain degree of intellectual sophistication to understand, is a relatively straightforward doctrine. It is not difficult to understand; it is difficult to live with. The world exerts an immense pressure, both overt and insidious, in order to force anyone attempting to hold to this doctrine either in the direction of an anti-traditional universalism, such as that of Robert Mueller or Barbara Marx Hubbard, where religious doctrine is not taken seriously, or toward an increasingly militant religious exclusivism. This pressure may even split a single individual in two, intellectually if not existentially, leading him to espouse *both* an anti-traditional universalism *and* an increasingly rigid religious exclusivism, just as libertinism and compulsive morality may co-exist in the divided soul of a religious leader who is addicted to secret vice. But to attempt to make a synthesis between Robert Muller and Osama bin Laden, and call this two-headed monster "the transcendent unity of religions," is doomed from the outset; this much should be obvious.

As religious believers, our first loyalty, and our first attention, must be toward God. In God the uniqueness of our various religious revelations finds its true purpose, and is relieved from the burden of the hopeless attempt to establish our various "religious identities" by determining how we are like others or different from others. God only blesses the uniqueness of our chosen revelation when we understand it as a way to Him, not primarily as a way to form or assert our own identities, individual or collective; He is actually quite jealous in this regard. This is not to deny that God has willed that certain races, cultures and geographical areas should act as seed-beds for particular revelations; if this were not the case, His revelations to man would have no way of existing on earth. But once these revelations have been established, anyone who uses them primarily to assert the religious identity of his own group, and of himself (necessarily) as a member of that group, rather than as a way of knowing and serving God (Who may or may not command us to assert the rights and identity of our particular religion in a given historical situation, and Who in any case will set His own firm limits to such assertion), is in fact a unconscious idolater. Given that *there is no god but God*, a person who sets up his own religion as an object of worship alongside God, instead of using it as a way provided by God to draw closer to Him and enter more deeply into His Will, may ultimately be among the losers (and God knows best). Religion is the best of pursuits and the worst of idols; when a King commissions a craftsman to produce a beautifully ornamented cup, the craftsman does not present the King with his tool-chest, but with the cup itself—otherwise he will be lucky if a lack of future commissions is the worst thing that happens to him.

Those who are occupied with God are standing in their own uniqueness, with no need nor any desire to assert that uniqueness before others, or even before themselves. Those, however, who spend most of their time and energy worrying about how they are like other people or different from other people resemble men who are always comparing their wives to other men's wives. If the comparison is negative, they have insulted their spouses; if it is positive, they have pandered to their spouses' vanity, and insulted them as well: a man who truly loves his wife does not love her because she is better than other men's wives, but because she is incomparable; as Shakespeare put it, "comparisons are odious."

It is the same with religion. There is no question that the religions must relate to one another, especially in today's world; cultural insularity, for better or worse, has become impossible to postmodern humanity. And as for the correct way for religions to relate to one another, given that insularity is no longer an option, another passage from Shakespeare says it best: "To thine own self be true, and it must follow as the night the day, thou canst not then be false to any man."

[NOTE: I owe the term "Neo-Perennialism" not to Ken Wilber, since I am not using it in his sense, but to Eric Galati, who confirmed my impression that Islamic Perennialists are beginning to identify Perennialism strictly with Islam, or at least to give Islam a certain preeminence in terms of religious universalism—possibly due to the fact, at least in part, that the Christian Perennialists Rama P. Coomaraswamy and Alvin Moore, Jr. are no longer with us.]

Five:

FRITHJOF SCHUON: LIFE AND TEACHINGS

[By Jean-Baptiste Aymard and Patrick Laude]

A Critical Appraisal

Jean-Baptiste Aymard and Patrick Laude have written the best book to date on Frithjof Schuon. Their *Frithjof Schuon: Life and Teachings* [SUNY, 2004] gives a balanced portrait of Shaykh Isa, both autobiographical and in terms of his spiritual character, situates his poetry and paintings in their appropriate spiritual and aesthetic contexts, and presents a synopsis of his teachings that is sufficiently rigorous, subtle and comprehensive to do them justice—which, in view of the almost unparalleled depth and comprehensiveness of those teachings, is no mean achievement. As I read Aymard and Laude's book, I breathed the clear fragrance of the Schuonian *baraka*, such as no book other than one of his own had ever transmitted to me.

However, since I am essentially a contrarian (by fate not by choice, unless fate represents a choice too deeply buried in pre-eternity to be recognized as such), I will concentrate on those parts of the book where I feel that the authors are in error. These errors fall into three categories: misunderstandings of Shamanism, misrepresentations of the doctrines of Ibn al-'Arabi, and certain departures— or the beginnings of them—from the doctrines of Schuon himself. It is one of the marks of an important book that its errors are almost as fruitful as its truths, because, in a sense, they represent the inevitable shadows cast by those truths. Consequently, in answering the errors

105

of *Frithjof Schuon: Life and Teachings*, I have been able to articulate almost everything I have always wanted to say *to* the Traditionalist/Perennialist writers, in response to all I have learned from them.

TROUBLE WITH THE LAW

Like many of us with a Christian cultural background, the authors seem to have trouble with the idea of a law revealed by God and incumbent upon human beings, though they do not explicitly deny the necessity of it (at least for some); this may in fact indicate—though I am uncertain here—that the notion that Christians are no longer "under the curse of the law" is still strong in the "unconscious" of the west, even among some who are formally Muslims. Furthermore, their trouble with the law is only one aspect of their trouble with "exoteric" religion in general. They define religious tradition, in the face of pure esoterism, as a "lesser evil" [p. 80], though lesser than what greater evil they never make clear. They speak of "the concrete need for a solid traditional framework", of the need to protect tradition more than ever against "any relativization that would blunt its effectiveness" [p. 82], and characterize the revealed religious law as "precisely a means of approximate conformity to Divine Qualities within the realm of terrestrial experience." But then they go on to define "gnosis" partly in terms of its "intrinsic independence of formal religion" [p. 88], to speak of "an intellective standpoint that is in a very real sense independent from the traditional and even the religious point of view" [p. 82], and to claim that "metaphysics [does not necessarily need] the context of the Islamic tradition, or any other tradition, in order to keep being alive. . . ." [p. 91]—directly contradicting Frithjof Schuon's position, as given in *Stations of Wisdom* [World Wisdom Books, 1995], that "intellection outside tradition will have neither authority nor efficacy." "Given the essentiality of esoterism," they say, "the question must be raised, is esoterism independent from the religion within which it manifests itself? To this question, a totally logical and consistent reader of Schuon's writings can only answer with a proximate 'no' upon which an indisputable 'yes' must however ultimately prevail" [p. 48].

In order to evaluate such statements, one would first have to know exactly what the authors mean by "independent". That metaphysical discernment, gnosis, and consequently esoterism *transcend* (in a "vertical" sense) the formal limits of the religions in which they appear is certainly the case. The question is, can they be expected to easily develop, survive intact, resist the degenerating influence of the secular mind-set, and find legitimate and spiritually effective ways of propagating themselves *outside* these limits? Here a very proximate "yes", based upon the principle that "the Spirit bloweth where it listeth", is immediately superseded by a clear and indisputable "no". To be blunt, I cannot think of a single historical example where an esoterism deserted its parent religion without eventually—or immediately—turning into a heterodox cult, a political cadre, a universalist pseudo-religion, or all three at once. Aymard and Laude speak of esoterism as if it must appear "within" a given religion; the question is, do they believe that it must in every case *remain* within the religion where it first appeared? It would seem that they do; on page 89 they explicitly deny esoterism's "independence" of exoterism in the sense of its ability to exist outside orthodoxy. They say: "Exoterism as a formal system is a practically necessary framework for the manifestation of esoterism, which befalls upon the former as the mistletoe on an oak" [p. 89]. Mistletoe is in no way "independent" of the tree it grows upon; you can't plant it in your back yard flower bed and expect anything to develop. It transcends the limitations of the oak since it grows on the highest branches, and because it is evergreen—making it a symbol of eternal life and truth—while the oak is deciduous, conditioned by time and the cycles of manifestation. But the "locus of manifestation" of the mistletoe is the oak, and nowhere else. Furthermore, given that esoterism is the very Life of exoteric religion, just as exoterism is the necessary protective context which allows that Life to manifest in this world, if esoterism is considered able to exist "independently" of exoteric religion in the sense of *outside* it, then how will those "solid traditional frameworks" that the authors consider so important be able to survive? Can the body live without the Heart? In light of this passage, it is clear that we should not take Aymard and Laude's use of the word "independent" in this sense—a point that we must never tire of reiterating, especially in light of the authors' other more ambiguous statements, and in the face of the contemporary claim made by some (such as the Ibn 'Arabi Society, or Sufi popularizer Idries Shah) that Sufism—or certain forms of Sufism—can exist outside of Islam entirely. (For Sufism to *subsume* Islam, and exist as the essence and epitome of it, is another matter.) Furthermore, it is one of the many ironies of the latter days that whoever claims that Sufism can be independent of Islam, in the sense of existing outside it, is of one mind with Islamic "fundamentalists" like the Wahhabis, who would certainly like to see Islam "purified" of Sufism, just as the Ibn 'Arabi Society would—in effect—like to see Sufism "purified" of Islam. (I must note here that the Ibn 'Arabi Society was very important in my own spiritual development, and their decades-long work in bringing the doctrines and writings of the Shaykh al-Akbar to the west has been wholly admirable. Nonetheless they do tend to see Ibn al-'Arabi as an exemplar of universalism as opposed to Islam, and clearly believe that an Akbarian or pseudo-Akbarian universalism can do the work of a traditional Sufi path—a point on which we seriously disagree.)

In some places the authors, as we have seen, are entirely clear on this point; in others, not so clear. In reading the passages in question we can feel the formidable pressure applied by This World in its unending attack on Tradition—the slow, interminable, muffled thud of its inexorable and insidious campaign to drive a wedge between *every* esoterism and its proper exoteric context, which can only result in the destruction of both—as when the authors complain that "Sufi metaphysics is pulled apart between its sublime non-dualism and its legalistic straps" [p.105]. But it is only pulled apart in this manner if—unlike the vast majority of the greatest Sufis of the past, including Ibn al-'Arabi and al-Ghazali—one accepts the non-dualism but rejects the law, thus bowing to the precise subversion of Tradition that This World demands. If esoterism fails to remain within the context of the religious traditions, what is to prevent it (all questions of heterodox and counter-initiatory developments aside) from disappearing from this earthly world of form entirely? The authors explicitly state that the plenary esoterism of the *religio perennis* cannot constitute a religious form in itself; but if not, then what form can it adopt that would allow it to continue to exist, concretely, in this world?

The authors speak of "pure esoterism" as focusing on "quintessential prayer, that is, jaculatory prayer" [p. 88]. Certainly the invocation of the Name of God, in the form of *dhikr*, has always been central to Sufi practice, as well as to Eastern Orthodox Hesychasm (as *mnimi Theou*), and has found an important place in Hinduism in the form of *japa-yoga*. And while I will allow that, for a very few, it *may* be possible for the entirety of their religion to effectively be reduced, and concentrated into this practice alone (given that "the Spirit bloweth where It listeth"), there are certainly many esoterists—those who, in an Islamic context, the authors refer to as "esoteric Muslims" rather than "Islamic esoterists"—who believe the canonical prayer, and the other pillars of normative Islam, to be both obligatory and spiritually necessary. Ibn al-'Arabi, for one, considers the obligatory practices of the religion to be spiritually higher than "supererogatory" practices such as *dhikr*: "God chose obligatory works as the best of works, because they result in the servant being the attribute of the Real—His hearing and His sight— while the love of supererogatory works yields the Real as the hearing and sight of the servant. Thus the supererogatory stands in a lower degree than the obligatory, since the obligatory possesses primacy" [*Futuhat al-Makiyya II* 173.8, appearing in William Chittick, *The Sufi Way of Knowledge*: SUNY, 1987, p. 330].

Aymard and Laude characterize Schuon's position—accurately, I believe—on the proper relationship between esoteric and the exoteric in these terms: "Schuon has repeatedly asserted that it can and must be viewed from two standpoints: that of continuity, following which esoterism appears as the inner core of a tradition, and that of discontinuity, according to which esoterism transcends exoterism and may even stand in opposition to it: 'If you would have the kernel, you must break the husk,' according to Meister Eckhart's formula often quoted by Schuon" [pp. 88–89]. My only caution here, and I believe it is a necessary one, is as follows: We must never forget that this "breaking of the husk" is an *esoteric* operation, not an exoteric one. We break the husk of exoterism by transcending its formal limits from within, not by attacking them from without, since to pull down the outer doctrinal and liturgical bulwarks of a given tradition, like Vatican II pulled down traditional Catholicism, can occur only by virtue of a satanic nihilism—either that or in the name of an "alternative" dogmatic theology, which, along with its liturgical expression, would necessarily be heterodox and sacrilegious. The husk that is broken from without may provide me with a savory nut, but once I've eaten that nut its nourishment applies to me alone, and its influence is short. On the other hand, if the nut is broken from within, by the processes of life and growth, it may become a tree that will satisfy the hunger of many, one whose influence will continue "until the consummation of the age". As long as Aymard and Laude are absolutely clear on this point, I have no quarrel with them.

The Traditionalists have always considered affiliation to a particular orthodox tradition as spiritually necessary, no matter how much of an esoterist one may consider oneself to be; and certainly the authors do not explicitly deny this requirement. However, the necessity for such affiliation, it seems, has begun to fade in some people's minds; this may explain why the term "Perennialism" (proximately derived, to some degree, from Aldous Huxley's "perennial philosophy"), as used by Aymard, Laude and others, has begun to replace "Traditionalism"—though, as the authors point out, Schuon's doctrine may be legitimately described by both terms.

René Guénon, and Frithjof Schuon, despite their differences in perspective, as well as Titus Burckhardt, all required adherence to one particular orthodox religious form. In the quotations below, Guénon's "exoterism" is not to be strictly identified with Schuon's "orthodoxy", given that the term "exoterism" cannot be equally applied to all religions; Islam, for example, is formally divided into exoteric and esoteric domains; Christianity is essentially an esoterism which has assumed the form of an exoteric religion; and Buddhism is, so to speak, an esoterism made explicit. Nonetheless, all three authors make it clear that no true esoterism can exist "outside" traditional orthodoxy:

Guénon:

Many people seem to doubt whether it is really necessary for one to aspire to initiation to attach himself first of all to a traditional form of the exoteric order and fulfill all its prescriptions; moreover, this is indicative of a state of mind peculiar to the modern West, for reasons that are no doubt numerous. We will not undertake to ascertain how much of the responsibility for this lies with the very representatives of religious exoterism, whose exclusivism too often tends to deny more or less expressly all that passes beyond their domain; but this aspect of the question is not what interests us here, for what is more astonishing is that those who consider themselves qualified for initiation should display a basically equivalent incomprehension, although here it is applied in an inverse manner. It is indeed admissible that an exoterist be ignorant of esoterism, although such ignorance does not of course justify a negation of it, but what is inadmissible is that anyone with pretensions to esoterism should ignore exoterism, even if only in a practical way, for the 'greater' must necessarily comprehend the 'lesser'. Besides, this practical ignorance, consisting as it does of regarding participation in an exoteric tradition as useless or superfluous, would not be possible without a theoretical misunderstanding of this aspect of tradition; and it is this misunderstanding that makes the matter all the more serious, for it can be asked whether someone with such a misunderstanding, whatever his other possibilities may be, is really prepared to approach the initiatic and esoteric domain, and whether he ought not rather to apply himself to a better understanding of the value and scope of exoterism before attempting to go further [from "The Necessity of Traditional Exoterism", appearing in *Initiation and Spiritual Realization,* Sophia Perennis, 2001].

Schuon:

From our standpoint, orthodoxy is the principle of formal homogeneity proper to any authentically spiritual perspective; it is therefore an indispensable aspect of all genuine intellectuality. . . . To be orthodox means to participate by way of a doctrine that can properly be called "traditional," in the immutability of the principles which govern the Universe and fashion our intelligence [from "Orthodoxy and Intellectuality" appearing in *Stations of Wisdom:* World Wisdom Books, 1995; p. 1].

The divine origin and the majesty of the religions implies that they must contain all truth and all answers; and there, precisely, lies the mystery and role of esoterism. When the religious phenomenon, hard-pressed as it were by a badly interpreted experience, appears to be at the end of its resources, esoterism springs forth from the very depths of this phenomenon to show that Heaven cannot contradict itself; that a given religion in reality sums up all religions and that all religion is to be found in a given religion, because Truth is one [from "To Refuse or to Accept Revelation" appearing in *From the Divine to the Human*: World Wisdom Books, 1982; p.138].

If every man possessed intellect, not merely in a fragmentary or virtual state, but as a fully developed faculty, there would be no Revelations, since total intellection would be a natural thing; but as it has not been like this since the end of the Golden Age, Revelation is not only necessary but even normative in respect to individual intellection, or rather in respect to its formal expression. No intellectuality is possible outside the language of Revelation, a scriptural or oral tradition, although intellection can occur, as an isolated miracle, wherever the intellective faculty exists; but an intellection outside tradition will have neither authority nor efficacy [from "The Nature and Arguments of Faith" appearing in *Stations of Wisdom*, p. 48].

Burckhardt:

There is no spiritual method without these two basic elements: discernment between the real and the unreal, and concentration upon the real. The first of these two elements, discernment or discrimination (*vijñana* in Sanskrit), does not depend upon any special religious form; it only presupposes metaphysical understanding. The second element, however, requires a support of a sacred character, and this means that it can only be achieved within the framework of a normal tradition. The aim of method is perpetual concentration upon the Real, and this cannot be achieved by purely human means or on the basis of individual initiative; it presupposes a regular transmission such as exists only within a normal tradition. For what is man? What is his puny will? How can he possibly adhere to the Absolute without first integrating his whole being into a non-individual (i.e., supra-individual) form? To be precise: there is no spiritual path outside the following traditions or religions: Judaism, Christianity, Islam, Buddhism, Hinduism and Taoism; but Hinduism is closed for those who have not been born into a Hindu caste, and Taoism is inaccessible [from "A Letter on Spiritual Method" appearing in *Mirror of the Intellect: Essays on Traditional Science and Sacred Art*: Quinta Essentia, 1987; p. 251].

The undeniable difficulty that Aymard and Laude have with the formalistic aspects of the religious traditions (and they are certainly not alone) is apparently based on the assumption that for an esoterist to adopt a "confessional" religious form must in every case represent a narrowing of his or her intellectual perspective—as if, in the case of a true *jñani*, "the metaphysical transparency of phenomena" did not apply as much to theological formulations and ritual forms as it does to natural forms and human characters. William Blake's expression is useful here: "I question not my corporeal or vegetative eye any more than I would question a window concerning sight: I look through it, not with it"—an expression that applies equally to the vision of human body and that of the "body" of a given religious form. Where the exoterist, or the one whose esoterism is limited by the horizon of a single religious form, confronts a wall, the *jñani* faces a window, or a door; as he looks through (not with) the window, so he is also free to walk through the door, into the Open, the Infinite.

Nonetheless, houses have their use. As Schuon made clear in so many places, forms have a double nature: they both hide and reveal the Essence. Without forms, the Essence could not communicate Itself; without the ability to transcend forms, we would remain mired in the dimensional reflections of the Essence, and be compelled to absolutize them, thus becoming idolaters. The overturning of these idols is not accomplished by destroying those forms (since, on the plane of form, they are legitimate and necessary, and if we

were to reject them, others—heterodox rather than orthodox—
would inevitably take their place) but by withdrawing our idolatry,
our ego-identification with them, thus witnessing them in their
metaphysical transparency. Even Islam, an archetypally an-iconic
religion, cannot do without the written words of the Qur'an, as well
as sacred architecture, beginning with the Kaaba—nor do these
things—given that a Muslim also entertains no prejudice against the
iconography of the non-Islamic traditions, in the understanding that
what is illegitimate within Islam may still be willed by God in terms
of other revelations—necessarily limit his spiritual perspective.

The inability to adopt religious forms without being intellectually limited by them is the mark of the exoterist, not the gnostic.
And the devaluation of religious forms, stretching in a continuum
from complete rejection to a subtle deprecation based on the adoption of a superior "gnostic" attitude, is the mark either of the anti-
traditional religious freelance, or of the *batini*, the man of the
Inner, but not of the plenary esoterist, the one who has actualized
the truth that God is both *al-Batin* and *al-Zahir*, both the Inner and
the Outer; in the words of Attar, "The *Zahir* is the shadow of the
Rose and the rending of the veil." This is not to ignore the fact that
exoteric religious forms, and more particularly exoteric attitudes,
can exercise a powerful constricting influence on anyone but the
plenary esoterist, particularly in today's world of politicized religion and militantly polarized attitudes. In the case of the soul
immersed in the world but sincerely seeking God, such constriction
may act as a salutary form of recollection (*jam*): one must say "no"
to dissipation in order to approach the Absolute, which is in Itself
the enemy of dissipation, intrinsically. In the case of the true but
not yet perfected gnostic, on the other hand, the constrictive aspect
of religious particularity will function partly as a contraction, a
veil—as if, out of a self-willed loyalty to one particular form, it were
possible to deny God in the name of God. But in the case of the
perfected gnostic, a particular religious form could not be a
constriction, of either the Intellect, the affections, or the will. If it is
not intrinsically a case of bondage and constriction to inhabit one
body instead of a thousand, to love one wife instead of ten, to live in
one house instead of several, then to remain formally within one

religion need not represent a limitation of one's intellectual horizon or spiritual understanding.

The sense of stifling constriction experienced by some people in their attempt to remain faithful to a single religious form will, if a person chooses to reject that constriction or flee from it, most often lead either to dissipation in a multiplicity of forms, or to what might be called a false Gnostic abstraction or rarefaction of the soul (taking the word "Gnostic" in its heterodox and sectarian sense only). Such rarefaction is a sign that one is not fully inhabiting or sufficiently aware of the totality of one's psycho-physical being, but is rather falsely identifying the subtler aspects of the psyche—which remain entirely subjective for all that—with the Spirit itself, which is intrinsically objective. As for dissipation (in the Sufi sense of *tafriqah*, "dispersion"), it may serve spiritual expansion in certain conditions of life or stages of the Path, insofar as it acts to dissolve negative crystallizations of the psyche, but it ultimately ends in contraction (*qabd*), dessication and a veiling of the Truth. Conversely, when dissipation is being overcome through recollection (*jam*), this may initially be experienced in terms of contraction and darkening: the Dark Night of the Soul. Nonetheless, the ultimate end of recollection is, precisely, spiritual expansion (*bast*) and unveiling.

To oppose plenary esoterism to the particularity of religious forms—as when Aymard and Laude speak of the "Islamic crutches" [p. 91]—is to render that esoterism subtly reified and abstract. To come into the presence of the Absolute is to realize, and invoke, the Infinite; to realize the Infinite is to grant each rung of the ontological hierarchy its right to be what it is. To devalue limitation in the name of the Limitless, or earth in the name of Heaven, is to fail to recognize that it is precisely because of its limitlessness that the Limitless can, and must, embrace the limited: "If I ascend up into heaven, Thou art there: if I make my bed in hell, behold, Thou art there" [Psalms 139:4]. Only the limited can be delimited by limitations; the Unlimited embraces limitations, perfectly hierarchicalizes them, and assigns each limited form its proper place and *raison d'être* in the context of the Universal Order. Thus the adoption of a particular religious form by the perfected gnostic, or his continuation within it, is not a concession to a certain weakness of will or limited power of discernment, nor the application of a particular *upaya* in the sense of "saving illusion" (in Schuon's phrase); it is, precisely, the seal of the universality of his outlook. Only those susceptible to a particular temptation need avoid it; only those who count among their passions the tendency to idolize religious forms must flee from them as occasions of sin; only those who believe that they *are* their clothing must go naked in order to be free. If we know that beneath our clothes we are always naked, then we are free dress as our contemporaries dress so as to become indistinguishable from them—or, conversely, to appear in public in our sacerdotal vestments, so as to witness to the truth of our tradition against the darkness of this world. We are also free to drop them at God's command—as al-Hallaj did, when the militant stupidity of an exoterism divorced from its own Secret was in danger of stifling the heart of Islam.

When Ibn al-'Arabi said "my heart has become capable of every form", he was speaking out of a realized Limitlessness which no limit could veil. Nonetheless, being a plenary esoterist if there ever was one, he realized the necessity and appropriateness of maintaining the particularity of the Islamic forms within dar al-Islam, as when he advised the ruler of Konya to limit the right of Christians to publicly call the faithful to worship—though it is certainly true that such a principle does not have the same quality or effect in our own religiously plural and largely secularized world. Furthermore, it is only within the context of such a world that to freely "adopt" a particular tradition becomes a choice, and a crucial one, confronted by many.

In more concrete terms, the use to the gnostic of his remaining (in *formal terms alone*) within a particular religious form, is, first, that it prevents him from giving scandal to those attempting to preserve and be spiritually formed by their sacred tradition—as when religious universalism is used either to syncretize religious forms, or devalue them in the name of a supposed higher "generic" metaphysic, two tendencies which are nearly inescapable in today's world. Secondly, it provides him with a set of perfectly adequate and providential forms by means of which he can communicate his influence to a given religious collective. And thirdly, it saves him from aiding and abetting the politicization of universalism itself, much of which is presently being co-opted, funded and directed by those globalist forces—some aspects of which perfectly fit René Guénon's definition of the "counter-tradition"—who want either to federate the world's religions under a single, non-religious authority, or actually to create a One World Religion in order to pacify the "particularist" tribes and stabilize the New World Order. [See *False Dawn: The United Religions Initiative, Globalism and the Quest for a One-World Religion* by Lee Penn; Sophia Perennis, 2005; ed. Charles Upton—a book that might have been sub-titled "The Counter-Initiation Documented"].

Frithjof Schuon, in his day, was not called upon to face such a danger. When Schuon was forming his worldview, one had to struggle to establish an intelligent and well-informed universalism in the face of the relatively self-enclosed confessional faiths. In our time however, religious universalism of one form or another is a cliché; the challenges of the present day include developing the ability to fully adopt—as a protection against syncretism or generic metaphysics as much as a spiritual path—a particular religious form without losing one's universal perspective. This is not to say that those teachers like Schuon whose teachings are not limited to a single religious form no longer have a place or a function (far from it!), nor that the stance of the plenary esoterist who chooses to adopt a single religious form is in every case superior to that of the teacher whose message is transmitted in a more universalist manner. God employs many modes of expression because He knows we are need of them. I maintain only that the *incapacity* to remain within a single form without being limited by it—in terms of one's intrinsic intellectual depth and comprehension, that is, not on the level where the form itself asserts its rights (given that, in themselves, forms are nothing but limits), is precisely that: an incapacity.

Ibn al-'Arabi mentions three classes among the Muslims: the "worshippers" or "common folk", the "Sufis" and the "People of Blame", with the last being the highest. The "Sufis" are subject to states, stations, unveilings, charismas, and the "breaking of habits"; they "stand out" among the followers of the Prophet as possessing special gifts. However, the People of Blame exhibit no such marks. According to the Shaykh al-Akbar,

The third group add nothing to the five daily prayers and the supererogatory exercises (*rawatib*). They do not distinguish themselves from the faithful who perform God's obligations by any extra state whereby they might be known. They walk in the markets, they speak to the people, and none of God's creatures sees them distinguishing himself from the common people by a single thing; they add nothing to the obligatory works or the Sunna customary among the common folk. They are alone with God, firmly rooted, not wavering from their servanthood for the blink of an eye. They find no favor in leadership, since Lordship has overcome their hearts and they are lowly before it. God has given them knowledge of the places of things and of appropriate works and states. They are veiled from the creatures and stay concealed from them by the covering of the common people. For they are sincere and purely devoted servants of their Master. They witness Him constantly in their eating and drinking, their waking and sleeping, and their speaking with Him among the people [*Futuhat al-Makkiyya III* 34.28 appearing in William Chittick, *The Sufi Way of Knowledge*: SUNY, 1987, pp. 373–374].

The People of Blame are those who are perfectly satisfied with the "outer" norms of the religion because they have seen and understood the limitations inherent in specialness and spiritual excess. Outwardly they are indistinguishable from the simple "common folk", so obviously it is not this group who "blame" them. So why are they called the People of Blame? They have earned this name because they draw blame from the "Sufis", who see their return to the outer norms of the religion as a betrayal of esoterism, forgetting that God is not only The Inner (*al-Batin*) but the Outer (*al-Zahir*), and that while *al-Batin* takes precedence over *al-Zahir*, the equilibrium between *al-Batin* and *al-Zahir* takes precedence over both. As St. Thomas Aquinas puts it, the contemplative life is greater than the active one, but the "mixed" life comprising both contemplation and action is greater still—a statement which Thomas Merton, in *The Seven Storey Mountain*, interprets to mean that the contemplative capacity of the one leading the "mixed" life must be great enough to insure that his action in no way compromises his contemplation, but is rather a direct expression of it. Such, within Islam, was the example of the Prophet Muhammad, peace and blessings be upon him.

MISUNDERSTANDINGS OF SHAMANISM

The authors are at great pains to justify Schuon's interest in Native American spirituality, which they identify primarily with Shamanism. And in the course of this justification, they criticize Guénon's "one-sided" characterization of the psychic or animic realm as almost exclusively demonic. In the face of Guénon's radical distinction between psyche and Spirit, they bring forth those aspects of Schuon's teaching that emphasize their continuity, although they do not hide the fact that Schuon also taught the need to clearly differentiate psyche and Spirit, and said that in the psychic domain the soul runs the risk of "drowning in its own nothingness."

The authors' metaphysical basis for the validation of Shamanism or white magic as legitimate elements of the kind of spiritual Path integral to a plenary esoterism is drawn in part from Schuon's essay "Summary of Integral Metaphysics", appearing in *Survey of Metaphysics and Esoterism* [World Wisdom Books, 1986]. According to him (and given partly in my paraphrase), there is a descending order of perspectives where the border between the divine or principial realm and the world of manifestation falls at several different points. In the first perspective, the line is drawn between *Atma* and *Maya*, between the Undifferentiated Absolute, *Nirguna Brahman*, and *all* differentiation, whether cosmic or *in divinis*. In the second perspective the line falls between Principle and Manifestation, between God and the World. Here God, as Pure Being, which in terms of the first perspective is seen as an aspect of *Maya*, is classed with *Atma* as its first and integral reflection. In the third perspective the line is between "heaven" and "earth", between the celestial order seen as composed of Beyond Being (*Atma* or *Nirguna Brahman*), Pure Being (God in Himself, identifiable with *Saguna Brahman*), and the Logos (God as Creator, seen as in relation to, and thus inseparable from, His creation), and the realm of cosmic manifestation, composed of the spiritual, psychic and material universes. The fourth perspective draws the line between the Logos—seen as the expression of all that is above it, both *Nirguna Brahman* and *Saguna Brahman*, but also as incorporating, according to the authors, the celestial realm of the "angels" and/or the "gods"—and the "outer world" now considered as relatively fallen, terrestrial and profane.

Here, however, the authors add a fifth level of distinction, calling it the essential principle behind Shamanism: that between the *visible* and the *invisible*, according to which, whatever is invisible pertains to the divine or principial realm, and only that which is visible as sense-experience to the earthly or profane one. They have apparently based this on a different rendition of the shifting border between manifestation and Principle that appears in Schuon's *Logic and Transcendence* [Perennial Books, 1975]:

> one may make a distinction between the material or visible world and the immaterial and invisible world; broadly speaking this is the perspective of the Shamanists, in which the animic powers are regarded as prolongations of the Divinity [p. 170].

One might wish at this point that Schuon has not spoken quite so broadly. Though there is certainly an element of truth in this depiction of Shamanism, it is nonetheless true that traditional doctrines relating to the phenomenology of the psychic plane, including those having to do with the *jinn* (in Islam) or "the Powers of the Air" (in Christianity), make it abundantly clear that the notion that anything which is invisible must necessarily pertain to the realm of the Principle, to the Good, the True and the Beautiful, by the simple fact that it transcends sense experience, is erroneous. It is, in fact, this very false belief that has validated in the public mind the ignorant and dangerous teachings of the spiritualists and the New Age "channelers", not to mention the phenomena of the sorcerers. Nor is it accurate to imply that Shamanism itself recognizes no distinction between helpful and demonic spirits. Mircea Eliade, in *Shamanism: Archaic Techniques of Ecstasy*, even quotes certain Siberian shamans—Siberia being in many ways the "heartland" of Shamanic belief and practice—as saying of themselves, "we are the ones God has sent to earth to fight demons". (That *Survey of Metaphysics and Esoterism* was published later than *Logic and Transcendence* indicates that Schuon may ultimately have rejected the idea that the invisible world can stand in a simple way as representative of the Principle vis-à-vis the visible one.)

As we descend the ontological hierarchy, we encounter worlds that are more and more subject to time; which is to say, worlds whose denizens are less and less capable of being strictly identified with eternal metaphysical principles. The quality of time in the animic plane, to which magic and Shamanism directly pertain, is less uni-directional and more multidimensional than the geological and historical times of earthly reality. Nonetheless, the *jinn* too have their histories, their clash of forces, their "political" regimes that rise and fall, even their trends and "fashions"; the quality and phenomenology of such histories, if not their actual events, are perhaps best expressed by J.R.R. Tolkien in his *Lord of the Rings* trilogy. In view of this, we need to emphasize that the animic realm is at present in a highly polluted and toxic condition. This is due both to the effects of the general degeneration of the cosmic environment in the Kali-yuga, as well as to the more direct influence of the collective psychic degeneration of humanity.

The human form, as possessor of the *kalifate*, is the central guardian, epitome and pole of earthly reality, both material and subtle; this is why the spiritual darkening, fragmentation and disorder into which that form has fallen in the modern world—which is only deepened and exacerbated under the enshrined psychic fragmentation known as postmodernism—profoundly affect those strata of the psychic plane most directly related to earthly reality and the natural world. Thus to simply recommend the "integration" of this world into the spiritual life, via Shamanism or white magic, in the name of the Unity of Being, is rather naive. Pious, powerful, integrated and good-willed shamans like Black Elk or Yellowtail, working within relatively intact Native American traditions, are the great exceptions in today's world; the shamans, or magicians, of the 21st century are much more likely to be disordered or subversive individuals whose appeal lies solely in their access to invisible worlds, whatever the *quality* of those worlds may be.

As for the identification of the psychic plane with the world of Shamanism and Shamanism with white magic, we must remember that even though Schuon himself, in *The Feathered Sun*, associates Shamanism with white magic, he says elsewhere—in *Light on the Ancient Worlds*—that, in relation to Native American spirituality, "the word 'magic' which is sometimes used in this connection is far too limitative, and even erroneous in the sense that it defines a cause in terms of a partial effect." Furthermore, Black Elk himself could not unreservedly praise the world of the traditional Lakota shamans of his time. Few are aware that he worked as a Catholic catechist among the Lakota for even longer than his term as a traditional medicine man, and that from the standpoint of the Catholic tradition he was able to recognize the problem of arrogance and self-aggrandizement that affected many of his traditional Lakota colleagues [cf. Michael F. Steltenkamp, *Black Elk: Holy Man of the Oglala*: University of Oklahoma Press, 1993].

It is nonetheless true, as the authors assert, that to make a strict separation between psyche and Spirit, thereby in effect turning the whole psychic plane over to the Devil, does militate against a realization of the Unity of Being. But the fact remains that the unity of psyche and Spirit, if it is not to open us to demonic incursions, must be effected from the Spiritual pole, not the psychic one. The soul immersed in worldly dissipation, glamour and identification must seek the Transcendent God, the One whose "kingdom is not of this world", and this can only be done through a strict differentiation between psyche and Spirit—in the words of the Prophet Muhammad, peace and blessing be upon him, through a "war against the soul." It is only when we disobey the commands and impulses of the unredeemed psyche through ascetical practice that we gain the power to *concretely* distinguish them from the commands and promptings of the Spirit; as Schuon says, the spiritual man is the one who dominates himself, and loves to dominate himself, in order to transcend himself. Only the will to place the Spirit first in our lives, to grant It precedence over all psychic and material concerns, will allow us—God willing—to ultimately realize our identity with It, an identity that is spiritual and transpersonal, not individual or psychic. And it is only when this identity is firmly established that the Divine Transcendence gradually—or suddenly—flowers into the Divine Immanence. Nothing less than the unveiling of the Immanence of God in His creation that can fully establish the seamless unity of Spirit and psyche, and the material world as well; weekend excursions into all the magical wonders of the psychic plane cannot. This is not to say that the contemplation of the secrets of God in the wonders of His creation, as well as the development of a healthy psychological self-understanding through a sober assessment of one's strengths, weaknesses and predilections, cannot even begin until the spiritual Path is nearing its end; these lessons are much better learned, gradually and progressively, during the whole course of that Path, on pain of falling into great psychic excesses, deficiencies and imbalances. It *is* to say, however, that magic, no matter how white we want to make it, and duly noting the rare exceptions to this rule, is emphatically *not* the path to either psychic self-understanding or the vision of the metaphysical transparency of phenomena. Ninety-nine times out of a hundred, no matter how "good" our intentions may be, it is the straightest path to Hell—and never more so than in these extremely dark times. The authors speak of Guénon's "prophylactic" need to counter "the phenomenism of the occultists and other neospiritualists, Guénon concluding that the obsession of the latter with all kinds of fanciful or dangerous psychic manipulations needed to be denounced unambiguously"—as if such manifestations were things of the nineteenth and earlier twentieth centuries, and not clear and present dangers confronting us today, dangers whose obvious power over the collective psyche has grown exponentially since Guénon's death. To ignore this truth, to assume that Shamanism can easily work as method of integrating the physical and psychic elements of the human constitution into the plane of the Spirit under present cosmic conditions— particularly for non-Indians who approach the world of Shamanism on the basis of curiosity, the hope of witnessing "wonders", or a raw hunger for power—is naïve to say the least. Certainly the authors will allow that "The matter is not to cultivate powers for the sake of power—for, as Schuon has judiciously and vigorously stated, one can go to Hell with all the powers one wishes—but rather to integrate the various levels of one's being so as to know God with all that one is." But how can the simple lack of a self-interested power motive protect the one who enters a plane of reality where the power motive is in full force, and whose denizens possess powers that he can neither wield, nor sometimes even conceive of? Can one expect to travel safely through a war zone simply because he enters it unarmed?

The authors characterize Shamanism, which they identify in part with esoterism, in the following terms:

> The key word of this perspective, that is common to all forms of Shamanism, is "transmutation." "Everything that is human is ours", and everything that is ours is to be transmuted by the Spirit. As opposed to exoteric or eso-exoteric perspectives that tend to proceed through exclusive asceticism or even, on a lower level, through puritanical abstraction, esoterism will tend to transmute animic reactions and states by identifying them with the Spirit or its Symbol. This is particularly important to underline with respect to the soul's receptivity to beauty, and specifically erotic beauty. The transmutation of aesthetic and erotic emotions through the means of a sacred symbol, like a Divine Name in *japa-yoga*, constitutes one of the fundamental aspects of psychic integration [pp. 100–102].

In my view, a number of steps and considerations are left out here, not the least of which is the fact that the shamanic "transmutation" more often refers to magical shape-shifting, such as the shamanic sorcerer's assumption of an animal form, than to the spiritual alchemization of the soul. To begin with, it is inaccurate to oppose "Shamanism/esoterism" to asceticism. Shamanism at its best is an operative expression of a greater esoteric perspective, not something—at least in this *yuga*—to be identified with esoterism per se. Secondly, one of the things that characterizes Shamanism the world over is, precisely, asceticism, though it may not be given the specifically puritanical twist that it has sometimes assumed within Christianity. The self-torture of the Shaman for the purpose of gaining theurgic power is perhaps our most extreme example of the "ascetical exploit"—as for example the Eskimo *angakok* who immersed himself, fasting, in a hole in the arctic ice for many days.

This aspect of ascetical self-torture, sometimes amounting to a true psycho-physical death-and-rebirth, is expressed in the Plains tribes through the fast, sometimes accompanied by self-mutilation, that is integral to the vision quest, as well as by the rigors of the Sun Dance, where a participant may dance for many hours in the hot sun, fasting and without water, with a splint of wood inserted through the flesh of his chest, tied to a leather thong secured to the central pole of the sacred area, a splint that is sometimes torn free during the course of the dance. All this is a far cry from the sacred eroticism of the Hindus (though certainly not from their own more extreme forms of yogic asceticism); the two spiritual universes are animated by very different geniuses. That Schuon was apparently able (though this remains open to question) to successfully integrate Native American spirituality, spiritual eroticism and sacred nudity into his own "plenary esoterism", as expressed in the "primordial gatherings" he conducted, in no way establishes Shamanism as a normative aspect of esoterism in our age, nor sacred eroticism (to say the least!) as a normative aspect of Shamanism; what is possible to the great spiritual Master is often impossible to others, particularly after the Master in question has passed on. Schuon himself characterized his primordial gatherings as the expressions of a personal predilection, not an integral aspect of his spiritual method, and after his death Martin Lings offered the opinion that the time for this particular manifestation had passed with the passing of the Shaykh. To take the exception that proves the rule as a rule in itself has been the origin of all too many heterodox and anti-traditional movements over the centuries.

The authors place Shamanism in the context of the undeniable need to integrate both *psyche* and *soma* into the spiritual life. They quote Schuon as recognizing the need for "integrating the psychic elements", and go on to say: "By contrast with Guénon, who tended to perceive the body as a distraction, Schuon's esoteric and integral perspective emphasizes the need to integrate the body into one's understanding and assimilation of reality." In other words, as they say, "everything human is ours," paraphrasing the famous statement of the Latin comic dramatist Terence, *Homo sum: humani nil a me alienum puto*: "I am human, therefore nothing human is alien to me". Dostoevsky, in *The Brothers Karamazov*, points out the dangers hidden in this glib assertion when he has the Devil say to Ivan, *Satan sum: et nihil humanum a me alienum puto*: "I am Satan, therefore nothing human is alien to me." Infernal psychic possibilities are also "human" in the sense that human beings may enter infernal states, but this emphatically does *not* mean that we should try to "integrate" them into our spiritual lives, or that they can be "transmuted by the Spirit" at any time before the final dissolution of the universe. The diversion of the human faculties from their proper ends can be made right through reorienting them to those ends, but truly infernal possibilities, entirely perverse and oriented only to destruction, in a sense have no right to exist. From the standpoint of *Mahamaya* or All-Possibility, evil as "the possibility of impossibility" (in Schuon's phrase) is inevitable as soon as the progressive ontological descent of manifestation reaches the point where it can appear; from the human standpoint, it must be rejected "quasi-absolutely". "There needs be evil," said Jesus, "but woe to him through whom evil comes". Even the alchemists, who put to use many aspects of the human psycho-physical entity that a simplistic spiritual idealism might lead us to reject, spoke of a *terra damnata*, a "damned earth" that cannot be integrated into the human form and the spiritual life but must be rejected definitively. The existence of a possibility in the universal order does not justify the attempt to actualize it in the human one; as Schuon says in *Gnosis: Divine Wisdom* [Perennial Books, 1990, p.61]:

> It is true that "evil", or what we call such, reduces itself in the last analysis to a tendency which cannot not be and is part of the universal equilibrium; but this does not prevent there being, on the plane of cosmic coagulations—whether it be a question of the "external" world or the soul—phenomena which are either conformable or contrary to pure Being (*Sat*, whence *sattwa*), or mean that creatures endowed with understanding should fail to recognize them; to affirm the contrary is to disavow all the sacred Scriptures, not to mention simple common sense. In metaphysics, as in every other realm, it is necessary to know how to put everything in its place.

I would only add that the ascetical perspective, at its best, also recognizes the need to integrate the body into the spiritual life, whence the phenomenon of the incorrupt corpses of certain saints, some of whom were among the most extreme examples of asceticism in the annals of sanctity. To overcome the passions is not to deny the body but to purify the psyche, the body being the site-of-manifestation of the various psychic tendencies, not their source.

René Guénon, in *The Reign of Quantity and the Signs of the Times* [p.182], characterizes Shamanism in the following terms:

> If we consider "shamanism" properly so-called, the existence of a highly-developed cosmology becomes apparent, of a kind that might suggest concordances with other traditions in many respects, the first with respect to a separation of the "three worlds," which seems to be its very foundation. "Shamanism" will also be found to include rites comparable to some that belong to traditions of the highest order: some of them, for example, recall in a striking way the Vedic rites, and particularly those that are most clearly derived from the primordial tradition, such as those in which the symbolism of the tree and the swan predominate. There can therefore be no doubt that "shamanism" is derived from some form that was, at least originally, a normal and regular traditional form; moreover it has retained up to the present day a certain "transmission" of the powers necessary for the exercise of the functions of the "shaman"; but as soon as it becomes clear that the "shaman" directs his activity particularly toward the most inferior traditional sciences, such as magic and divination, a very real degeneration must be expected, such as may sometimes amount to a real deviation, as can happen all to easily to such sciences whenever they become over-developed.

MISCHARACTERIZATIONS OF IBN AL-ʾARABI

The authors seem uncomfortable with the doctrines of Ibn al-ʾArabi (as Schuon also was, in certain places), possibly because the Shaykh al-Akbar is in many ways the closest thing to a great Sufi—

on the level of metaphysical expression, perhaps the greatest—who was also an "esoteric" universalist, while at the same time remaining firmly within the Islamic fold. Schuon made a distinction between "esoteric Islam" (or esoteric Christianity) and "Islamic (or Christian) esoterism"—between those Muslim and Christian gnostics whose esoterism remains within the confines of a particular revelation as its inner Secret, and those Muslims (or Christians) whose esoteric horizon embraces all the divine revelations rather than being limited to one of them. (In Christian terms, we might characterize Jean Borella as an esoteric Christian, and James Cutsinger, at least in his earlier career, as a Christian esoterist.) We have already addressed this distinction above, and seen that the position taken by the authors, based on Schuon's own, is that of Islamic esoterism, not esoteric Islam. It may be that, in relation to Schuon, Ibn al-'Arabi tends to appear to them as not as an Islamic esoterist, but as that more limited type, an esoteric Muslim, whose horizon is bound by the revelation that encloses him and whose esoterism is necessarily transcended and comprehended by Schuon's more plenary esoterism.

Be that as it may, I must take issue with two of the authors' characterizations of Ibn al-'Arabi's teachings: their view of his doctrine of the Names of God, and their explanation of his reasons for including among the Names of God *al-Mudhill*, "The Misguider", which they see as placing the origin of evil on the level of the Will of Allah, Who in Schuon's doctrine is identified both with the Personal God and with Pure Being.

To begin with, Aymard and Laude strictly oppose Schuon's doctrine of the Names or Qualities of God as "the Self-determinations of the Absolute" to Ibn al-'Arabi's view that these Names represent relations between the Absolute and various created beings; this opposition, however, is not warranted. According to the central doctrine of the Shaykh al-Akbar, which has come to be known as the Transcendent Unity of Being (*wahdat al-wujud*), God is, strictly speaking, the *only* Being, the only One to Whom Being can be attributed intrinsically. Therefore all His creative manifestations are, precisely, Self-determinations and nothing else. Furthermore, since The Transcendent Unity of Being envisions all manifestation as remaining *essentially* within God (as the Mahayana Buddhists also do, though in a very different way), the distinction between the Divine Names as relationships between God and created things, and those Names as the Self-determinations of the Absolute within the close embrace of the Divine Nature (Schuon's *Maya-in-divinis*; Ibn al-'Arabi's *ahadiyya al-jam*), effectively disappears. And to the objection that the Transcendent Unity of Being therefore collapses the ontological hierarchy, thus making it necessary to envision evil as originating directly from the Divine Will rather than (as Schuon explains it) from the ontological attenuation of the Infinite in the course of God's progressive Self-manifestation, the answer is that according to Ibn al-'Arabi, the Names of God, though each is a Name of the Absolute Reality and nothing else, are arranged in hierarchical order according to how complete or how limited a manifestation of God they designate. In line with the *hadith qudsi* "My Mercy has precedence over My Wrath," the Shaykh al-Akbar places the Names of Mercy higher than the Names of Rigor as being more comprehensive and accurate expressions than those lower Names of the fundamentally inexpressible mystery of the Essence—a doctrine that is essentially equivalent to Schuon's "emanationist theodicy." The lower the Name, the more limited the view of Reality it represents; the more limited the view of Reality held by those created entities who spring from a given Name, the closer they are to the experience of Rigor (for which read "evil"), and the further they lie from Mercy or felicity. However, I would nonetheless agree with the authors that Schuon's image of the progressive attenuation of the Infinite due to the necessity of Its Self-communication, till the point is reached where evil must manifest, is clearer and more satisfying as a theodicy than those formulations of Ibn al-'Arabi of which I am aware.

As for God as *al-Mudhill*, "The Misguider", the authors take as their source for this attribution a passage from William Chittick's *Imaginal Worlds: Ibn al-'Arabi and the Problem of Religious Diversity* [SUNY, 1994; p.142], which they quote in a footnote: "The Shaykh [Ibn al-'Arabi] explains why disobeying the prescriptive command may lead to wretchedness by referring to the implications of some of the implications of *wujud*. God is not only the Guide, He is also the

Misguider (*mudhill*). Although not mentioned in the well-known lists of ninety-nine names, this name is implied by thirty-five Qur'anic verses where God is the subject of the verb 'to misguide'. In certain circumstances, God's misguidance may dominate over His guidance, leading to disobedience in this world and wretchedness in the next."

In order to understand what William Chittick is getting at here, we need to place the quote from him given by Aymard and Laude in a larger context. On the next page [p.143], Chittick continues:

> To ask why God misguides people is like asking why *wujud* is *wujud*, or why reality is reality. The answer is simply that reality is what it is, and cannot be otherwise. To say that God is the Misguider is simply to assert that *wujud* allows for the possibility of misguidance and wretchedness and that entities representing this possibility will have to exist. This is why the Shaykh insists that, in the last analysis, God misguides no one. Rather, people follow their own natures, which is to say that they manifest their own immutable entities. No one can blame the gardener when an apple tree fails to yield grapes, and no one should blame God when a sinner fails to do good works. The sinner can blame only his own reality. This, says the Shaykh, explains Satan's answer to those who will complain to him at the resurrection that he had misguided them: *Do not blame me, but blame yourselves* (14:22).

I understand and partly share the authors' difficulty with formulations like this, which appear not to allow us to apply to God the Names Al-'Adl (the Just) or Al-Ghafur (the All-Forgiving); the sinner, at this point, might seem justified in retorting, "I am certainly willing to blame myself, if You will allow that I created myself." As it stands, this way of stating the matter does not seem to fully absolve God from a sort of arbitrary, Calvinist predestinarianism. In response to this difficulty, under the influence of Ibn al-'Arabi's doctrines but in my own words, I would explain things as follows: In this world, choice and destiny necessarily appear as polarized. But in the Unity of the Names of God, on the level of Divinity known in later Akbarian doctrine as *wahadiyya* (apparently synonymous with

Ibn al-'Arabi's *ahadiyya al-jam*), the synthetic unity of all the Divine
Names which is denoted by the name *Allah*, choice and destiny are
one, this being the esoteric meaning of Heraclitus' saying, "character
is fate." The choices I freely make during life, when seen *sub specie
aeternitatis*, are indistinguishable from my pre-eternal character,
since they are precisely how that character appears when refracted
into the moments of passing time. But if who I am determines my
choices, my choices equally constitute who I am. In time, my choices
form my identity, my particular relationship with God, and my
post-eternal destiny; in pre-eternity, when the Breath of the Merciful
conferred existence upon my permanent archetype *in divinis*, I
freely chose to be precisely who I was destined to be, to the exclusion
of all else. Thus, in Schuon's phrase, I am "condemned to freedom".
Eternity underlies the moments of our lives rather than simply coming before or after them; therefore my eternal choice does not negate
my free will, nor strictly predetermine my daily choices in passing
time, since it can with equal validity be seen as the final sum of them.

God does not directly will evil, but rather "wills what is". He wills
the actualization of the *ayan al-thabita*, the permanent archetypes,
which together constitute what Frithjof Schuon calls "All-Possibility." According to Schuon, All-Possibility must include "the possibility of impossibility", or evil, and this is substantially the same
doctrine as Ibn al-'Arabi's assertion that God cannot change the
nature of the permanent archetypes, but only bring them into existence. He cannot change them because, as All-Possibility, they are the
necessary expression of the Infinity of His Essence; this means that,
on their own proper levels, the possibilities known as evil and privation must manifest. We might say that it is God's very *lack* of privation, in terms of His intrinsic Infinity, that makes the manifestation
of privation necessary, in terms of the inevitable radiation of His
Infinity in the direction of non-entity. In any case, neither Schuon
nor Ibn al-'Arabi assert that God, as Pure Being, wills evil. When
the Qur'an says *I take refuge in the Lord of Daybreak from the evil of
that which He created*, it is not implying that God creates evil or is
partly evil Himself (He could not "create" evil since it is essentially a
privation, not a positive expression of any essence whatsoever), but
that creation, insofar as it departs from God, necessarily becomes

subject to evil—not through God's Will, however, but by virtue of its exile from Him. And Ibn al-'Arabi agrees with Schuon in declaring that evil is a privation, possessing no positive existence: "Evil is the opposite of good, and nothing emerges from good but good; evil is only the non-existence of the good. . . . Hence all existence is good, since it is identical with the Sheer Good, who is God" [*Futuhat al-Makkiyya* I 47.2, appearing in William Chittick, *The Sufi Way of Knowledge*: SUNY, 1987, p. 290]. So for Ibn al-'Arabi as much as for Schuon, God is the Sovereign Good, and the Sovereign Good cannot, in any positive sense, will evil.

In inaccurately claiming that by the use of the Name *Al-Mudhill* Ibn al-'Arabi situates evil on the level of the Will of the Personal God, thus making Him in some sense "partly good and partly evil" (not, as Schuon characterizes Him, the Sovereign Good, Pure Being, Who is "beyond of good and evil" precisely because He is All-Good, totally without privation, neither composed of parts nor paired with any opposite), Laude and Aymard seem to treat Ibn al-'Arabi as if he were a sort of doctrinaire Asharite. The Asharite school of Islamic *kalam* denies secondary causes and attributes everything—all forms, all events, even all *choices*—to the sovereign Will of God, going so far as to assert that events are not even proximately attributable to natural law, or to antecedent causes within the realm of creation, but are produced directly by God through His continuous re-creation of the entire universe, instant by instant— the famous doctrine of "occasionalism". Asharite doctrine would thus seem to deny free will. It is nonetheless clear from the Qur'an that the absolute denial of free will is in no way Islamic. On almost every page of the Holy Book warnings and exhortations appear, which, if there were no such thing as human free will, would be meaningless.

Ibn al-'Arabi incorporates Asharite *kalam* into his doctrine, but absolves God from the accusation—inseparable from strict occasionalism—that He is an arbitrary tyrant, damning some and saving others for his own inscrutable purposes (or for no purpose at all, since to the Asharite form of theological extremism, for God to even have a *purpose* in relation to His creation might seem to limit Him by making Him "subject" to it). He does so by virtue of the formulation "the determined determines the Determiner." God does not overwhelm us, forcing us to do this or to choose that; rather, he seconds us in our own choices, guiding those who submit to Him and leading astray those who rebel against Him. In the words of the Noble Qur'an (14:4): *And We never sent a messenger save with the language of his folk, that he might make (the message) clear for them. Then Allah sendeth whom He will astray, and guideth whom He will. He is the Mighty, the Wise.* If we choose to follow Him, the knowledge and strength we require for His service are attributable only to Him, not to us, just as our very being is not attributable to us, but is freely given out of the store of His Being. That knowledge and strength are drawn from Him in his names *Al-Nur* (Light), *Al-Hadi* (the Guide), *Al-Muqit* (the Nourisher), and *Al-Mujib* (The Answerer of prayers). Likewise if we choose to disobey Him, the impulse to transgress is drawn only from Him, in his names *Al-Jabbar* (The Compeller), *Al-Muqtadir* (the All-Determiner), *Al-Mudhill* (the Abaser), and *Al-Darr* (the Punisher); since God is omnipotent, our power to rebel against him is granted to us only by His leave. No choice made by man, free though every choice most certainly is, has the power to depart from the Will of God, which embraces all actions and all choices. God does not reward or punish us in *recompense* for our actions, but *by means of* them.

The authors also assert that, while Ibn al-'Arabi sees the inevitably limited perspectives on Reality of existing creatures, as well as transgressions of God's law, as the twin sources of evil, he provides no criteria that allow us to understand the difference between these two factors, nor why "some limitations are adequate extentiations of archetypes, while other limitations are privations or subversions that not only limit the Reality of God but also constitute negations of his qualities". Aymard and Laude allow that "Law . . . is precisely a means of approximate conformity to Divine Qualities within the realm of terrestrial experience," but complain that, although Ibn al-'Arabi names the law as the source of human felicity in this world and the next, "the relationship between the nature of prescriptions and proscriptions on the one hand, and their ontological connection with happiness on the other is not really explained." In light of Ibn al-'Arabi's doctrine, but again in my own words, I would explain that relationship, as well as the nature of the distinction between limitations as "adequate extentiations of the archetypes" and limitations as "privations or subversions", as follows: Obedience to the law leads to felicity precisely because the law is sent by God for the purpose of guiding us to felicity. Religious laws are not imposed upon us arbitrarily by some divine tyrant—though their later degeneration into various pharisaical legalisms may make it seem as if they were—but are more on the order of "it is unlawful to cut your fingers off" or "it is unlawful to put your eyes out." On the simple moral level (though not so clearly on the ritual one), nothing could be more obvious than that the development of the virtues and the avoidance of murder, theft, drunkenness, adultery etc. are directly conducive to human happiness. The origin and essence of the law is the primordial human form, *al-fitrah*. In this world, the law exists to prevent us from betraying our essential humanity; *in divinis*, the law is nothing less than God's eternal vision of the human form, a vision which in fact constitutes that form. Who we think we are must always be partly inaccurate, since while we remain identified with our limited selves we cannot attain to a global comprehension of those selves; on the other hand, who God knows us to be, whether or not we consciously participate in that knowledge to any significant degree, is who we really are. And who God knows humanity to be, according to *al-Rahim*, God's particular, prescriptive and saving mercy, is the source of the law incumbent upon humanity, as well as its final end.

In the case of humanity, the one "primordially given" limitation that is an "adequate extentiation of our archetype" is our *fitrah*, our original form as manifested by God through His universal creative mercy, *al-Rahman*. The human form is the cosmic point where *al-Rahman* reaches its destined limit. As expressions of that limit, it is our duty to ourselves—if we are to realize felicity and avoid wretchedness—to dedicate our lives to God's particular and prescriptive Mercy, *al-Rahim*, manifest as *sirat al-mostaqim*, the path of return to the human archetype *in divinis*. If we do not embark upon this path, we will necessarily be swept along by the creative current of *al-Rahman* beyond the point where it manifests as Mercy, and into the outer darkness where it must appear as Wrath—though even this Wrath ultimately serves Mercy, since it may manifest as a salutary warning as well as a subversive seduction. In other words, all use of human creativity—sometimes erroneously named "co-creativity" in our day—outside of *al-Rahim*, must lead to limitations in perspective that represent subversions of the archetypes rather than adequate extentiations of them. The human passions, the "achievements" of secular civilization based on the expression and worldly sublimation of those passions, man's destruction of the world around him, man's destruction of himself—all, from God's perspective, are "perfect" extentiations of the archetypes in terms of the level on which those archetypes are now manifested, entirely lawful operations of the Names of Rigor. But from the perspective of the human form and the natural world as God created it, they are subversive, and lead only to wretchedness. In terms of *al-fitrah*, only those limitations that fall under the Name *al-Rahim*, those that are the necessary expression of the things God requires of us— including all those "saving illusions" that Schuon (though a bit grudgingly at times) allows as salutary and necessary—represent adequate extentiations, not subversive distortions, of the permanent archetypes. This, at least, is what any *Traditionalist* would claim. (For a different perspective on this question, see *The Fall of Lucifer: A Synthesis of Emanationist and Volitional Theodicy*, below.)

Lastly, the authors seem to balk (though I may be wrong here) at Ibn al-'Arabi's assertion that the whole purpose of the religious enterprise is to lead man to *felicity*—as if, after his immense metaphysical excursions, he ultimately fell back, exhausted, on a simple, pietistic "love God and obey Him, and you'll go to heaven." However, "going to heaven" is not such a bad proposition, after all, in my humble opinion—especially in view of the fact that Schuon speaks of the Paradise of individual "felicity" as being like a reflection of the Paradise of the Essence, as psyche is a reflection of Spirit, the latter embracing the former but not negating it [see "The Two Paradises", appearing in *In The Face of the Absolute* and *Form and Substance in the Religions*]. And Aymard and Laude themselves remind us of this principle when they say that "spiritual realization in no way contradicts the crystallization of the immortal soul. The extinction of the self that constitutes the ultimate goal of the esoteric path is in a sense proportional and simultaneous with the existential actualization of the personal archetype" [p.90]. One of the things that some people find most difficult to understand in Ibn al-'Arabi is his resumption of all the norms and pieties and *anthromorphisms* of exoteric religion, not in opposition to metaphysical esoterism, but precisely in light of it. His perspective is far beyond that of those simple believers to whom Paradise is no more than as extension of this world, a kind of higher and purer material nature, filled with sensual delights given by God as a reward for earthly obedience. The true and highest Paradise is the Paradise of the Essence, infinitely beyond all possible form and conception. And yet, in his doctrine of imaginal theophanies, all those higher worlds of form that constitute the "mythological" aspect of religion come back again. This time, however, they are not seen as "literal" realities—though they most certainly are real experiences—but are rather witnessed in their metaphysical transparency: if, as Schuon asserts, the Infinite, as All-Possibility, must communicate Itself, then there is nothing to prevent It from legitimately manifesting, on one level, as the pavilions, the couches, the feasts, the *houris*, the fountains of wine and of camphor, the *gardens beneath which rivers flow*. Religious literalists may conceive of God as a man like you and me, only infinitely wiser, more powerful and more beautiful. This rudimentary conception is left far behind by the understanding of the *batinis*, who know God in terms of Spirit, not of form. And yet the level of the *batinis* is itself left behind in such theophanies as the appearance of God to Ibn al-'Arabi at the Kaaba in the form of a beautiful youth. That youth was not *literally* God; he both was and was not God; he was an *apparition* of God—a theophany, not an incarnation. Once again, only those in danger of being bound by form are required to distance themselves from it.

CONCLUSION AND ELEGY

In a way, I can't blame anyone for having serious difficulties with "organized religion", given the terrible state of all the religious traditions at the tail end of the Kali-yuga. And there are certainly valid reasons, both practical and based on spiritual efficacy, for simplifying the Islamic *shari'ah* in these times, particularly in non-Islamic nations; according to the prophetic *hadith*, "Those who neglect a tenth of the law in these days will be damned, while those who keep a tenth of it in the last days will be saved." And yet, just as everyone alive on this planet has a body, everyone *will* have an "exoterism" whether they like it or not. If their intellectual, moral and emotional context is not provided by one of the religions in its more-or-less traditional form, it will be provided by "the World"—this postmodern world of militant secularism, militant religious exclusivism, various compulsory fantasies and distractions (not the least of which is the smorgasbord of counter-initiatory "religions"), politically co-opted religious universalism, social chaos, violence, fragmentation and fear, as well as the mores and folkways of this or that more limited province of the postmodern world—academia, for example. Of course all these things affect the traditional religions as well. Yet if "I am with thee always, even to the consummation of the age," then the possibility that one's worldview and social context might remain fundamentally religious rather than secular will never entirely disappear—until this world itself does.

For over twenty years I have been both an eager student and a sort of friendly critic of the Traditionalist world, "in it but not of it." My present impression, however, is that soon I may not be able to be *in* it either any more, because the greater Traditionalist world appears to be in the process of breaking up (though Schuon's Maryamiyya Tariqa is still an entirely viable organization as of this writing). Certainly a number of dedicated Traditionalists still exist, many of them doing good work and breaking new ground; but as for the "School", it is clear to me that any sort of Traditionalist consensus that would make people think twice before they purvey anti-Traditional ideas in the name of "Perennialism" is largely a thing of the past. Frithjof Schuon always said that true esoterism cannot be opposed to religious orthodoxy, nor can it contradict the plain meaning of scripture, though it may open up layer-upon-layer of the symbolic depth that underlies that meaning; and certainly when I was first drawn into the orbit of the Traditionalist School it was generally understood that one of the intrinsic functions of their sophisticated metaphysics was to defend the orthodoxy of the revealed religions when that orthodoxy was attacked either by external forces (worldly

138 FINDINGS IN METAPHYSIC, PATH AND LORE

skepticism) or by internal ones (heresy). But today, one is just as likely to encounter "Traditionalists" or "Perennialists" whose meta-physical sophistication is being directed toward replacing orthodoxy rather than defending it—though I do not necessarily include Aymard and Laude among this group.

So clearly the Traditionalist world is not what it once was. The European Guénonistes have spawned a large Neo-Fascist offshoot that has little to do with Guénon's actual doctrines. And Guénon's best-selling book in North America is *Crisis of the Modern World* [Sophia Perennis, 2001] probably more because it is of interest to certain conservative intellectuals who wish to see themselves as an elite than because most of them have any real interest in traditional metaphysics. Schuon's followers are now increasingly divided between the "Traditionalists" who believe that adherence to a single orthodox revealed tradition is the *sine qua non* of Traditionalist/ Perennialist practice, and "Primordialists" who increasingly believe —either explicitly, or in simply in obvious effect—that Schuon's "quintessential esoterism" allows one to depart from orthodoxy in the direction of a universal metaphysics, that it is possible for us to live as Primordial, Adamic human beings, following no religious dispensation other than God's first revelation—the universe itself— here at the tail-end of the Kali-yuga, with supports that include a sensitivity to the beauty and spiritual significance of sacred art and Virgin Nature, invocatory prayer practiced outside the context of any particular revealed tradition, access to Native American rites, and the books of Frithjof Schuon. And then there are those who see Shaykh Isa as "a sin of their youth", either because they have become religious exclusivists—often of the maximalist variety—or because they have dumped his doctrines entirely to pursue this or that diversion provided by the postmodern world, whether or not said diversion appears in religious garb. For the most part, people have taken from him what they were destined and able to assimilate, and formed their spiritual lives around those elements of his doctrine that were most congenial to them; they seem fixed in the courses. As I see it, the hope (which I at least entertained) that those who have emphasized different aspects of the body of Traditionalist/ Perennialist doctrine might be able help each other to a greater understanding through dialogue and constructive criticism seems unlikely to be realized—unless somebody proves me wrong. And perhaps that hope was merely my own unwillingness to accept that the times are as they are, and that, in the last analysis, nothing happens that is contrary to God's will. The dissolution of sacred forms may be tragic, but tragedy is also providential.

The central difficulty may be that Traditionalism/Perennialism has become a "thing," an academically-recognized "school of thought"; it is no longer so much an introduction to the traditional metaphysics and esoterism of the world religions as an independent body of doctrine drawn from these sources. It always had this tendency, of course; Ananda Coomaraswamy did comparative religion largely from the standpoint of the traditions themselves, while Guénon—though his Hindu studies, particularly *Man and His Becoming According to the Vedanta* [Sophia Perennis, 2001], were entirely traditional—also relied upon a more "generic" metaphysics, as for example in *The Multiple States of the Being* [Sophia Perennis, 2001] and *The Symbolism of the Cross* [Sophia Perennis, 2001], this being an important aspect of his work. As one correspondent remarked, "my only problem with the Traditionalists is that they are not very traditional." This is undoubtedly an exaggeration; but to the degree that it is true, Traditionalism/Perennialism is in danger of becoming part of This World, whatever its founders and earlier exponents may have originally intended.

Guénon, in *The Crisis of the Modern World* and *East and West*, expressed the hope that an elite of western spiritual intellectuals might, under the influence of a relatively uncorrupted East, return the West to its own spiritual tradition; but by the time he wrote *The Reign of Quantity* after WWII, that hope seemed to have largely evaporated. The generation of Traditionalists centered around Schuon understood that they could not expect to have a wide influence on western culture, though as it turns out they have had a considerable influence among Islamic intellectuals, largely through the work of Martin Lings and Seyyed Hossein Nasr. The understanding among the last generation of Traditionalists that they were in a certain sense a "remnant" was inseparable from their telling critique of the modern world. Now, however, it seems that many in the

Traditionalist/Perennialist camp want nothing more than to be accepted and validated by the same modern world that their forebears repudiated; this explains why the Traditionalist critique of modernity has by and large not been updated to include a critique of postmodernity, nor has it dealt with the great advances made by the counter-traditional "spiritualities" toward the centers of global power.

The earlier Traditionalists—René Guénon, Ananda Coomaraswamy, Frithjof Schuon, Titus Burckhardt, Martin Lings, Marco Pallis—whether or not they held doctorates, were by and large *amateurs*, not academics; their work was carried on not as a profession but in response to a vocation, in the traditional sense of that word. The present Traditionalist/Perennialists, however, are represented mostly by professors, at least in the English-speaking world: Patrick Laude, Seyyed Hossein Nasr, William Chittick, Vincent Cornell, Harry Oldmeadow, James Cutsinger et. al. These scholars have done much admirable work, and it may be true that only academic acceptance will prevent the body of Traditionalist doctrines from disappearing from human memory. Nonetheless, the days when the lone spiritual seeker, haunting obscure bookstores, would come upon a volume by Guénon or Schuon as if by an act of Providence, and find their own vague and unformed intuitions miraculously answered and expanded and confirmed by profound and explicit metaphysical doctrine—suddenly to feel that they were no longer alone in their quest—may be largely over: if you've first encountered Traditionalist ideas as part of the curriculum of "Metaphysics 101", it's just not the same. Academic exposition of traditional doctrines, no matter how thorough and accurate it may be, necessarily casts them, rightly or wrongly, as one of the many intellectual choices available to the "wise of This World." Nonetheless, the Truth remains the Truth; in its intrinsic nature, metaphysical Truth cannot be altered to the slightest degree by worldliness—only veiled by it.

As one of the presenters at the 2006 Edmonton conference on *Tradition and Modernity*, hosted by *Sacred Web*, said to me on the plane home, "there is no longer any room in the world for non-academic intellectuals like Frithjof Schuon"—which is simply another way of saying that the *mass* transmission of traditional esoteric and metaphysical doctrines to the western world, that began some time in the middle of the last century, is now largely over. Schuon, for all his elitism, was an important part of that transmission, whether he knew it or not; it was as if he partly represented a higher, more intellectually rigorous, more quintessentially esoteric octave of the same spiritual influx that produced the hippy/New Age counterculture, as witness his interest in the Divine Feminine, his "sacred nudity," his appreciation for Native American spiritualities, his interest in a "pure metaphysics" transcending the limitations of "organized religion", etc. But it is equally true to say, with Gai Eaton, that though Schuon was born in the twentieth century, he was in some ways like the last and greatest of the great nineteenth century "geniuses"—a genius in the field of religion. In any case, he might well be described as the great "summer-up" of the traditions and revelations of this *manvantara*—a function that, in a much more diffuse, popular, and polluted way, the counterculture also fulfilled. He and the counterculture were poles apart, of course, in their actual relationship to Tradition (not to mention in their relation to drug-use, which Schuon strictly prohibited); Shaykh Isa was one of the great re-enunciators of the world's orthodox wisdom traditions, while the hippies and their successors for the most part took these traditions out of context, falsified them, trivialized them, and ultimately devoured them like locusts. But the fact remains that the hippies were generally more attracted to traditional spiritualities than most people are today; they represented perhaps the last chance for traditional metaphysics and esoterism to be disseminated on a popular level (for good or ill) in the West. But those days are over, and we must now admit that for the most part the seed of the Lost Word has already been scattered: some of it to fall and die on rocky ground (hardness of heart), some to be eaten up by the birds of the air (in Schuon's phrase, by "mental passion pursuing intellectual intuition"), and some to strike root in fertile soil. The precise location of such soil, however, may be harder than ever to determine: the era of the latter-day unveiling of the Primordial Tradition has now given way to the era of the hidden saints.

PART TWO:
FINDINGS

HE IS THAT HE IS

[This chapter first appeared as an article
in *Parabola*, vol. 33, num. 2, summer 2008]

GOD IS THE SOURCE and First Principle of all things: Absolute, Infinite and Perfect. As such, He also absolutely transcends the definition "Source and Principle of All Things", since to define Him as the Source of all things is to define Him in terms them, and He will not submit to such definition. He is both Pure Being—the personal God to Whom we pray, Who answers our prayers, and Who necessarily presents to us a personal face, since we ourselves are persons—and the Impersonal Absolute, beyond even Being itself, out of which the personal God eternally arises into Being, and into which He eternally returns, in a single motionless act. And there is not the shadow of a duality between God as Being and God as Beyond Being. He is Beyond Being by the fact that He is neither this nor that; by the fact that, since He *Is* by His Own Essence alone, He is therefore not one among the various things that *possess* Being; and by the fact that He is neither contingent upon some other Being, nor "contingent upon Himself". He has not created Himself and so need not maintain Himself. He need not *be*.

To us westerners the word "impersonal" often denotes something on a lower level of being than personhood, like "the Force" in the Star Wars mythology, something on the order of electricity or magnetism or nuclear energy; thus the "impersonal" Absolute is actually better described, for us at least, as *transpersonal*. That One transcends all we know as personhood in the same sense—though to an infinitely greater degree—that you or I, as persons, transcend a rock. God is indeed a Person, but if we say He is *only* personal, we are in danger of implying that He is no more than we conceive Him to be, of imprisoning Him on our human level of understanding, of denying that He opens out "behind", onto the Infinite. But of course we do the same thing in our habitual ways of seeing other people, and ourselves; we treat others as if they were no more than our ideas of them, and ourselves as if we were limited to our own shifting self-images. We forget that *all* persons are, precisely, personal faces of the Transpersonal Absolute: if, like God, we were not also *more* than persons, we would not be persons at all.

God in His Essence is ultimately unknowable, though it is only by virtue of that Essence that anything whatever is known. But in relation to His creation, God appears to possess various Attributes, to be namable by various Names. However, as Ibn al-'Arabi taught, God's Names and Attributes are in no way divisions in His Essence: God is absolutely One. Rather, they are the unique Faces He shows to each and every created entity; they are not His parts, but His relations. And given that the symbolic number of manifest existence is *four* (the four directions, the four seasons, etc.), the primary faces that God shows to manifest existence are (on one level), also four: The Eternal Lawgiver, the Intrinsic Nature of Things, Infinite Life, and the Universal Self.

God is the Eternal Lawgiver. The Torah, the Laws of Manu, the Islamic *shari'ah* were given to humanity not as a arbitrary impositions of tyrannical rules, but as mercies—which is why ancient peoples looked on lawgiving kings and sages as among the supreme benefactors of the race. Given that humanity had fallen from Eden, from the direct perception of Divine Reality, law became a necessity. A sacred law is an expression of the true shape of the human culture, and ultimately the Human Form, to which that law applies. By the divine act of lawgiving, God creates a given culture in space and time: not through an arbitrary decree, but through His vision of that culture as an eternal facet of the Divine Humanity within His own nature. To command, "thou shalt not kill, thou shalt not steal, thou shalt not commit adultery, thou shalt not forget to acknowledge the Divine Source of your life" is like ordering us not to cut off our arms or put out our eyes. As a safeguard of our integral humanity, the sacred law is beholden to that humanity. It is shaped to fit us; we are not, as in the myth of the bed of Procrustes, cut to fit it. As Jesus said, "the Sabbath was made for man, not man for the Sabbath." Revealed law is necessary because we find ourselves within time, and so need a vehicle whereby eternal principles can be applied to changing situations.

God is the nature of things. A recognition of the nature of things, which the Chinese call *Tao*, the Hindus *Rta*, and the ancient Egyptians *Maat*—the manifestation of Necessary Being in the cosmic order—is the basis of contemplative spirituality. The way things naturally are, the realm of natural law, manifests as appropriateness, beauty and inevitability; through it we can contemplate the Divine Names or Platonic Ideas, the eternal archetypes within the mind of God. Contemplation is like space. Empty in itself, it shows us the pattern whereby all things are related to one another outside time, from the point-of-view of Eternity. Law enters time, and so manifests as speech and spoken scripture; contemplation, being of the nature of space, is better symbolized by the Hindu mandala, the sacred calligraphy of the Qur'an, or the Eastern Orthodox icon. Law speaks; contemplation listens.

God is infinite life. The vast profusion of the "ten-thousand things" eternally overflows into manifestation out of the Divine Infinity. God sends sacred laws, but He is greater than they. He manifests as the cosmic order, but He is not limited by it. There are no barriers in God to the infinite radiation of His Being, and this is His perfect freedom, a freedom which does not begin to be exhausted by universe after universe, bursting with life.

God is the Absolute Subject, the *atman*, the transcendent and immanent Self, the *imago dei* within each of us. By virtue of this *atman*, we are, at the deepest level of our being, both unique and universal. The Self within us is pure, impersonal, universal Being, without attributes; It is also Beyond Being; it can never be an object of consciousness subject to human definition, even as pure Being, since (as the Vedanta declares) "the eye cannot see itself." But because God is unique as well as universal, this Self is also the principle of our unique human integrity, the way in which we are not simply humanity in the abstract, but actual human beings, commanded by God to be precisely ourselves, no greater, no less, and no other. And yet this very uniqueness is also universal, since it is shared by all human beings, and in fact by all things. Self as the principle of uniqueness is not other than Self as the principle of pure Being: *I Am That I Am.* And what God can say of Himself, we can also say, certainly not of our limited human personalities, but of the God, the *atman*, within us. In St. Paul's words: "It is not I who live, but Christ lives in me."

According to Aristotle, "essence" is *what* a thing is, and "being" is *that* a thing is; consequently God can be defined, in Aristotelian terms, as That, and That Alone, in which being and essence are one. Thus when God spoke to Moses at the burning bush, and named Himself as "I Am That I Am", He was in effect saying: "My unique Essence is not other than My pure Being; it is My unique Essence, and eternal good pleasure, to *be* pure Being."

As we have already seen, God may also be defined, following St. Thomas Aquinas, as Necessary Being—as That, and That alone, which cannot not be. Only God *must* be; everything else *might* or *might not* be; if God is Necessary Being, then everything other than God possesses only possible or virtual being. Aquinas also defines God as "Pure Act". In the world of creation, of becoming, of possible being, things come into existence by moving from possibility to actualization, from "potency" to "act". But in God, all possibilities are actualized "already"; He does not harbor some "divine potential" that He might or might not realize later on. As Pure Act, God does not choose between alternatives, but rather wills what is. He does not wonder what might have happened if He had taken a different road. As Pure Act, He is without what we see as "activity," which is in reality the realization of possibilities, the passage from potency to act, a motion that can take place only in the projected *reflection* of God in the sea of space and time. We, who are involved with possible being, and consequently with relative and limited frames of reference—such as a human life, a historical age or a material universe—must experience God as choosing the actions He will perform, as doing some things and leaving others undone, as saying "no" to some petitions and "yes" to others. But in His own nature, His Action is indistinguishable from His Being. He has already performed all conceivable actions; He has already answered all conceivable prayers. In His Mercy to us, the Book of Existence is still open; more may yet be written into it, or else effaced from its pages. But in His own nature, the Book of Being is closed for all eternity: *I Am That I Am.*

THE JÑANIC ASPECT
OF DIVINE LOVE

IT IS IMPOSSIBLE for me to love God as He deserves. If I, the individual self, am the lover, and God is the Beloved, then all I really love is my own image of Him, my shadow cast across His Face—an image that is perishing, and will ultimately die.

In *jñana,* Divine Knowledge, the Knower is God, and God appears nowhere among the things of this world, nowhere among all things knowable. Likewise in the *jñanic* aspect of Divine Love, the Lover appears nowhere among all things lovable, nowhere among the beloveds. In the words of Rabi'a al-Adawiyya, "when the Heart is fully awake, it needs no Friend."

When I am the lover and God the Beloved, I cannot love Him as He is or deserves. But when God is the Lover, He *can* love the things of the universe as *they* are. I cannot appear as even a drop in His vastness, but He can fill every one of His creatures—fill them to overflowing.

I cannot love God, nor His creatures, as they deserve, but I can love the creatures with God's own love. Divine Love is not my love for God based on my own separate individuality, a love which is inadequate and misdirected—nor my love for the creatures, which can never encompass them because I am only one among them. It is not even what little I can truly receive of God's love for me, which I cannot accept as it deserves to be accepted—while I am still "me".

My point of true contact with Divine Love is God's love of His creatures *through* me—a Love that creates and destroys the entire universe in a single moment—a Love by which the universe is known not as the face of any beloved other than me, and thereby related to me, but the Face of the Lover Himself. God within me is Formless; the universe itself is the ensemble of His Forms—His very Face in the Mirror. But the Lover Himself, in His own Essence, is totally beyond that Face, eternally hidden beyond Being itself.

In God's love for His creatures—and what He loves in them is

149

none other than the One Who loves—my infinitesimal love for Him as a separate Object, or for His creatures only as individual sentient beings according to my conception of them, is blotted out. God is Absolute Love; there is no room in that Love for my partial, interested love—even if that interest be the fervent longing for union with Him. His Love pours through me, like light through an open door, because I myself—a shadow no longer—am no longer standing in the doorway.

NECESSARY BEING

"With God all things are possible?" No: With God, all things are *necessary*. Necessity is Reality, and God is the Real. If I am considered to be the doer, then all things *are* merely possible: I might choose this action or that one; a given action of mine might succeed or it might fail. But with God, all actions are complete from beginningless eternity; whatever He conceives, IS. (This is the real meaning of "With God all things are possible": that He has the *power* to realize—immediately and eternally—His every conception, and does in fact realize them, every one of them. There is no "might be or might not be" when it comes to God.)

The realm of possibility is the illusory world where the ego is apparently the doer; the realm of Necessity is the Real world where God alone is the Doer. God in His Own Nature is Necessary Being and Pure Act—which means that, when we realize that only God is the Doer, all events are seen as absolutely necessary: the world of possibility, of what might have been, disappears; it was never there. God is *necessarily* the Absolute and Unchanging; the world of relativity and multiplicity, His reflection, is *necessarily* quasi-absolute change. Precisely because God is the Unchanging, every moment of change is unique, necessary, and a direct act or reflection of Him. And to live in this knowledge, without longing to escape into the illusion of possibility, is true freedom.

In certain fairy tales, like the Grimms' tale *Jorinda and Joringel* or the Persian fairy tale *The Bath Badgerd*, when questers or seekers enter the sacred precinct unprepared, they turn to stone. Why is this? It is because they have gone into the realm of Necessity still adulterated with possibility; thus they falsely experience Necessity as the enemy of possibility, the tyranny of Fate, the regime of the Gorgon Medusa: they are petrified with fear in the face of it.

To worshippers of possibility, freedom appears to be based on the presence of many different *alternatives*—but unfortunately, in a given situation, to choose to actualize one of these alternatives to

151

the exclusion of all others appears to destroy that very (illusory) freedom. Freedom therefore becomes falsely identified only with *potentiality*—that is, with *illusion*, with something that would lose all its glorious and illusory freedom if it ever became real. But Necessary Being *is* Reality—and so, when the idol of possibility enters the kingdom of Necessity, where all potentialities are actualized, this very actualization is experienced, by the ego, as imprisonment and petrification. The ego is the realm of the merely possible: the Divine Spirit, the realm of true Necessity. In close proximity to Necessity, possibility—which seemed so much like freedom—is shown for what it really is: the bonds of the indefinite, the hell of chaos, the prison of unreality.

But in reality, *Necessity* is freedom: what is inevitably and purely Itself, what is completely actualized, has overcome all internal conflict and—because whatever is fully self-actualized is, in a sense, its own environment—all external constraint as well. Whatever is incompletely formed is at odds with both the universe and itself; to such an unrealized potentiality, the appearance of Necessity—that which completely forms and perfectly finishes everything it touches—is both the doom of all mere potentiality, and the dawn of the Mercy of Self-realization, the paradise of the Absolute.

THE NATURE OF
ONTOLOGICAL PERSPECTIVES

For Marco Toti

FRITHJOF SCHUON'S DOCTRINE of the Transcendent Unity of Religions is based, in my view, on the principle that while we human beings can compare, contrast and evaluate realities lower than we are on the Great Chain of Being, we cannot do so when it comes to those that are higher. Religious revelations are higher than humanity because they are sent by God, which is why they have a right to command our allegiance; and because they are higher than we are, we cannot encompass them or pass judgment upon them on their own plane of existence.

Facts are objective realities which occupy a lower ontological plane than human beings; we can evaluate them, but they cannot evaluate us; this is why we can pass judgment as to the truth or false-hood of statements presented as factual. Lee Harvey Oswald was either a lone assassin or a member (or dupe) of a conspiracy whose aim was to assassinate President Kennedy. One of these statements must be true, but both cannot be true; there is no way that these two contradictory statements can be resolved in some higher unity.

Religious revelations, on the other hand, are objective realities that occupy a higher ontological plane than we do; there is no way we can place them, as it were, on the table in front of us so as to compare, contrast, evaluate or judge between them. They are not laboratory specimens; we will never be able to construct an experiment capable of exhaustively determining their actual properties. It would be truer to say that *we* are *their* experiment; though we will never be able to test them, they are already testing us.

Religious revelations might be characterized as "ontological per-spectives"—God-given perspectives that allow us to entertain certain valid views as to His nature. But since God is Absolute Reality, no single view can encompass Him; in the words of the Qur'an

[6:103, Rodwell translation], *No vision taketh in Him, but He taketh in all vision.* And because He is Infinite Reality as well, no number of valid views, even if they are revealed by Him, can "add up" to a complete understanding of Him. Nothing other than He can encompass Him in knowledge, which is why all theological formulations must fall short of defining Him—even if, in relation to the particular ontological perspective we occupy, they are necessarily true, and therefore (in Schuon's phrase) "relatively Absolute."

Ontological perspectives are not subjective beliefs or impressions, but objective realities. They are not views we choose to adopt on our own authority, or are influenced to adopt by social or psychological or genetic factors: they are views that God Himself both permits us and commands us to adopt, as ways of knowing Him. We are used to thinking of "views" as collective or individual *opinions.* And it is true that when speaking of beliefs, impressions, or conclusions based on human experience—rather than of the necessary conclusions of logic which partake of the objectivity of the Transcendent, as both Schuon, in *Logic and Transcendence,* and C.S. Lewis, in *Miracles,* conclusively demonstrate—we are dealing with perspectives on Reality that, though they may attain a certain degree of objectivity, can never entirely escape from the subjective bias of those entertaining them. Ontological perspectives, on the other hand, are not based on belief or experience; they are not dependent upon psychology, or history, or culture, either individual or collective; they are not opinions. Like the view of a stationary object from a given distance while facing a given point of the compass, each is entirely objective—as real as (or rather, much more real than) the rocks on the hillside or the stars in the sky. And since they have radiated directly from Absolute Reality, they are ontologically superior to us. We can never encompass them; they have already encompassed us. Consequently, though we can compare certain reverberations of them as they appear in psychology, or history, or culture, we cannot compare them to one another on their own plane of existence, because each Divine revelation, each act of God, is incomparable—unique. Realities superior to us on the Great Chain of Being are in fact *more* unique, and thus more fully incomparable, than the realities of our human world; this is what St. Thomas Aquinas was alluding to when he taught that *each individual angel is a species unto himself.* (Furthermore, what appears as a doctrine or system of ideas in this world may in fact be a conscious, living entity in another world; as the Shi'ite theosophers teach us, the Platonic Ideas, in that higher spiritual world which is proper to them, are, precisely, angels.)

Lee Harvey Oswald cannot have been both a lone assassin and a member (or dupe) of a conspiracy; logic is logic, and facts are facts. But when it comes to questions like "Was Jesus Christ the Son of God (the Christian view), or was he only a prophet, though among the greatest of them (the Muslim view)?", exclusionary logic no longer applies. Such logic can certainly be applied to facts that are ontologically lower than us; we can compare them with each other, and evaluate in relation to one another, because we transcend them. But it cannot be used to evaluate perspectives that are ontologically higher than we are. Consequently, as soon as we admit that more than one Divine revelation is true and valid, we can no longer compare one revealed religion with another on the plane of essence. And we cannot accept one Word of God and reject another without denying God's veracity, and consequently destroying the very basis upon which we claim to invoke His authority, even insofar as it validates the particular Word we are willing to accept. Nor can we stand outside of two Divinely revealed propositions— "Jesus is the Son of the God" and "God has no son", for example—so as to compare, contrast, evaluate and judge between them, since to do so could only be based on the false belief that we can encompass the revelations of God with our human understanding, which clearly we cannot. And we can't say "Jesus both is and is not the Son of God" either, since to do so would be to place in a false relationship two unique Divine revelations which, on the plane of form, "quasi-absolutely" exclude each other. Formal reverberations can be compared; transcendental essences cannot.

This seemingly insoluble dilemma is only resolved by an intuition of the overwhelming vastness of God. We agree that God is "Absolute, Infinite, Perfect, the Sovereign Good"—and then we treat Him as if He were like the king in a game of chess, moving in response to our own will and intelligence on a board of 64 squares we can survey in a single glance. But that is not how it is. I have said that we cannot encompass the reality of God—but we *can* encompass the necessity for this very inability. God is not intelligible to us, but His unintelligibility is—and this, precisely, is our point of intimate contact with the Divine Transcendence. As Abu Bakr said (peace and blessing be upon him), "To know that God cannot be known is to know God". And the resulting certainty that God is infinitely beyond our power to encompass Him is the root of the further certainty that every perspective upon His nature that has in fact been revealed by Him, not concocted by human cleverness, is objectively real, necessary in its own terms, superior to us, and incomparable in essence to any other such perspective. No two religions are "equivalent" to one another, any more than two human individuals can be equivalent, or an eagle equivalent to a lion. If more than one religion is true—just as the lion and the eagle are both beautiful, both awe-inspiring, both sublime—this is because all Divinely-revealed religions are unique and incomparable, and because God's Truth, which is a Name of His Essence, is Infinite. Infinite Truth has the power to *make* true (and therefore spiritually efficacious), certainly not every idea we may entertain about It, but whatever objective perspectives upon Its Reality It may grant us of Its own volition—even if, from our limited, subjective perspectives (a limitation which is no less necessary than is God's Infinity), they contradict each other. If God's unknowability imposes, at one level (though certainly not all), a necessary quality of paradox upon all statements made about Him, this same unknowability also makes His Self-revelation necessarily contradictory, to one degree or another, on the plane of form; in the words of Ibn al-'Arabi, "there is war between the Names of God". In His own Essence, God cannot contradict Himself—but the incapacity of form to fully embody the Formless Absolute makes contradiction a necessary element— though certainly not the only one—in His cosmic Self-revelation. If we are unable to accept this truth, we are in effect demanding that the world of form encompass God, or actually *be* God—something that is both impossible in reality, and idolatrous in effect.

From a different but equally-valid perspective, however, two things that cannot be compared with one another cannot contradict each other; they can never come to blows because they can never occupy the same field. A Divinely-revealed ontological perspective is a saving ray of Light that, if we truly and existentially enter into the stream of it, will sweep all other perspectives away, and concentrate us upon God Himself, upon the Divine Reality from which it flows. The two propositions that "Jesus is the Son of God" and "God has no son" can never be resolved on the plane of form; no degree of human ingenuity can make peace between them. They are, however, truly resolved in a higher Unity—the Unity of God Himself. And so, if we wish to avoid the seemingly inevitable conflict between two objective, ontological perspectives on the Divine Nature that contradict each other, the only way is to renounce comparisons entirely, and follow the stream we have chosen (and that therefore must necessarily first have chosen us) to its ultimate Source—in the understanding that a unique, incomparable, Divinely-revealed, "relatively absolute" perspective on the nature of God has no other purpose in the Divine economy than to lead us back to that Source. Once our initial orientation is complete, such a perspective is not to be speculated upon or theorized about; it is to be put to work.

THE FALL OF LUCIFER

A SYNTHESIS OF EMANATIONIST
AND VOLITIONAL THEODICY

IN *Survey of Metaphysics and Esoterism* [World Wisdom Books, 1986, p.18], Frithjof Schuon says:

> It is in the nature of the Good to wish to communicate itself: to say Good is to say radiation, projection, unfolding, gift of self. But at the same time, to say radiation is to say distance, hence alienation or impoverishment; the solar rays dim and become lost in the night of space. From this arises, at the end of the trajectory, the paradoxical phenomenon of evil, which nonetheless has the positive function of highlighting the good *a contrario*, and of contributing in its fashion to the equilibrium of the phenomenal order.

In Schuon's metaphysics and cosmology (at least as I understand them), the Formless Absolute (*Nirguna Brahman*; Godhead; Beyond Being) "emanates" the Personal God (*Saguna Brahman*; Pure Being; the Creator), Who in turn brings into outward manifestation the possibilities latent in All-Possibility or *maya-in-divinis*, and thereby creates the spiritual, psychic and material universes. God does not positively will evil, and He possesses the power to abolish any particular evil; however, in the nature of things, He could not negate the existence of evil as such without annihilating creation itself, which only exists by virtue of the ontological level it occupies, where evil is an inescapable possibility, woven as it were into the fabric of things. If the universe did not contain the possibility of evil, it would not be the universe, but God Himself.

So universal Emanation necessarily contains within it, as a subset, the possibility of particular Creation, which in turn introduces the possibility of a Fall. Neither Emanation nor Creation, however, *are* the Fall. Creation introduces the possibility of a Fall, but does not actualize it; only rebellious free will can do that. One might argue that it is inevitable—in more or less "actuarial" terms—that some among an indefinite multitude of beings endowed with free will would choose rebellion, but this does not negate the reality of freedom in each individual case, nor the justice of the grim consequences earned by those who misuse it.

According to Schuon, The Real, the Sovereign Good, must communicate itself to (and as) celestial and cosmic manifestation, by virtue of the fact that what is Absolute is also necessarily Infinite, and no bound can be set to the Infinite. And it is certainly true that celestial and cosmic manifestation arise from the necessary and Infinite overflow of the superabundant Reality of the Absolute. But insofar as this manifestation is also a veil, the possibility of Satanic subversion is latent within it. For God to communicate Himself to cosmic existence is only good, but it is a limited good, not the unlimited reality of the Sovereign Good; the Supraformal necessarily manifests Itself in terms of form, and every form is a limitation. But insofar as existence is good in itself, such limitations are neither evil nor subversive. And yet they harbor the possibility of evil and subversion, by the very fact that limited forms are always paired with imperfect knowers, sentient beings who are limited in perspective just as the forms they perceive are limited in scope. And as soon as limited forms as perceived by limited knowers make their appearance, the possibility of idolatry arises, which I will define here as the tendency to "willfully mistake" a limited form for the reality of the Absolute which has manifested it, and which subsists within it as its essential Reality. There can be no evil in the Divine realm; the seeds of evil do exist in the celestial realm, but they remain latent since they have no context for deployment; it is only in the psychic realm that evil actually constellates as a subversive force. Schuon is right that evil only makes its appearance at the end of the trajectory of cosmic manifestation—not at the ultimate end, however, which is matter, but rather on the psychic plane, where "worlds" constructed with the ego rather than God as their proximate cause first become possible. Nonetheless, the existence of Lucifer testifies to the fact that the subversive privation which is, or will become, evil, has its beginnings at the apex of the celestial order; otherwise he could not have fallen "from heaven".

Lucifer represents not the descent from Principle into manifestation, but the potential, on every level of the ontological hierarchy, for delusion, privation, and subversion—the concrete manifestation of which, however, is only made possible by that very descent. As the "light bearer" he is symbolic, in his unfallen mode, of the *Nous*, the First Intellect, the first eternal motion of God's knowledge of Himself as "other". In his fallen mode, he symbolizes the possibility of spiritual subversion and metaphysical error on the highest possible level—in terms of the human microcosm, the subversion the *Nous* (which appears, in the Qur'an, as the refusal of Eblis to bow down to Adam). The *Nous*, the Uncreated Intellect within man, cannot be subverted in its essence, but it most certainly can be counterfeited and veiled.

According to Schuon, for the "volitional and affective" man, the ego is "I" and God is "He", while for the "intellective" man, God is "I" and the ego is "he." Applying this distinction to Lucifer, we can imagine his fall as made possible by a descent from the intellective or *jñanic* station to the volitional/affective one, coupled with *a refusal to accept the necessity* of this creative descent—the later consequences of which God, in Genesis, looked upon and called good. If he had accepted the necessity of the descending radiation of the Absolute in the direction of manifestation, Lucifer would have been able—in his own case—to redress its potential deficiencies. Instead, he opposed it. In holding on to a "higher" conception of God as the Formless Absolute, he failed to understand that God's celestial and cosmic manifestation is in no way a departure from His Essence, but rather a veiling of that Essence for the very purpose of revealing It. In other words—like the sectarian Gnostics—he looked upon God's creative act not as a positive Self-manifestation, but strictly as a Fall. And by this very rejection of cosmic existence, which was both an intellectual error and a willful rebellion, he *transformed* it into a Fall; this is the "primordial irony". Lucifer failed to understand that "If I ascend up to heaven, Thou art there; if I make my bed in hell, behold, Thou art there." The ambiguity of existence, which is the ambiguity of *maya*, is: that while manifestation must

depart from the Essence, the Essence can never depart from Itself—
and what is manifestation, on every level, but the revelation of that
very Essence?

Lucifer looked within himself and saw the image of the *atman*,
the Absolute Divine Witness, but he saw it as an object of *his* knowledge, not himself as an object of Its knowledge. This primal *limitation* placed upon Intellection—or rather, this primal appearance of
Intellection apart from the Absolute One, an Intellection capable
for the first time of knowing the One as an object—can still be
defined as a stage of the descent of the Absolute into manifestation,
not as a subversion of that manifestation, not as a Fall. Lucifer's
intellectual *error*—which, in terms of his free will, was also an act of
rebellion—was *to identify his now limited selfhood with the Absolute
Reality he saw within him*, rather than submitting to It and worshipping It, which was now required of him given the present stage-of-
descent of Divine manifestation. As soon as manifestation descends
from the purely intellective station to the volitional/affective one—
in other words, as soon as free will is born—then the will is required
to submit, and the affections, to love. This act of immediate submission to the new and more limited condition—*not* the will to
reject it by holding on to the *memory* of the former and higher
one—is the only way back to that higher one.

If Lucifer had retained the higher level of consciousness represented by the *atman*, he would have remained rooted in the Absolute Witness which witnesses only Itself, and would consequently
have been able to witness the cosmic unfolding, by virtue of the Eye
of God within him, as a positive Divine manifestation, not a Fall. As
soon as he saw that Reality as an "object", however, no longer as the
Witness by which he witnessed, and which also witnessed him, then
the Fall became possible. This was the primal intellectual
limitation—a limitation which, because it posited God as an object,
equally posited Lucifer as an independent entity. As an apparently
independent entity, he found himself possessed of an independent
will, which could either submit to and adore this newly-arisen
objective God, or else deny Him and worship itself instead. Unwilling to redress the consequences of his intellectual limitation
through submission and adoration, which would have immediately

unveiled the *atman* once more, and effected—for him—the reinte-
gration of the Personal God into the Formless Absolute, God into
Godhead, Lucifer held on to the memory of that higher state in
which himself as subject, and God as object, had not yet polarized—
a state which, at this stage of the cosmic unfolding, *he could now
identify only with himself*, not with God. He saw the objective Personal God as a veil covering the Essence (which It is) but not as a
theophany of that very Essence (which It certainly also is). Thus, in
the name of the "preservation" of the level of consciousness of the
atman, he barred the only effective road of return to that *atman*,
rejected God, entered into a state of self-worship, and fell: and the
etiology of the fall of Lucifer is, precisely, the etiology of the ego. We
can understand by this that the possibility of self-idolatry, of the
egoistic denial of God, was present from the first moment of the
unfolding of universal manifestation. But it was present only as one
possibility within the embrace of All-Possibility ("the possibility of
impossibility" as Schuon has called it), not as a necessity on the
level of free will (since if it were present as such a necessity, then the
will would not be free). As soon as form is born, both potential obedience, resulting in a vision of the metaphysical transparency of all
forms, and potential rebellion, based upon the idolatry of these
forms, are born along with it.

Universal manifestation can also be viewed in terms of the Hindu
doctrine of *Maya*, which is substantially identical with Schuon's
"emanationism" (and, in many ways, with Neo-Platonic emanationism as well), with the notion that Reality must, by Its nature,
communicate Itself in an descending order of celestial and cosmic
manifestations, each lower ontological plane being both more
attenuated and more opaque and solidified than its higher predecessors. But this truth does not license us to ignore the ontological
level upon which, and subsequent to which, evil must progressively
be defined in terms of the abuse of free will by angelic, animic and
human entities. When the Noble Qur'an says *I seek refuge in the
Lord of Daybreak from the evil of that which He created*, it is not saying that God deliberately created evil, or (as Carl Jung maintained
in *Answer to Job*) that He is somehow half evil Himself; if this were
true, there would be no refuge in Him. As Schuon repeatedly points

out in his writings, God is the Sovereign Good, and as such He cannot positively will evil, seeing that evil is not a positive reality on any level, but precisely a privation.

As Schuon teaches, in *Gnosis: Divine Wisdom* and elsewhere, *Maya*, as the "magical" manifestation of the Absolute, presents us with a universe that is neither real nor unreal, a world that is not strictly non-existent, but is nonetheless not what it seems. Insofar as *Maya* manifests a cosmos apparently composed of limited forms arranged in various relations to one another, and subject to natural law, it is *avidya-maya*, or "ignorance-appearance"; insofar as it presents us with forms which by their very existence testify to the Real, and which, by their essential qualities, exist as reflections of the Names or Qualities of God, it is *vidya-maya* or "wisdom-appearance." Thus *Maya* cannot be strictly identified with the evil Demiurge of the sectarian Gnostics, who recognized cosmic manifestation in its aspect of *avidya-maya*, but not in its aspect of *vidya-maya*. To the Gnostics, the crystalline spheres of the circling heavens were an ingeniously-contrived prison ruled by oppressive spiritual powers; in no way could they "declare the glory of God", nor could "the earth show forth His handiwork".

The Devil is not evil because, like the Gnostic Demiurge, he *creates* this cosmos of heaviness and material limitation, but rather because he subverts it. The goal of all cosmic manifestation, the "lowest" point where God can be reflected as integral Being, is the human form. And as every religious tradition teaches, either openly or "esoterically", the centrality of the human form, despite the heaviness and opacity of its material manifestation (whether or not this be considered as the product of a "Fall"), gives it a potential spiritual precedence over even the highest angels, since it is the direct, though distant, reflection of God in the material cosmos, while the angels are the higher, but relatively peripheral, reflections of the various Names or Qualities of God. Man alone exists as a synthesis of all the Names—a "stewardship" or "Trust" that he is free to either realize or betray.

(Man at the limit of cosmic manifestation, imprisoned in a material existence transformed from a theophany into a veil, in relation to which he has lost the power to see material forms in their metaphysical transparency, is well symbolized by Prometheus bound to the rock, his liver being eaten by the eagle of Zeus. The liver—related to the *manipura-chakra* of the Hindu Tantra—when alienated from man's higher faculties becomes the seat of a "Promethean" self-will, a reckless willfulness that steals the fire of Zeus—the Intellect, the *Nous*—and transforms it into blind impulse. Man in the state of self-will represents the lowest point of cosmic manifestation—matter itself being incapable of rebellion, and thus fundamentally innocent—at which point cosmic existence must either begin its return to God, via the sacrifice of self-will, or else fall into an infernal or *titanic* state, which is no longer a veiling of God with a view toward His outward manifestation, but a plunge into chaos and non-entity. And the sole path of this return is the path of *intellection*, either actual or virtual: the eagle of Zeus is a symbol of the *Nous* in the process of devouring the fallen self-will, thereby transforming it back into Intellection again. The "punishment" of Prometheus, being precisely purgatorial, is the beginning of his salvation.)

So the Absolute, by virtue of Its Infinity, radiates Itself through the descending eschelons of celestial and cosmic manifestation until it reaches the human form—which, by virtue of the possibility of spiritual realization and Liberation, is the point where the return of universal manifestation to its Origin begins. (This entire cycle of radiation and return is encapsulated in the *Basmallah* that begins every *surah* but one of the Noble Qur'an: *Bismillah al-Rahman al-Rahim*; "In the Name of God, the merciful, the Compassionate." *Al-Rahman* is the "universal Mercy" that allows all beings to come into separate existence, the Mercy of Creation; *al-Rahim* is the "particular Mercy" that provides the criteria and established the spiritual Path by which each being, insofar as it *chooses* to avail itself of them, may return to Allah.) But, due to the freedom of the human will, without which God's own freedom could not be mirrored in humanity, the expansion and attenuation of the Absolute's cosmic manifestation does not end at the human level, but may also (as we have seen) sink below it. In Hindu terms this "sinking" is the result of the action of the *guna* named *tamas* (the *gunas* being the three modes of Universal Substance or *Prakriti*) which, in terms of its positive function, materially stabilizes the cosmic environment in which earthly, incarnate man must exist, but which also, in terms of its negative or subversive function, veils the face of God, thus introducing "materialism" in all the senses of that word.

That man has a body is not evil, though that body is subject to many evils. That he lives in a material world is not evil, though matter and material concerns are a heavy veil. The nature and activity of the Devil must not be sought in these mere facts of earthly man's existence, but in the satanic subversion of the true significance of them. In one sense they are the product of a fall, of the loss of Eden which made it necessary for humanity to don these "garments of skin" [Genesis 3:21]; in another, this very fall was a *felix culpa*, destined not to confirm and solidify Satan's kingdom, but to overturn it definitively. In light of this we can understand our present physical forms not as a punishment for Adam's sin, but as a product of God's mercy, who willed a partial redress of the effects of that sin on a lower level of being, thus opening man to the possibility of Redemption.

When cosmic manifestation, in its expansion and attenuation, falls below the human form, because the human being has failed to recognize God in the totality of that manifestation—and thus, by that act, to return cosmic manifestation to its Origin—it enters the realm of what René Guénon calls the "infra-psychic", which is, precisely, the kingdom of Satan. Ontologically lower, but also subtler, than gross matter, the infra-psychic possesses all the darkness and opacity of matter without its nobility and stability, as well as the all swiftness, penetration and ingeniousness of pure Intellection without its orientation to Divine Truth: the "possibility of impossibility" with a vengeance! (We might term the tendency toward heaviness and opacity "Satanic", and the quality of ingeniousness and lightning-swiftness "Luciferian".) It is here, not in the bare facts of material existence, that the nature and "function" of the Devil are to be found.

Though evil is a *privatio boni*—a depletion of, or limited access to, the Good, on a particular level of being—it is not a "mere" insufficiency. Certainly evil is a privation and nothing else, a privation of both Divine Reality (in ontological terms) and the Sovereign Good (in "moral" ones)—as well as, in terms of both the possibility of spiritual intuition and an understanding of the doctrines derived from revelation, a privation of the Truth, a veil over spiritual knowledge. But what is often poorly understood by many who espouse a more-or-less emanationist view of Divine manifestation is that evil, privative though it be, does not manifest simply as a kind of weakness or lack, but also as *attack, subversion,* and *counterfeit.* Where sound doctrine is wise, evil (as error) is not simply stupid, but also infernally ingenious; where love is strong, evil (as hatred) is not only weak, but demonically cruel; where universal manifestation constitutes a Cosmos, an Order composed of a descending hierarchy of orders within orders, the kingdom of Satan also has its infernal modes of organization, its "lowerarchies" (to use the humorous term coined by C. S. Lewis), its dark *agendas.* Hell is not a neutral chaos, but an inverted order; not a loveless indifference, but an active attack upon Love; not a stupid impermeability to metaphysical Truth, but a swift, ingenious and infernally "intelligent" war upon that Truth. As a parasite on order, evil forms its own counterfeit order, chaotic in essence but nonetheless marshaled into a semblance of order through naked power. As a parasite on love, it tempts us to give our love to that which is in the process of destroying us, as the drunkard loves his bottle or the addict his drug; as a parasite on Truth, it forms its own inverted metaphysics, and inverted morality as well; it forges its own counter-tradition and counter-initiation with scraps and fragments of doctrines stolen from the Primordial Tradition, and from the various Divine Revelations that are its branches. It prepares, is presently preparing, and is at this moment acting, to subvert, attack, destroy, counterfeit and supplant whatever remains of this Tradition—whether doctrine, institution, moral standard, faithful believer or metaphysical sage—in this earthly world. Only when it has succeeded in destroying the last vestiges of the Primordial Tradition, thus bringing this cycle of manifestation to a close, will it itself die, and die by starvation, since it has no principle of life within itself, but can exist only as a parasite on the Real.

And so evil is not a "mere" privation, any more than starvation is a "mere" lack of food. It is all too easy, however, for those who hold to the true doctrine that evil is a privation, not a positive force, to see it as a "mere nothing" that can be safely ignored—particularly those who in their spiritual life overly concentrate on the intellective pole, the realm of metaphysics, to the detriment of the existential pole, the realm of sanctity. Such people may foolishly believe that it is relatively easy, at least for those with a degree of metaphysical discernment, to "rise above" evil, that there is really no such thing as "spiritual wickedness in high places". Such complacency is not derived from true metaphysical insight, however—which includes the gift known as "discernment of spirits"—but from that state of spiritual delusion which the Buddhists name *deva-loka*, in reference to the *samsaric* world of the long-lived gods, where the realities of impermanence and karmic rigor are hidden under a veil of aesthetic refinement and false spiritual elevation—until it is too late.

In order to understand the doctrine of evil-as-privation in any effective way, and avoid its potential pitfalls, we need to hold to a metaphysic—as well as to the intrinsic moral standards which exist as reflections of it—that both grants evil its true place in the universal order, so as to free God from the twin slanders that He is either good but too weak to prevent evil, or all-powerful but too evil, or too nihilistically indifferent, to will the good, and one that also grants evil its full gravity, while providing access to the complete panoply of traditional powers and skills by which it may be combated—doctrinally, ascetically, and theurgically. To settle for anything less is to reduce metaphysics to an abstract, academic exercise, a parlor game for people who want to entertain themselves with religion instead of saving their souls by means of it.

This world, filled with suffering though it may be, is a creation of Divine mercy, not a product of infernal subversion. In human terms, the possibility of the subversion of a merciful creation—at least in the present *Kali-yuga*—arises first from our mis-perception of that creation as material only, opaque to the light of God, and secondarily from the many ill-conceived actions that flow from this primal error. Subversion is based in *possibility* on the necessary "departure" of creation from God via emanation, so that the universe may exist in its own right—but it is only realized *in act* by the misuse of free will, which—again in human terms, and ignoring the angelic rebellion which preceded us and still affects us—begins when we succumb to the *temptation* of ignorance, and ends when we express this ignorance concretely through transgression and sin, further reinforcing it by means of them.

Jesus encapsulates in a single line [Luke 17:1], both the necessity of the *possibility* of evil in terms of emanation, and the *actualization* of evil in terms of the misuse of free will: "It is impossible but that offenses shall come, but woe to him through whom they come!" A truly plenary esoterism, in view of the metaphysical truth that limitation is necessary for divine manifestation, does not ignore perspectives more limited than itself, but rather embraces them as providential, and grants them their precise position and function in the universal order.

ON HUMOR

For James Cutsinger

HUMOR, in the highest sense, is the perception of the incongruity between the eternal truths that Intellection reveals and the habitual attitudes of the ego, in the firm confidence that Intellection, since it serves the Truth and radiates from the Truth, will "laugh last". There is the seriousness of the ego and the seriousness of the Spirit. The holy humor that pokes fun at the seriousness of the ego is wit; the demonic humor that pokes fun at holy things is levity, and levity is always cruel, whereas holy humor is always compassionate. (You can always tell levity from wit by the fact that levity resorts to sneering and posturing, precisely because it lacks any real sense of humor.) When Socrates said that nothing in this world deserves to be taken seriously, not even sacred things, he undoubtedly meant that even sacred things—*especially* sacred things—are degraded by association with the heavy humorlessness of the ego. But they are also degraded by the demonic levity of the ego. (There is even a particular class of demons—the *imps*—who tempt us to such levity; their insidious danger lies in the fact that they seem relatively harmless, especially in a profane culture like ours that considers holy seriousness "pompous" and "uncool".) Levity, insofar as it is the profane and nihilistic reaction to the often formidable paradoxes of metaphysical expression and the spiritual life, inverts the true scale of values that wit fights to establish. And both Christ and the Qur'an, in any case, demonstrate that while holy humor can balance, serve insight, alleviate burdens and explode illusions, only holy seriousness can save—that's why Platonism lives on in any spiritually effective sense only within the Christian and Islamic revelations. On its own, deprived of grace, it degenerates into a loveless, supercilious, academic sport: "This day thou shalt be with Me in Disneyworld." Only *fear* places sport above seriousness in holy things: the fear of that one after whom our *yuga* is named, Kali—

who, in Disneyworld, is simply an animatronic device or holographic image.[1]

Plato's *boyish* culture was affected by a deeply unconscious fear of the Divine Feminine. It was partly a case of whistling past the graveyard, an intellectual tightrope walk over the abyss where the Great Goddess of the late Minoan age still ruled—as Persephone, as Hecate, as the Demogorgon whose name could not even be pronounced without running the risk of overturning the whole complacent, tittering, Olympian order of things. (There was certainly more to the Olympian worldview than this, but it definitely did include a certain element of dangerous childishness, especially in its degeneration—a degeneration which, as Rodney Blackhirst shows in his *Primordial Alchemy* [Sophia Perennis, 2008] Plato lamented, and tried to redress.) The god-realm of Olympus had many affinities with the Buddhist state of delusion known as *Deva-loka*, the realm of the long-lived gods where ignorance is bliss, a world that is complacency incarnate. And—as I'm sure many of us have seen or suspected at one time or another—*complacency is fear.*

Below is a treatment of the spiritual dimension of humor from my book *Hammering Hot Iron: A Spiritual Critique of Bly's* Iron John [Quest Books, 1993; Sophia Perennis, 2005]:

> The question of the correct balance between trickster energy and holy seriousness is a complex one. In certain American Indian cultures, for example, the role of the Sacred Clown is of great importance. Given a collective sense of awe and holy

---

1. The Kali-yuga is traditionally associated with the male demon *Kali*, the Tenth Avatar of Vishnu. His name means "black", whereas the name of the Great Goddess Kali means "time"; the "confusion" of these two names is often dismissed as folk etymology. The Goddess Kali, however, is most often pictured as black, and her role as All-Devouring Time, *Shakti* of Shiva the Destroyer, well fits her to preside over the last *yuga* of the *manvantara*, in line with René Guénon's doctrine that time devours space in the final period of the cycle, which is characterized by the veiling of the Absolute manifest as Essence—the masculine pole, the realm of *quality*—and the unveiling of the Absolute manifest as Substance—the feminine pole, the realm of *quantity*. Folk etymology, sensitive as it is to the symbolic or qualitative affinities between words, is often wiser than academic etymology, which only considers their historical derivations.

seriousness in the face of the Mysteries, the Clown, who pokes fun at the whole ritual process, can be devastatingly effective—funny, but also terrifying, as if an awkward, Buster Keaton-like figure were to almost slip on a banana peel and almost drop the jar he is carrying, which in fact contains real nitroglycerine. In any intact sacred tradition, the Clown figure is always a foil to the sense of holy dread. His or her shock function is to carry us beyond the form of the ritual and into the living reality beyond. Han Shan served this function for the good temple monks in the Cha'an Buddhist tradition; Nasruddin did so for the exoteric mullahs in Sufi legend; the institution known as the Feast of Fools in medieval Christianity, where an ass dressed up in a bishop's robe would bray instead of say Mass one day out of the year—all were vehicles of liberating shock, designed to mitigate the heaviness of the solemn Mysteries and let the worshippers see beyond the sacred form to the higher reality which any sacred form always both manifests and veils. But in the absence of the solemn mysteries, in a society like ours where literally nothing is sacred, the Clown function tends to play into the hands of spiritual blindness and social repression. . . .

Without Sophoclean tragedy, then, the comedy of Aristophanes lacks any viable social purpose; without a collective vision of human dignity, the Clown is not liberating, and finally not even funny. This is because, while there is nothing more worthy of parody and satire than false, narcissistic dignity or pompousness, true dignity is a projection of the Absolute into manifest existence, and since there is no incongruity in the Absolute, there is no humor. Incongruity, and consequently both liberating hilarity and bitter irony, exists on the border between the Absolute and the contingent, and nowhere else (the contingent minus the Absolute being deadly serious, like Marxism). This is why the American Indian figure of Coyote, who, like Nasruddin, is always tricking and always getting tricked, is rarely if ever identified with the Absolute, the Great Spirit, the Great Mystery. When a metaphysical role is assigned to him, it is usually that of a secondary creator or demiurge, who, as it were, slips on a banana peel and creates the universe. Coyote thus illustrates the esoteric principle that, in Rumi's words, "this world goes on by reason of heedlessness." In other words, manifest existence itself is an imbalance in the face of the Absolute. That this imbalance is ultimately destined to be righted before falling out of balance again is called in Hinduism the *mahapralaya* and in the Abrahamic traditions "The Day of the Lord" or "The Day of Judgement."

Nowadays "spiritual" humor is often identified with "esoteric" spiritualities—possibly because it is one of the ways in which a truth that cannot be adequately translated into literal or discursive terms can still be conveyed, at least in part. But the "trickster" quality is certainly not to be exclusively identified with esoterism, any more than the quality of seriousness should be limited to "mere exoterism". And the *unthinking* identification of trickery with the esoteric—the whole half-conscious notion that "wisdom is sneaky"—is the misconception that produced the panoply of spurious "Spiritual Tricksters" and "Crazy-Wisdom Gurus" we were treated to in the late twentieth century. The ultimate form of this false identification is the idea that to practice esoterism, because it is intrinsically involved with "secret knowledge", is necessarily to lie.

When esoterism degenerates, it becomes mystification; the arcane is transformed into the clandestine. This process often begins with esoteric groups who have been forced underground due to persecution; what *cannot* be said, because it is a mystery, thereby becomes confused with what *must not* be said, on pain of persecution, because it is a *secret*. (The true history of the involvement of various esoterists or occultists in espionage, intelligence-gathering and the work of secretly influencing mass belief would make a whole book in itself.) This is not to say that certain valid esoteric groups cannot legitimately operate in a clandestine manner in order to spread their teachings and fulfill certain other functions, only that when secrecy becomes an end in itself, the resulting addiction to deception and manipulation necessarily opens the door to self-delusion and demonic influence.

There have undoubtedly been consummate tricksters in the history of the spiritual Path—beings like Lear's Fool, or the Jacob of Genesis who, by the Grace of God, have served Wisdom by their tricks. But to attempt to employ *Maya* as a conscious teaching method most often results, as we have seen in the case of Coyote, in the trickster himself getting tricked. And if he remains *unaware* that he is getting tricked, and thus incapable of repenting of the *hubris* that led him to believe he could control the mystery of God's Self-revelation for his own considered ends, then he is one short step from outright Satanism.

So if we undertake to laugh, let us pray that we, not the Devil, will laugh last—with a laughter which, as an aspect of *Maya-in-divinis*, rests in the beauty of holy seriousness and pious discretion, in the hidden heart of God.

A DIALOGUE ON MAGIC
with Kamal Southall

K: A FRIEND AND MYSELF want to run these thoughts past you, for your feedback. We wonder if we are "on the right track" here.

It seems to me that in some ways we live in a "ghost-haunted world". How many people who hear voices today are schizophrenic? I have a few friends, mostly women, who state that they suspect some mild "mental illness" on their part, but prefer to think that the voices they occasionally hear, or the things they occasionally see, are actually spiritual or psychic matters from another world.

These friends do not seek psychiatric aid and for the most part are usually drawn to "earth spirit" types of spirituality; one friend of mine believes that all schizophrenics are actually psychic and that our culture simply doesn't know how to handle them.

C: I always say that "you can't see something that isn't there." And it's certainly true that many schizophrenics are very psychic; Jungian analyst Marie-Louise Von Franz wrote that this is one of the things, the temptations, that makes schizophrenia so hard to treat: the schizophrenic doesn't want to lose his or her "powers."

K: I think of other matters in which people seem to be massively confused, dictated to, spoken to, in ways that result in real horrors: like the massive numbers of serial murders, gross child rape and abuse.

C: Yes; demonic possession in many cases—if not the effect of deliberate suggestion and mind-control produced by the "wizards" employed by various government-sponsored mind-control programs like MK-Ultra—as well as by *wizards* in the literal sense of the word.

K: Then there are the mundane phenomena in which most people, most of the time, have some song or other constantly running through their heads, or sharply intrusive thoughts, and desires, obsessions. Much of this is likely simply the result of living in a hyper-paced society out of balance, but I wonder how much is prompted "from outside causes".

C: It's extremely hard to differentiate subjective "psychological" causation from what you call "outside causes"; they almost always operate together. When the "psychic immune system" is depleted, outside psychic influences, some of them demonic, can more easily enter. In some ways demonic possession is like an "opportunistic infection." And like I say, sometimes the "outside causes" come down to deliberate and clandestine manipulation by human agents.

K: A close friend of mine, and I, both have some past attachment to the occult. My friend was once attracted to neo-pagan streams of thought though by the grace of Allah he has entered Islam, after a previous attachment to a Traditionalist form of Catholicism. Both of us, it turns out, were quite familiar with certain schools of thought, in particular European neo-Right forms of Pagan Traditionalism, inspired in part by Julius Evola. Over the years he has increasingly discovered the writings of Schuon and our discussions have dwelt on these topics more and more.

We have speculated on the nature of a dead tradition, and why it is impossible to resurrect European Paganism. Apart from the loss of the detailed knowledge of the rites, necessitating a reconstructive work that is purely the work of man, and the inability to authentically verify any "inspiration", the very vital force that animated these traditions long ago departed leaving simply dead shells. One thing that I have noticed is the increasingly respected merging of neo-gnostic streams of thought, some focusing on "Dagobert's Revenge"/"Da Vinci Code" types of themes, with a politicized neo-paganism partially inspired by Evola (and I would argue by MIS-READING and misunderstanding of Evola, who in spite of my distaste for some of his ideas, seemed more rooted in a knowledge of tradition than many others).

C: If only those shells were merely dead! Many of them are actually "animated" by what Guénon called the "infra-psychic".

K: Is it possible for human beings to act as accumulators of subtle forces? Like batteries? The more I examine magic, or rather sorcery, the more it dawns on me that unlike the popular view in modern occultism that the Magician works with his own personal power may not be accurate.

If the powers worked with in magic are decidedly of a psychic nature, and far from impersonal forces, such forces may simply be subtle modalities of beings possessed of will, intent, and individuality, though in a non-physical way.

C: Certainly: familiar spirits. The magician believes that because he can expose himself to these beings they are thereby his slaves—and they like to foster this illusion. The magus can open Pandora's Box, but once the cat is out of that box, those beings have more control over him than he does over them; they produce phenomena that allow him to believe he is the author of them only to draw him further into their power.

K: The Greek Neo-Platonic idea of *henosis* seems very much like the *fana* of the Sufis. But what modern writers pass off as works of theurgy seems to be far from this; *henosis* was a matter of self-unification with the divine source, is this correct? Whereas the sort of apotheosis of the self than many modern magicians seek, in particular self-identified "luciferians", is far from this.

C: Right. Theurgy in essence is not the power of the magical ego to command the presence of a god, but an intellective recognition of the eternal presence and quality of the particular Name of God that the god in question symbolizes. And each Name of God, recognized and embraced, DECONSTRUCTS a particular element of the ego, permanently. When an ego-attachment is released, through the resulting gap in our ongoing, obsessive, unconscious self-definition shines a ray of the Divine—an "angel".

K: The subtle forces evoked and invoked may essentially be "the Jinn" who, beyond being of a subtle nature, are also possessed of free will and their own agendas, just as I may compel a human "force", say a servant, to run to the White Castle and pick me up a hamburger, in this manner a discrete human being is a force affecting a change of sorts. . . .

C: The Jinn have vastly greater power than the human ego; why should they serve us, except to trap us by pandering to our power-motive? According to the Qur'an, Solomon was the only one given power over the Jinn by God—the only one, that is, in this world-age. Primordial, unfallen humanity was not just the virtual but the realized *khalifa*; he commanded all the spiritual forces of the universe,

including the Jinn; since he was the epitome of universal manifestation, they were in some sense his elementals. But he didn't command them by force; he had precedence over them by transcending
them and encompassing them; they were the reflections of the
Names of God of which he was composed. This is what led Blake to
say "the gods should sacrifice to man, not man to the gods." The
memory of this unfallen state is one of the justifications for the
belief that the magician, posing as al-*insan al-kamil*, can command
the Jinn. But under present cosmic conditions, especially when the
magician is attempting to deify his ego rather than transcend it, this
is hardly possible.

K: In modern Sigil magic, the magician "charges" the sigil with
what he believes to be his own power, but I wonder how much this
is really the case. . . .

C: If anyone is deluded who doesn't recognize that ultimately
God is the performer of every act and the source of every event,
how much more deluded is the magician who thinks he can command forces that, in terms of personal power, vastly transcend him?

K: In Indonesian, Vietnamese, and other Southeast Asian forms
of magic, often times the magician acquires what is called a
"Helper" or a *khodam*. The *khodam* (in Indonesia) is a magickal
force that displays real intelligence and serves the magician, after he
acquires it through various trials and austerities. There is a biography of a Vietnamese traditional healer, who now lives in Maine, that
recounts his early learning of traditional sorcery in which he under-
went trials quite similar to those of the Indonesian magician, and
acquired his own "helper".

C: Indeed; that's how the Philippine psychic surgeons work (who
operated on me many times, both in the Philippines and California). They perform true white magic. They don't attempt to dominate the Jinn or *daimones* they work with, but rather partner with
them under the common tutelage of (as the Christian surgeons
describe it, and most of them are Christians) the Holy Spirit. But
these practitioners are operating on the very edge of what is possible
under current cosmic conditions; psychic surgery, even if entirely
well-intentioned (which most of it is) may have unintended consequences, such as post-operative "infections" on the psychic plane.

After the last time I visited the surgeons, I dreamt of *al-Dajjal*, so I stopped seeing them.

The *surah* on The Jinn from the Qur'an, the point is made (if I read it right, knowing no Arabic) that for us to worship the Jinn actually corrupts them, turning them away from the worship of Allah and tempting them to think of themselves as gods worthy of human worship. That's one of the perennial dangers of working with "spirit helpers."

K: Are thought-forms and magical energies actually simply impersonal subtle forces, like Ch'i, or are they more along the lines of actual entities who exist outside of the magician and have their own agendas?

C: I don't know. But I suspect that thought-forms might be described as impersonal energies configured in such a way that they invoke conscious entities

K: My meditations on Guénon's writings, and some of your previous replies to my emails, and what little knowledge of ceremonial magic I have leads me to believe that what remains of traditional magic, and sorcery, as practiced by various peoples, may have a "double sided" aspect in which the practitioner simply carries out what remains of more ancient rites as transmitted to him, and takes refuge in the forces evoked or invoked for protection against other subtle forces—but this reminds me of paying "protection money" to a gangster to protect you from other gangsters.

C: Precisely. One shaman interviewed by anthropologists, when they asked him why he became a shaman, replied that it was out of fear of the other shamans.

K: But in doing so is it possible that subtle modalities of our being are somehow being "marked" or "tattooed" or "branded" in a way?

C: Sure they are—as they are indeed by all experiences undergone in less than full consciousness, especially if they are of great psychic intensity. Heedlessness over-writes the soul with unconscious impressions; it is the function of the spiritual Path to purify us of such impressions so that, like the Prophet Muhammad, peace and blessings be upon him, we become "unlettered"—a blank page waiting to be written on by God alone.

K: I think of the manner in which Reiki healers undergo an attunement ceremony in which certain sigils or Japanese characters seem to be incorporated into their beings.

C: Yes; I've experienced Reiki many times. And I know that the Church of Joh-rei, which invokes similar energies for healing, uses amulets with Japanese characters. But faith in God, prayer, and invocation of His Name, are greater.

K: Whatever powers and benefits one may acquire may also lead one open to being "ridden" in the way that a voodoo *loa* rides a voodoo practitioner.

C: Yes. But Allah doesn't ride us—He carries us.

K: In this way I wonder if channelers and mediums may become locuses of manifestation for subtle influences who are able to act out through the mediums in far more profound ways than simply talking through them.

C: Of course. On the level of mere material phenomena, this includes psychic surgery, materializations, immunity to fire, etc. God only knows what effects are being produced on subtler levels!

K: If sacred geometry takes advantage of the correspondences between certain places, and subtle "places" in turn possess a correspondence with higher, or lower planes, and if these correspondences could only be sensed by a humanity whose subtle psychic senses, if not spiritual senses, were attuned to a degree that is unusual for modern man, then these "ley lines" may be carriers of subtle forces, the locations upon which ancient sites were built may have taken advantage of the more subtle modalities of the place.

C: Right: Mecca; Medina; Jerusalem.

K: The Roman sense of the *genius loci* shows an awareness of the subtle forces that may naturally tend to accumulate in a place. If the "degenerate" remnants of older traditions still carry out certain rites to propitiate, serve, and consult with, subtle forces that are mistaken for spiritual forces, is it possible that the rites they perform may have a dual purpose of gathering and accumulating even more forces there that can then be "tapped" and used—contrary to the will or even knowledge of the magicians using those sites and rites?

C: Sure. Unless the local psychic forces are under the rule of a living religion—a working channel of divine grace, not merely a psychic technology—they become available for evil uses. And it stands to reason that more powerful and more hidden magicians, as well as dark spiritual forces of a non-physical nature, might appropriate energies accumulated by the "little" magicians—seeing that all psychic operations not under the firm control of a living religion revealed by God are predatory in nature. The ultimate "predator" in this process, occupying the top of the magical food-chain, will be *al-Dajjal*.

K: Could the Shaman, seeking knowledge and the protection of his people, unwittingly serve others of whom he is unaware—not to speak of the naive Western neo-occultist?

C: The Western occultist is playing with a fire he can't even see. And plenty of shamans are undoubtedly messing with forces they don't understand, especially today. God willing there are still humble, powerful, well-intentioned, wise and balanced shamans working under the protection of the Great Spirit.

K: Much of what I understand in African Magic, and the magic of my ancestors in the "African diaspora" in the new world, seems to be of a degenerate nature, and dangerous, from the folk Hoodoo of the "Root Doctor", much of which is defensive in nature, protection from the evil eye or other sorcery (what my Grandmother used to call "Casting Roots at someone") to Santería in the New World, and the role of the *brujo* in South America. The practice of Brujería in some parts of South America seems to be benign, and even respected, but in other parts feared and despised.

C: It all depends on the *brujo*. I once knew an Irish-American Dominican nun who, after quitting her job as the mother superior of a convent in Mexico, started working with a local "white" *bruja* to undercut the power of the evil *brujos* of the area; the women were training young men as herbal doctors so the people wouldn't have to patronize the evil *brujos* every time they got sick (*brujos* who might in some cases have been *making* them sick in order to secure that patronage).

Voodoo shows signs of a very sophisticated theosophy and cosmology, syncretizing elements of Egyptian religion and esoteric (probably Ethiopian) Judaism with other sub-Saharan African influences. But the whole thing fell from mystical intellection—

which is where everything begins—through theurgy, to sorcery; the Pethro rites, for example, are entirely satanic. African religion is mostly degenerate probably because it is so incredibly ancient; it's had a long time to degenerate. A cave-sanctuary was recently discovered in Africa containing the sculpted image of a python 70,000 years old—apparently the same god still worshipped by the tribes of the region.

I have nothing against the protective "sacramentals" of the revealed religions—holy water, etc. But protective magic becomes dangerous when it starts to fight fire with fire. Spiritual protection has to come from a higher level of being than the evil magic it protects us from, otherwise we get slowly drawn into various magical conflicts where the remedy partakes of the disease.

And *miracle* is higher than all these. As I see it, everybody is always practicing magic of one kind or another, in that we are constantly working to achieve certain outcomes and prevent others. *Islam* is the only thing that can raise us from the pit of magic, the world of the *nafs al-ammara*; if we turn our will over to His Will— while still fulfilling all our responsibilities—then the outcome is in His hands, and whatever He wills is the best outcome. Through the door of submission to His Will comes the miraculous—*insha'llah*— and in the presence of Miracle, we can no longer posit ourselves as the originators of any action or event. Only God is the Doer.

K: Then there is the "Skin Walker" with certain Native American peoples.

C: Yes. But why think about them? Because they're hard NOT to think about; they know how to command our attention, and divert it from the remembrance of God. According to some Sufis, a person who has advanced to a certain point on the path, and then abandoned it, may become a *saher*—a sorcerer—someone who has opened the psychic plane but not transcended it. If you've been involved with occultism, you may not be able to go back to what Guénon calls "ordinary life"—if any of us can any more—but only *on*, until God takes you.

I have somewhere the text of some teachings by an African Sufi, who tells his mureeds (in line with the Qur'an) that in order to embark on the Sufi path they have to give up their "protectors". The threat of magic tempts us to counter-magic, and so we are led to seek out protectors from among the Jinn. But, as you wonder above, will we end up *paying* protection? This is very likely. The problem with even protective magic is that it is based on the lack of faith in God, and acts to undermine it. If we really knew that *He is Witness over all things*, we wouldn't turn to mere spooks for protection and power.

EXPERIENCE VS. BEING
IN THE MYSTICAL LIFE

A MEDITATION ON PSYCHEDELICS

Our companions warm themselves up with hashish. That's the
devil's imagination.
Even an angel's imagination is no great thing here—much less
the devil's imagination.
We would not be satisfied with the angel itself, much less the
angel's imagination.
　　　　　　　　　　　　　—Shams Tabrizi

Enter houses by their doors.
　　　　　　　　　　—Muhammad

THE RENEWED TALK in some circles about the use of psychedelics
to stimulate "mystical experience" has led me to ask whether or not
"experience" is really central to the mystical life. It may be that the
tendency to define mysticism in terms of a central "ultimate"
experience—as, for example, in the writings of Evelyn Underhill—
has subtly falsified our conception of that life, divorcing it from the
practice of virtue, the need to conform to tradition, and the understanding of metaphysical principles.

　If earlier generations made virtue or confessional orthodoxy into
idols—if, that is, the real nature of orthodoxy and the true goal of
virtue were imperfectly understood—the last two or three generations have certainly done the same for "experience." The test of the
validity of any religious commitment, or any human relationship for
that matter, is now seen in terms of experience, no longer in terms of
honor or duty or strength of character. A marriage based on duty
rather than affection is obviously far from ideal, but so is one based
on the sort of affection which neither develops out of nor flowers
into any sense of duty whatsoever. Without affection it is hard to

184 FINDINGS IN METAPHYSIC, PATH AND LORE

be dutiful, but with no sense of duty or responsibility affection is ultimately reduced to a shared narcissism.

I believe that the greatest danger of psychedelics—greater than their potential for damaging the mind or opening the soul to demonic activity, both of which are very real—is their power, in certain instances, to produce "valid" mystical experiences: true insights into the nature of God and our relationship to Him. To some, this may seem like an absurd conclusion: Is not the direct experience of God, the "beatific vision," the crown of the spiritual life? And if such a vision is admitted to be valid, then how could it be dangerous? How could it be wrong? If God is the Sovereign Good, how could witnessing that Good, by any means available, be anything but the greatest good life can offer?

I will answer this objection with an assertion: *The essence of the mature spiritual life is to love God's will above His gifts.* One might catch a glimpse through a window of a beautiful women disrobing, but if She has not granted us that glimpse then we are violating her dignity, not to mention breaking the law. I believe that the same principle *strictly applies* to the mystical life.

I will return to this point in a moment. For now, I wish to point out that the quasi-deification of experience is inseparable from the idolatrous worship of the human subjectivity. Duty is something we owe to someone or something beyond us, which is why fulfillment of duty is always potentially an approach to self-transcendence. Experience, however, is not something we "give," but something we "get."

In terms of Sufi doctrine, spiritual "stations" are acquired through the fulfillment of spiritual duties, which is another way of saying that we develop them through the actualization of the virtues. Courage, humility, patience, zeal, contentment with God's will are spiritual stations; they are acquired through labor. Spiritual "states", however, are not acquired—they are given. Since no amount or any quality of human action can "add up" to a theophany of Absolute Truth—though such action can, up to a point, remove barriers to our receptivity to that Truth—such theophanies, such instances of mystical experience, are necessarily free gifts of God. This means that the attempt to "get" these experiences, to have them

for our own, to savor them for our personal pleasure and enlightenment, is tantamount to robbery. And to rob God is not to come
closer to Him, but rather to become estranged from Him—perhaps
for all eternity.

The mystical life has first to do with Being, and only secondarily
with experience. Our duty is to come into a real, viable, relationship
with Absolute Truth, a relationship which holds true *whether or not
we presently experience it.* As Beat Generation poet Lew Welch once
wrote, "I seek union with what goes on whether I look at it or not"—
not with the subjective experience of the thing, that is, but with the
very thing itself. In the words of St. Paul, *faith* is "the presence of
things hoped for, the evidence of thing not seen." In the mystical
life, experience is the product of faith, not faith of experience.

There is no mystical life, of course, without experience—because
God is generous, because the Absolute Truth, by Its Infinite Self-
manifesting Radiance, must communicate Itself. We ourselves, in
fact, are actual instances of that communication. Experience, however, is inseparable from the subjectivity whereby it is experienced—
that is, from our ego—while the entire *raison d'être* of the mystical
life is to transcend this ego. Thus the Sufis hold that specific spiritual states are given us by God not as permanent goods in themselves, but rather in order to deconstruct or annihilate specific
aspects of our ego, which is why the fully-realized Sufi is described
as being "beyond states and stations."

Mystical experience which is actively sought for itself alone, not
in obedience to the One who sends it—and He may or may not
choose to send it at any given moment—is experience sought by the
ego. Consequently it can in no way deconstruct that ego; it can only
inflate it—*even if the initial experience is one of ego-transcendence.*
Therefore it is entirely possible that mystical experience such as that
produced by psychedelics may actually *drive us away* from the Reality we have caught a glimpse of, *to the degree that this glimpse is
actually valid.* It's as if the beautiful woman we have seen disrobing
realizes that she's being spied upon and calls the police. The net
result of such an encounter is obviously not to bring us closer to
her. It may turn us into stalkers, but never into lovers. (This is not
to say that every artificially-produced glimpse if higher realities

must always estrange us from them, only that every such glimpse must eventually be paid for.) And to identify certain experiences of ecstasy, or clarity, or brilliant insight, or overwhelming love as "special, therefore of God", and other experiences—heavy, painful, or simply tedious—as "ordinary, therefore not of God," is to limit God to our own human conceptions, and also (in effect) to attempt to control Him, to make Him be, and do, what *we* want Him to. And nothing is more likely to produce this sort of partiality and idolatry than the overwhelming intensity of psychedelic experience. According to the Sufis, God sends *all* states: both expansion *and* contraction, both recollection *and* scatteredness, both drunkenness *and* sobriety. If we can recognize the hand and presence of God in each state that comes upon us, and submit to it as such, then we have begun to know Him as He really is—not merely according to a few of His Names (our special, favorite Names), but as His Unnameable Essence manifesting as the perfect synthesis of *all* His Names: *Allah*. To realize God in this way is to become *al-insan al-kamil*, the perfect or complete man.

There is, of course, the level of reality where Being and Knowing are revealed as One, the level of the Transcendent Intellect, beyond which is nothing but the Unnameable Essence, the Absolute Self. But in order for Being and Knowing to unite, "experience" and the "experiencer"—which are all that keep Being and Knowing (apparently) apart in the first place—must be annihilated. God does not "have experiences": He Knows, and Is; He Knows Who He Is, and He Is What He Knows. In the words of the Prophet Muhammad, peace and blessings be upon him, "pray to God as if you saw Him—because even if you don't see Him, He sees you."

> When the king came in to see the guests, he saw there a man which had not on a wedding garment:
> And he sayeth to him, Friend, how camest thou hither not having a wedding garment? And he was speechless.
> Then said the king to the servants, bind him hand and foot, and take him away, and cast him into the outer darkness; there shall be weeping and gnashing of teeth.
>
> —Matt. 22:11–13

[NOTE: Although the term "entheogens" is beginning to replace "psychedelics" to denote the drugs in question, I believe that the earlier term is the more accurate. Drugs may have the power to "expand (and thus attenuate, if not fracture) the psyche"; they do not have the power to "generate God within."]

HUSTON SMITH, YELLOWTAIL, & ANNE CATHERINE EMMERICH ON PSYCHEDELICS

HUSTON SMITH, following mycologist Gordon Wasson, believes that the sacred Soma plant of the Vedas was the psychedelic mushroom *Amanita Muscaria*. And, just conceivably, there might have been a time in which the "mass theophanic consciousness" of the Golden Age was still a living memory, a time when the collective veil over the Divine was thin enough to be temporarily lifted by psychedelics without invoking a demonic reaction. But we are certainly not living in those times. In Michael Fitzgerald's biography *Yellowtail, Crow Medicine Man and Sun Dance Chief* [University of Oklahoma Press, 1994], Yellowtail speaks of the superiority of the Sun Dance to the peyote "sacrament" of the Native American Church. Peyote is a limited path, but the Sun Dance can take one all the way—it is a path that has no end. However, Yellowtail stopped short of branding peyote and other psychedelics as possible vectors of demonic influence. [NOTE: Peyote, perhaps the most "sober" of the psychedelics, has apparently done some good on the reservations, especially in the treatment of alcoholism. However, it can definitely be used in sorcery as well, as I can confidently state from personal experience. The only two clear acts of sorcery I ever committed (*white* sorcery of course—as if we could tell black from white while practicing sorcery) were performed under its influence.]

The Christian visionary and stigmatist Anne Catherine Emmerich, however (1774–1824), gives unwitting evidence of the demonic potential of psychedelics. In her book *The Life of Christ and Biblical Revelations*, based on her visions, (as recounted to Clemens Brentano), she mentions an early non-Biblical patriarch called *Hom*, who was either named after, or provided a name for, a particular plant he considered to be sacred. This plant, in my opinion, is the *Haoma* plant of the ancient Persians, equivalent to the Vedic *Soma*.

According to Emmerich, the lineage that sprang from Hom—which included one Dsemschid (undoubtedly the legendary Persian king Jamshid) became polluted with Satanic fantasies. And although we will never know if, or how much, Clemens Brentano may have contributed to Emmerich's writings, she herself—she was a nearly illiterate Westphalian peasant—would have been highly unlikely to have known anything about Persian history or Zoroastrian lore. And it is equally unlikely that either she or Brentano would have known a great deal about psychedelics.

So it may well be that the "sacramental" use of mind-altering substances, at least in the present Kali-yuga, represents a truly ancient deviation in humanity's relationship with God—a Luciferian attempt to "take heaven by storm", to *access* God's hidden Wisdom rather than obeying the norms laid down in His revelations, and then standing in wait for whatever He may be pleased to provide or withhold. And from what we now know about the dissemination of LSD to both the intelligentsia (via Timothy Leary) and the masses (via Ken Kesey) as part of the CIA's sinister MK-Ultra mind control program [see the work of investigators David McGowan and Peter Levenda, as well as the archive of Beat Generation poet Allen Ginsberg now housed at Stanford University], we are led to ask: Are certain sectors of the ruling elite actually practicing Luciferians—people who have gone beyond the rudimentary ideas of Social Darwinism to the level of "Spiritual Darwinism"? Do they in fact hold to the notion that the universe itself is a kind of predatory food-chain, to a conception of God not as the intrinsic Reality of all things, a Reality both transcendent and immanent, but merely the most successful Predator to date—a Predator Who might conceivably be toppled from His throne by a victorious Luciferian revolution? (Art Kleps, in *Millbrook*, his book about Timothy Leary's famous "psychedelic manor house" in upstate New York, presents the well-known counterculture LSD-alchemist, Stanley Owsley, as an individual who ate only meat because he saw the universe precisely as a *food-chain*, and wanted to eat as high on the hog as possible.) And is the perversion of the revealed religions and wisdom traditions via psychedelics, as well as the use of these substances to influence mass belief, part of a conscious Luciferian agenda?

In light of this distinct possibility, the fact that a major North American Traditionalist journal, within the past few years, published a positive review of a book advocating drug-induced "mysticism" (something that would have been simply inconceivable in the case of the original *Studies in Comparative Religion*, for example), clearly points to a highly-successful attack by the Counter-Initiation—either through conscious agents, simply via the *zeitgeist*, or (as is most likely) by means of both—upon the Traditionalist/Perennialist School in North America.

A THREE-WAY COMMUNICATION ON PSYCHEDELICS AND THE SPIRITUAL PATH

THE FOLLOWING QUOTATION is taken from the text of an e-mail I received while writing this book; the speaker is Shams Tabrizi, spiritual master of Jalaluddin Rumi, from William Chittick and Annemarie Schimmel's book *Rumi and Me* [Fons Vitae, 2004]:

> Our companions warm themselves up with hashish. That's the devil's imagination. Even an angel's imagination is no great thing here—much less the devil's imagination. We would not be satisfied with the angel itself, much less the angel's imagination. What is a devil, after all, that there should be its imagination? Why indeed don't our companions have a taste of our pure, infinite world? That stuff makes people understand nothing and become stupefied.

> He objected, "The Koran forbids wine, but it doesn't forbid hashish."

> I said, "Every verse had an occasion, and then it came down. In the time of the Prophet, the Companions didn't eat this hashish. If they had done so, he would have commanded that they be killed."

My correspondent went on to say:

> [Shams] mentions hashish on a few other occasions as well; one time he advises Rumi's son, Sultan Walad, to stop eating hashish; another time he says, "In the Beloved's lane there's a kind of hashish. People eat it and lose their intellects. Then they can't find the Beloved's house and they fail to reach the Beloved." In the latter instance he appears to be speaking of a figurative intoxication in the Beloved's lane, comparable to the

stupefying effect of hashish. He lays a clear denouncement on it in every case.

Sultan Walad apparently had marital problems, which might well have had something to do with his hashish-eating. THC, the active ingredient of cannabis, is chemically similar to estrogen. When a man ingests cannabis, it subtly saps his manhood, to the point that—after a while—his woman may no longer approve of him, though in a traditional Muslim culture she might decide to keep her mouth shut. (No matter; looks are enough.) And when a man feels he's lost his wife's respect, he may react with abuse, if not violence. The following is a passage from Ibrahim W. Gamard and A.G. Rawan Farhadi's translation of *The Quatrains of Rumi*, which I edited [Sophia Perennis, 2008]; Rumi is writing to his daughter-in-law, who complained to him about how his son was treating her:

> He [Rumi] wrote that her sorrows were his sorrows, as well as her concerns. He expressed the highest respect for her (deceased) father, saying that he was so indebted to him that he was unable to pay for it. "Only the treasury of God Most High will be able to pay the gratitude for it." He told her that his expectation from her was that she should not conceal any suffering, so that he could help her as much as possible. He said that if his son continued to trouble her, he would detach his own heart from him, not answer greetings from him, and not wish attendance at his own funeral from him—or from any others who supported him against her.

In view of the fact that sorcery was introduced into North American mass culture by Carlos Castaneda, whose first two books, *The Teachings of Don Juan* and *A Separate Reality*, emphasized the use of psychoactive substances, the following passage from the Noble Qur'an [Rodwell translation, 2:96] is relevant:

> *And they followed what the satans read in the reign of Solomon: not that Solomon was unbelieving, but the satans were unbelieving. Sorcery did they teach to men, and what had been revealed to the two angels, Harut and Marut, at Babel. Yet no man did these two teach until they had said "We are only a temptation. Be*

not then an un-believer." From these two did men learn how to cause divisions between man and wife.

Those of my generation who lived *consciously* through the depressive, heartbreaking, feminist Seventies in North America— the decade when the cultural effects of the mass use of psychedelics came horribly due—will hopefully understand the full import of this passage.

At the very same time I received the above e-mail, I was also in e-mail contact with a practitioner of Sufi *ruhaniya*, which he described as "theurgy", "thaumaturgy" and "white magic" (terms which are entirely appropriate as descriptions of Shamanism, for example). He considered the use of psychedelics legitimate within an "initiatory context", and spoke of their application by *ruhani* "maguses". (I must apologize to any Sufis who may practice a form of *ruhaniya* which does not fit this description.) While the use of psychoactive substances may (or may not) be justifiable in a traditional Shamanic context, and allowing that the state-of-heart of the magi he spoke of may be blameless before God (and may God keep their secret), the use of intoxicants is not compatible with Qur'anic norms, no matter how long it may have been practiced in Islamic nations—undoubtedly, in many cases, before the advent of Islam. (And drug-use is certainly not the norm among Sufi orders; most of them strictly prohibit it.)

Theurgy in the pursuit of our human ideas of the good is certainly not to be identified with sorcery and black magic. And yet, to the degree that human "good will" replaces prayer-of-petition, we are attempting to *employ* God instead of submitting to Him, and— at that precise instant—opening the door to every possible rebellion. Furthermore, prayer-of-petition itself is only valid and effective at the moment when God says, "petition Me". My informant agreed, however, that magical self-will is a form of *shirk*, the sin and heresy of associating partners with God; I only hope that he and his colleagues in *ruhaniya* are truly free from that sin, which can take extremely subtle forms.

To many people, even many religious people, submission to God's will seems like a kind of weakness, an abdication of human responsibility. And certainly there are those whose false mask of submission conceals only cowardice and spiritual despair. What both the cringing spiritual coward and the powerful, self-willed magus fail to realize, however, is that submission *is* power—the greatest power imaginable, because it calls upon *al-Qadir*, upon "God Almighty" Himself. Who but God possesses both the Absolute Power to effect his Will, and the Absolute Wisdom to will the best possible outcome in every circumstance?

Why settle for less?

SUFI MANIFESTO

THERE IS NOTHING essential in Sufi doctrine that is not ultimately a commentary on the Noble Qur'an and the prophetic *ahadith*—the flawed scholarship of the orientalists and the fantasies of the anti-traditional pseudo-esoterics notwithstanding. Those so-called Sufis who try to separate Sufism from Islam, no matter how sincere they may be, are like cut flowers in a vase. Until the water that sustains them evaporates, they bloom and give off fragrance—but in reality they possess only the semblance of life, and the power to reproduce is forever denied them. God in His Mercy may save them in view of their sincerity, because He has the power to save whoever He will—but the norms He Himself has laid down for the soul's return to Him will form no part of that saving act. To reject the religion brought by Muhammad, peace and blessings be upon him, is to cut the *silsilah* that stretches back to him, and from him to Gabriel, and from Gabriel to Allah—to deprive it of all meaning, and of any effectiveness except (perhaps) a temporary and fading one.

Sufism is not a revelation in itself—a truth that some Sufis may lose sight of in view of the fact that the basic practices and some of the lore of *tasawwuf* clearly pre-date Islam. The Christian practice of the Prayer of the Heart, carried on by the Eastern Orthodox Hesychasts and referred to in several places in the New Testament, as when St. Paul recommends that we "pray without ceasing", or when St. Peter speaks of the moment when "the day-star shall arise in your hearts," is almost identical in form to the Sufi *dhikr*. Certain indications in the Old Testament also appear to refer to the practice of the invocation of God's Name, such as passages from the Psalms like "our heart will rejoice in Him because we have trusted in His Holy Name" [33:21] and "unite my heart to fear Thy Name" [86:11]. And certainly some Sufi lore and practices came into the tradition from pre-Islamic Central Asia. The question is: Did lore and practice from the ancient Near East and Central Asia enter Islam so as to become part of Sufism? Or did Sufism depart from Islam to seek that lore and practice in foreign lands and religions? The answer is obvious: the pre-Islamic and non-Islamic lore and spiritual practices were the guests, but Islam was the host. And it is the host who provides the nourishment. To say that Sufism is not intrinsically Islamic is no different from saying that the Dalai Lama is not really a Buddhist, since many of the practices of Tibetan Buddhism originally derived from the shamanic religion of Bön. Certainly Vajrayana Buddhism drew upon Bön, but whatever entered Buddhism from that religion became *essentially* Buddhist, not just accidentally so. No spiritual lore or practice is spiritually effective unless it sits at the table of one of God's great revelations to humanity; to attempt to carry on such practice outside one of these revelations is to turn it over to the self-will of the ego, to the *nafs al-ammara*. As every Sufi *silsilah* attests, living contact with God's *baraka* comes through His revelation to humanity in the Noble Qur'an and the way of the Prophet Muhammad, peace and blessings be upon him; every special unveiling or grace given and received in the course of spiritual practice and attainment, even in the case of the greatest Sufi masters, is only effective in that context. It may seem as if the existence of spiritual seekers and masters who reached high stations outside, or between, the great revelations—such as Waraqah the Hanif or Uways al-Qarani—proves that such revelations are unnecessary and can be ignored with impunity. Such is not the case. Waraqah was a Christian, and was waiting for the new revelation destined to come through Muhammad, which he gladly embraced. And although Uways al-Qarani, who is sometimes given as an example of a "Sufi" master outside Islam, never met the Prophet, he did embrace Islam when news of it came to him; this is undoubtedly what Muhammad meant when he said, referring to Uways, "I feel the Breath of the Merciful coming from the direction from the Yemen". When God opens a clear path, and we still foolishly think we can invent our own path or find a better one, then God help us.

Many Sufis who emigrate from nations with oppressive Islamicist regimes go to pieces in the comparative religious freedom of the west. They are so relieved not to be under the thumb of the Wahhabis, the Ayatollahs, the religious police that they gladly dump the *shari'ah*, even the Five Pillars, and revel in their new-found liberty. It is one thing to abbreviate the *shari'ah*, sometimes radically, so as to make it possible to practice it in a balanced way in non-Islamic nations; it is quite another thing to abandon it entirely. I cannot think of a single historical example where an esoterism such as *tasawwuf* deserted its parent religion without eventually—or immediately—turning into a heterodox cult, a political cadre, a universalist pseudo-religion, or all three at once. And though it is understandable that some Sufis in the west would want to publicly distance themselves from Islam—particularly after 9/11—the fact remains that the persecution faced by Muslims in western nations is nothing compared to the persecution faced by Sufis in certain Islamic nations. Whether or not they openly admit it, some Sufis who immigrate to the west feel relieved to be "freed" from Islam itself, forgetting that they *are* Islam, that as traditional Sufis they are much more truly Islamic than the Islamicists ever could be. What they don't seem to realize is that in drifting aimlessly away from Islam over the seas of western secularism, they are actually obeying the orders of the Wahhabis, the Ayatollahs, the religious police. Those heartless oppressors would like see Sufism ejected from Islam entirely—and those westernized Sufis who separate Sufism from its Islamic roots are blithely and unwittingly doing their work for them. The Islamicists slander Sufism by calling it heterodox and anti-Islamic, and then the westernized Sufis prove them right by transforming themselves into the very image of the heterodox, non-Islamic Sufi, perfectly validating the Islamicist ideology upon whose false image of Sufism they have patterned themselves. Westernized Sufis sometimes justify dumping the *shari'ah* by pointing to the all-too-common example of those Muslims who become obsessed with it, who use the law as a whip against others rather applying it to themselves in an attempt to become true human beings. But whether the ego of the exoteric Muslim obsessed with the law or that of the so-called Sufi who prides himself on being above the law is the hungrier beast, God only knows.

The Sufis of the west should stand against the Islamicists, not obey them. They should not abandon Islam to the Wahhabis and the other anti-Sufi Muslims, but should claim it for their own. This need not be done in a politicized or "activist" way, with public

demonstrations and denunciations; all that is required is that western Sufis should stand in the tradition of their own great exemplars
of the past, in the lineage stretching back to the first Sufis, in the
days when Sufism was a reality without a name, not a name without
a reality—to Ali ibn Abi Talib and the Prophet Muhammad himself,
peace and blessings be upon them. It is in the west alone that they
are almost entirely free to do this; it would be a tragedy if they did
not fully avail themselves of that freedom, while it still exists.

If there is one thing that immigrants to the west from dar al-
Islam need to understand—something that under present conditions it is very difficult for them to get a clear picture of—it is the
history of the west's religious opposition to its own secularization,
and of the relentless ejection of religious doctrines and values from
the arena of public discourse. They do not realize that religious freedom, which is a good thing in itself and a necessary aspect of any
humane, religiously-pluralistic society, is inseparable in practical
terms from a militant secularism that devalues *all* religion, relegat-
ing it to the "private" realm alone—and that religious freedom in
the west has already begun to be seriously curtailed by the very
"democratic" secularism that brought it into being. To the degree
that Sufis abandon their Islamic roots, and are content to occupy
only the shapeless "interfaith" zone designed by the secular globalists as a sort of theme-park to keep the traditional religions pacified,
subject to a false sense of security calculated to blind them to their
increasing marginalization under the "oppressive tolerance" of the
west, they will not be able to stand together in any effective way,
either vocally or silently, with their brothers and sisters of the other
world religions, against the forces of militant secularism and official
denial of God that menace them all.

Sleepers, awake.

THE SHEPHERDS, THE BAPTIST
AND THE ESSENES

A RESPONSE TO *THE LIFE OF CHRIST*
AND BIBLICAL REVELATIONS
BY ANNE CATHERINE EMMERICH

THOSE "shepherds keeping watch over their flocks by night" mentioned in Luke 2:8 were undoubtedly the leaders of secret or esoteric spiritual schools, "night" being a symbol of both outer secrecy and hidden matters of the Spirit. Such esoteric groups could also have actually made their living as shepherds, which would have allowed them to carry messages, gather intelligence and spread their teaching over a wide area, shepherds being relatively mobile as compared to town dwellers, and thus able to travel without arousing suspicion.

The Essenes, or some other esoteric brotherhood (possibly the Nazarites), could have maintained a clandestine presence among the people by this means. This is in line with Anne Catherine Emmerich's assertion that some among the lower classes knew about the prophecies of Christ's impending birth that the religious authorities were unaware of [see *The Life of Christ and Biblical Revelations*: TAN, 1979; p.134; new edition upcoming by Sophia Perennis]; it would also explain Jesus' reference to Himself as the "Good Shepherd". She also maintains that some of the followers of the Three Kings, who met with the shepherds, opted to remain behind with them after their masters returned home. But if the shepherds who attended the birth of Jesus had simply been ignorant sheep herders, why would privileged servants of the Kings, who were priests and spiritual dignitaries, have wished to remain with them? It's as if they had received some spiritual initiation at the hands of these shepherds (or vice-versa); they might also have joined them so as to maintain a Judean link with the Kings and their co-religionists in their original homelands.

Given that Isaiah 53:7 speaks of the coming servant of God, identified with the Messiah, as one "brought as a lamb to the slaughter", and that John the Baptist called Jesus "the Lamb of God" [John 1:36], it is symbolically logical that a clandestine brotherhood awaiting the coming of the Messiah should make their living as shepherds; only our modern ignorance of the weaving of spiritual symbolism into everyday life, common in all traditional societies, prevents this from being obvious to us. Such a brotherhood would probably have traced its origin to the patriarch Abel, who was both the archetypal shepherd and the first "pure victim"; they would thus have re-enacted the perennial theme of the Pure Nomad vs. the Corrupt City-Dweller—Cain, the agriculturalist, having been both the founder of the first city and the first murderer.

Jesus Himself lived as a nomad after he began His ministry, having no fixed abode. Furthermore, the Sufis of Islam, whose name means "wool-clad", may in fact have derived that epithet from their identification with an earlier spiritual brotherhood of shepherds in the Near East, the Nazarites. The Prophet Muhammad himself worked as a shepherd in his youth, and among the Sufis there are those who specially dedicate themselves to a life of spiritual nomadism—the Qalendars. The Sufis also call themselves *al-fuqara*, the "poor"—immediately reminding us of Jesus' saying, "blessed are the poor in spirit, for they shall see God."

The Three Kings or Magi are most often assumed to have been Zoroastrians, and it is likely that the Essenes maintained ongoing Zoroastrian connections. Among the Dead Sea Scrolls, attributed to the Essenes, the so-called War Scroll presents a picture of the final eschatological combat in terms that bear a close resemblance to the Zoroastrian account, and it is well known that Jewish (and later Christian) eschatology owes much to the Zoroastrian influence. The Book of Esther in particular demonstrates just how close the cultural ties were, at certain periods, between the Jews and the Zoroastrian Persians.

The ancient "Gnostic" sect of the Mandaeans, based in southern Iraq, trace their origin back to John the Baptist, and are also sometimes identified or associated by scholars with the Essenes. It is believed that some Essenes might have taken refuge with them at the time of the Jewish Revolt. The scriptures of the Mandaeans have a distinctly Zoroastrian flavor; also, southern Iraq was a part of Greater Persia at that time; during and after the Revolt many Jews took refuge within the borders of the Sassanid Persian Empire.

If the Mandaeans were Essenes or descended from them, this would make their founder John the Baptist an Essene as well. (The Gospel of Luke calls him a Nazarite, but there is no reason why he could not have belonged to both brotherhoods.) John preached and baptized within sight of the cliffs of Qumran, the major known Essene stronghold. Those scholars who deny that John could have been an Essene point to his violations of Essene ritual purity: his use of animal skins as clothing and—if the "locusts" he ate were the pods of the leguminous carob tree (called "locust" in the King James Bible), not the insects of the same name—his consumption of beans. But it is also possible that John's violation of Essene purity laws might have had a symbolic significance, seeing that it was his mission to preach to the people at large, not to remain secluded in a monastic setting like Qumran. He might have considered himself a "graduate" of the Essenes, no longer bound by their laws; and Anne Catherine Emmerich does in fact maintain that John, like Jesus, had been educated by the Essenes [see *The Life of Christ and Biblical Revelations*, p. 203].

It is also possible that John's open transgression of Essene ritual taboos might have been understood, by certain more esoteric Essenes, as placing him among what the Sufis call the *malamatiyya* or People of Blame—those who openly violate group norms, either to mortify their social pride, or to indicate that true spirituality must at one point transcend the limits of the Law, as Jesus demonstrated when he healed on the Sabbath and cast the money-changers out of the Temple. The Mandaeans, however, hate Jesus to this day because, they claim, he publicly revealed their esoteric secrets. This would point to a schism among the Essenes themselves in the face of Jesus' ministry; some of them would have accepted Him as the Messiah, while others rejected Him. The Gospel account of Jesus' baptism by John in the third chapter of Matthew would thus have been directed to, and accepted by, the first of these two groups, but denied by the second.

The shepherds who attended Jesus' birth might well have been members of the Nazarite Botherhood. A certain "Nazarite shepherd" is mentioned in the Talmud, and the Prophet Amos, who was himself a shepherd, laments the persecution and degeneracy of the Brotherhood. Some scholars believe that the characterization of Jesus as a "Nazarene" (an inhabitant of Nazareth) is actually a veiled reference to his being a Nazarite. The Nazarites (like Samson) took a vow not to cut their hair, and Jesus is traditionally shown with long hair. They also vowed to abstain from wine (like the Muslims after them), which would explain the criticism leveled against Jesus as a "wine-bibber"—a charge that would have been meaningless if applied to an ordinary Jew, but not to a Jew who lived in open violation of his Nazarite vows. Jesus, then, might have been of the *malamatiyya* in relation to the Nazarites, as the Baptist could well have been a *malamati* vis-à-vis both the Nazarites and the Essenes.

MYSTERY OF INIQUITY,
MYSTERY OF MERCY

A MEDITATION ON THE OCCASION OF THE
PUBLICATION OF THE GOSPEL OF JUDAS

For Rama Coomaraswamy

[NOTE: Though I have been a Muslim for the past 20 years, my first initiation was into the path of Catholicism—Baptism, Confirmation, Eucharist—before the Second Vatican Council all but dismantled it. It is out of this initiation of my childhood that I have written this piece.]

When the publication of the Gnostic *Gospel of Judas* was announced, precipitating a flurry of mindless affirmation and almost equally mindless criticism, something began to move in my soul. *The Gospel of Judas* portrays Judas not a Jesus' betrayer, but rather as His confederate in "setting up" the crucifixion. (Gurdjieff said the same thing.) But this ancient perversion of the Gospel account, which degrades Jesus from the status of the only-begotten Son of God to that of a worldly conspirator and swindler, set up its own counter-motion within me. In the face of the faithless tendency to excuse Christ's betrayer, which is only one instance of a much wider tendency in the post-Vatican II and post-pedophilia-scandal Catholic Church, and elsewhere, to self-servingly deny original sin, deny the gravity of personal sin, and posit the universal salvation of each individual soul, whether holy or corrupt, I suddenly understood, and became subject to, the Mercy of God—a ruthless, harrowing Mercy which called up all the darkness in my own soul. I saw that repentance, which is instantaneous, initiates an ongoing process of purgation, whereby those faculties of the soul that had been diverted from their true purposes, according to the human form as God created it, are progressively reoriented toward, and remarried to, those purposes.

I also saw that there are certain things in the soul, certain totally perverse tendencies, which cannot be rejoined to their true purposes because they have none. They are purely infernal, purely satanic, and as such have no right to exist. These tendencies cannot be redeemed; they can only be annihilated. As such, they cannot be the objects of the purgation initiated by repentance, if we define this purgation as the redemption of the human faculties. They are, as it were, perpetually and *essentially* in Hell; therefore only the annihilation of Hell itself can do away with them. In light of this insight, I understood that the doctrine of *apocatastasis*, the restoration of all things in God, which has been so problematical in the Christian tradition, cannot and must not be identified with the salvation of every individual soul on its own plane of existence, which is an affront to the Justice of God, as well as being clearly heretical. The only correct way to understand it is as the resorption of both Hell and Paradise into the Absolute Divinity at the end of time, at the point between (speaking in universal, cosmic terms) the passing away of the old heaven and earth, and the coming of the new heaven and the new earth. If heaven and earth can pass away, certainly hell also can pass away—after which nothing remains but the Word by which God names Himself and knows Himself, from all eternity.

We sometimes say that the true greatness God's Mercy can only be understood in relation to the gravity of sin: If we are convicted of sin and understand its enormity, only then we will understand the glory of God's Mercy and Forgiveness. But it is even truer to say that we cannot understand the enormity of sin except in close proximity to Mercy. Sin hides in its own darkness, until the coming of the light. Only then can we see—can we *bring ourselves* to see—the horror of the prison we have just escaped.

God's Mercy is an aspect of His Truth. Any doctrine which asserts that Mercy absolves us of the duty to confront our own darkness, that God wills to forgive us without our participation, and (as it were) behind our backs, is false. To hope and believe that God will *excuse* us by virtue of an *indiscriminate* Mercy, a Mercy without Intelligence and without Truth, is an expression of spiritual despair. It is to believe that if the true gravity of sin were dragged into the light, God could not forgive it. By this belief we attribute to God, under the name of cruel judgment, what is in reality our own faithlessness, our fear that if we were ever confronted with the enormity of our own sin, we—like Judas—would despair of God's Mercy. And this is precisely what Satan wants. Satan is not only the Accuser but also the *Ex*cuser. He excuses our sins in order to suggest thereby that our debts are too great for God to actually forgive, thus denying the efficacy of the Atonement and claiming that the final import of God's Mercy is not to *forgive* our sins but simply to let us weasel out of them through the back door—through denial, through mendacious rationalizations, through self-serving and sentimental false pieties, and finally (when these fail, as they inevitably will) through seeking the "all-excusing" oblivion of death—as if death were not in fact the *end* of all worldly oblivion, either to our great good fortune or to our irretrievable loss. And as soon as we have accepted the lame and lying excuses Satan suggests to us, blasphemously identifying them with the Mercy of God, then he changes with lightning swiftness from indulgent Excuser to merciless Accuser, tearing down all the cruelly permissive excuses he has just provided us with, and confronting us with the enormity of our sins *in the absence of Mercy*: because to identify God's Mercy with the kind of lame excuse that wouldn't stand up in any court is to throw that Mercy out the window. Moral permissiveness is thus nothing but cruelty; to excuse evil is to embrace despair.

The realization and acceptance of God's Mercy is the very power which enables us to confront the darkness in our souls, and dispel it. Repentance is the acceptance of Mercy. But according to scripture, Judas did not accept God's Mercy; he despaired of it and committed suicide. To imply (as some proponents of *The Gospel of Judas* have done) that Jesus in the Gospel accounts refused to forgive Judas is to cleverly hide the fact that Judas was damned because *he* refused that forgiveness. Jesus commanded us to love our enemies; to say that He had no love for Judas, that He did not *by His very being* extend forgiveness to him, is to accuse Jesus of not practicing what he preached. Of course He extended forgiveness; by His death and resurrection, He *is* forgiveness. It's simply that Judas refused to accept what was offered. You may freely hand me a $20 bill, but if, out of pride (which is another name for despair), I won't take it, then I don't *have* it. It's as simple as that.

In this life, our will is free to choose. In the next life, what we have chosen is fixed; God places His final seal of confirmation on what we have freely chosen, until the end of time. And at the end of the cosmic aeon (not just this earthly one), in the *apocatastasis*, when God takes both Paradise and Hell back into the mystery of His Essence, He also takes back the human forms he has given us, and along with them our human free will. This is the moment when God overwhelms both Heaven and Hell with His Absolute Reality, which is infinitely beyond both of them.

The end of our individual lives is encompassed by the particular judgment; the end of this world, by the general judgment; and the end of universal manifestation, of creation itself, by the *apocatastasis*. To confuse these levels is to fall into grave error. In particular, it is a great and terrible mistake to identify the eternal destiny of the soul on the plane of form with the supraformal eternity of God Himself, realized by the *apocatastasis*. That the doctrine, or the intimation, of such a tremendous and definitive Divine "event" should be used to deny the gravity of sin, to justify both self-betrayal and the betrayal of God, is an immense blasphemy, and also an immense stupidity—as if a child were to hope that the world would end before his mother discovered that he robbed the cookie jar—as if a serial murderer were to attempt to destroy the whole world in order to drown the tawdry memory of his crimes. God is just; if He were not just, He would not be good; if He were not good, He could not be merciful. And God is not mocked. He does not give us the gift of free will only to let us return it to Him again the moment we realize we have abused it, and that the consequences of such abuse are terrible. If He did, He would in effect be admitting that His creation of the human race with the power of sovereign free will was a joke, a farce, or a mistake. To expect Him to simply and glibly excuse the abuse of His greatest gift is to slander Him, to make Him less than God. (And if rays from the universe-dissolving power of the *apocatastasis* unexpectedly break into Hell, and Heaven too, since they emanate from a degree of eternity that is higher that the dark perpetuity of Hell, higher even than the formal eternity of

Paradise, then who are we to deny their power to do so? And who are we to either expect it, claim it, or foolishly rely upon it?)

Hell is a necessary doctrine, a doctrine made necessary by the nature of God and the freedom of the human will. And though we may hope that Hell may be emptied, or that a given soul may be rescued from it, in the mystery of God's Will, to take such action for granted would be like setting one's house on fire and then locking oneself in, in hopes that a windstorm would arrive in a minute to tear off the roof, and rain pour down quench the blaze. It would be the height of presumption, more abysmally and inconceivably foolish than anyone who claims to believe in God has any right to be.

Hell is fundamentally different from after-death purgation. Purgation is for those who have accepted God's Mercy and Forgiveness, who have resisted Satan's temptation (as Miguel de Portugal expresses it) to *choose* Hell because they have despaired of Forgiveness and therefore—in a perversion of Justice, as any Justice cut off from Mercy must necessarily be perverted—think that they *must* go to Hell because they are evil. Purgation, on the other hand (as Dante so well portrays it) is a motion of love, joy and gratitude—a love like that for one's Beloved, for whom one would gladly suffer any torment, a love which is also confirmed by the sure hope of reaching the Goal. But if we are not to be overwhelmed by the enormity of our own sins at the moment of death, such that we believe Satan's lie that the only way to wipe them out, or hide from them, is to choose an eternity of hellfire, we had better become familiar with them in this life, and familiar as well with the tremendous Divine Mercy in light of which they are as nothing. If we hope to enter into purgation in the next life, we must begin it in this one.

When Hell is ultimately emptied, it is not emptied by spiritual hope such as those know who are laboring in after-death purgation. Purgation is for the ones who have chosen Mercy, and are in the process of allowing that Mercy, with their willing cooperation, to plough and harrow their souls. Hell is for those who have willed to reject Mercy, and flee from God into the darkness of death, which in reality is only the darkness of their own flight. To fail to distinguish between the saved undergoing purgation, and the damned who are precisely in terror of purgation and in headlong flight from it, is a tremendous error. In Hell, no purgation is possible, neither is it desired. And though Hell may be made necessary by God's justice, in Hell itself there is no justice. The damned have neither the power nor the wish to do justice to one another, nor can they expect any, certainly, from the dark Prince who rules it. Hell is, precisely, a never-ending flight from God.

And this is why, in the ultimate *apocatastasis*, Hell too must die. For a flight-from-God to eternally exist side-by-side with God Himself is a Manichaean affront to His Goodness, His Absoluteness, and His Infinity. And this, precisely, is why revenge is not sweet. For revenge—which in God's terms, is Justice—to be truly sweet, the transgressor must be fully confronted with the horror of his own crimes. And this, precisely, is what cannot happen in Hell, because the enormity of evil can only appear in the light of Mercy, and Hell is closed to Mercy. How often have we seen sexual abusers or serial killers, monsters in human form, interviewed, grilled, cross-examined by various "researchers" in an attempt to discover *why* they committed such crimes, *how* they were able or willing to perpetrate such enormous atrocities. But these dedicated investigators never seem to get any answers that satisfy them—and they never will, because evil is inherently absurd. Frustratingly, maddeningly, to those trying to make sense of him, the unrepentant Hell-bound criminal can never grasp the evil of the horrible actions he so freely wills, nor can he ever reach this understanding, though we kill him and bring him back to life a thousand times. Where there should be conscience, there is merely a meaningless, sucking void; where there should be repentance, there is often an insidious, infernal mirth, as if the joke were on anyone stupid enough to look for *meaning* in Hell, and not on the one who deliberately sought meaninglessness, as if it were something to be desired, as if it were somehow a way out. To be strictly accurate there is some truth in both jokes, but the one who sought and found meaning, not the one who fled from it, is the one who laughs last.

But the day will come, when the *apocatastasis* dawns, when all the worlds of form, all the heavenly mansions and the infernal pits, are emptied and dissolved, when Justice will at last be satisfied. On that day, those who have chosen Mercy will be taken through and beyond Mercy, while those who have chosen punishment will be dragged through punishment, and beyond it. On the day when the gift of free will, eternally sealed in its final choice, infernal or para-disiacal, is definitively withdrawn, because everything other than God is withdrawn, the abysmal flight from God will at last encounter the overwhelming Reality of God, and be annihilated in the face of it. On that day, Hell will no longer be an option. The ultimate consequences of an aeon's flight from Reality will be confronted, and penetrated, and burned away, by the fires of that Reality. On that the day the souls will both suffer the full consequences of their sin—because they are damned—and *understand* the full consequences of it in the light of God's Mercy, *as if* they were saved. The ultimate Mercy and the ultimate Punishment will be one; and that will be the end of them. Only a moment like this, when the exquisite agony of Hellfire is made infinitely more exquisite and intense and soul-shattering by the ruthlessly penetrating Light of Absolute Truth and Mercy, can satisfy Divine Justice. After this point, no flight-from-God, no souls in torment rolling in a lake of fire, will remain. All will be Love; all will be Truth; all will be God. Heaven and Earth will pass away, but His Word will not pass away.

CHRIST AND QUR'AN

CHRIST, by His sacrifice, gathered together, summed up, spiritually transformed, and ended the whole regime of sacrifice, both animal and human. Ever since then, His sacrifice has been THE sacrifice.

The Qur'an, by its being-sent-down, gathered together, summed up, spiritually transformed and ended the whole regime of theurgic poetry, magic spells, legitimate curses and words-of-power. Ever after, that Book has been THE Book.

The Self-sacrifice of God eats up all other sacrifices: *Take up your cross and follow Me.*

And the Word of God eats up all other words: this is why the story of the rod of Moses that, transformed into a serpent by God's power, devoured the serpents of the Pharaoh's magicians, is told repeatedly in the Qur'an. All things in the created world are words spoken by God—but when the Word of God Itself comes down, all words go back to That Word:

Shall not all things return to Allah?

THE RIDDLE OF THE CAVE

And now have We brought them the Book:
with knowledge have We explained it;
a guidance and a mercy to them that believe.
What have they to wait for now but its interpretation?
    [Q. 7:50–51, Rodwell translation]

ONE DAY, as I was reading the *surah* of *The Cave* in the Rodwell
translation of the Noble Qur'an, the answer to the riddle posed
therein—i.e., the exact number of the Youths known as the Companions of the Cave—came to me. And after a short internet search,
I was fortunately able (to my great relief) to confirm to my own satisfaction what at first had been no more than an intuition. Here is
the pertinent passage according to Rodwell, Q. 18:8–26 [Pickthall,
18:9–28; Muhammad Asad and Yusuf Ali, 18:9–27]:

> *Hast thou reflected that the Inmates of the Cave and of al-*
> *Rakim were one of Our wondrous signs?*
> *When the youths betook them to the cave they said, "O our*
> *Lord! grant us mercy from before Thee, and order for us our affair*
> *aright."*
> *Then struck We upon their ears with deafness in the cave for*
> *many a year:*
> *Then We awaked them that We might know which of the two*
> *parties could best reckon the space of their abiding.*
> *We will relate to thee their tale with truth. They were youths*
> *who had believed in their Lord, and in guidance had We*
> *increased them;*
> *And We had made them stout of heart, when they stood up*
> *and said, "Our Lord is Lord of the Heavens and of the Earth: we*
> *will call on no other god than Him; for in that case we had said a*
> *thing outrageous.*

These our people have taken other gods beside Him, though they bring no clear proof for them; but, who more iniquitous than he who forgeth a lie of God?

So when you shall have separated you from them and from that which they worship beside God, then betake you to the Cave: Your Lord will unfold His mercy to you, and will order your affairs for you for the best."

And thou mightest have seen the sun when it arose, pass on the right of their cave, and when it set, leave them on the left, while they were in its spacious chamber. This is one of the signs of God. Guided indeed is he whom God guideth; but for him whom He misleadeth, thou shalt by no means find a patron, director.

And thou wouldst have deemed them awake, though they were sleeping: and We turned them to the right and to the left. And in the entry lay their dog with paws outstretched. Hadst thou come suddenly upon them, thou wouldst surely have turned thy back on them in flight, and have been filled with fear at them.

So We awaked them that they might question one another. Said one of them, "How long have you tarried here?" They said, "We have tarried a day or part of a day." They said, "Your Lord knoweth best how long you have tarried: Send now one of you with this your coin into the city, and let him mark who therein hath purest food, and from him let him bring you a supply: and let him be courteous, and not discover you to anyone.

For they, if they find you out, will stone you or turn you back to their faith, and in that case it will fare ill with you forever."

And thus made We their adventure known to their fellow citizens, that they might learn that the promise of God is true, and that as to "the Hour" there is no doubt of its coming. When they disputed among themselves concerning what had befallen them, some said, "Build a building over them; their Lord knoweth best about them." Those who prevailed in the matter said, "A place of worship will we surely raise over them."

Some say, "They were three; their dog the fourth:" others say, "Five; their dog the sixth," guessing at the secret: others say "Seven; and their dog the eighth." Say: My Lord best knoweth the number: none, save a few, shall know them.

Therefore be clear in thy discussions about them, and ask not any Christian concerning them.

Say not thou of a thing, "I will surely do it tomorrow;" without, "If God will." And when thou has forgotten, call thy Lord to mind; and say, "Haply my Lord will guide me, that I may come near to the truth of this story with correctness."

And they tarried in their cave 300 years, and 9 years over.

Say: God best knoweth how long they tarried: With Him are the secrets of the Heavens and of the Earth: Look thou and hearken unto Him alone. Man hath no guardian but Him, and none may bear part in His judgments:—

And publish what hath been revealed to thee of the Book of thy Lord—none may change His words,—and thou shalt find no refuge beside Him.

Rodwell's translation of part of his verse 22, *and ask not any Christian concerning them*, appears to be an extrapolation based on the fact that the legend of the Seven Sleepers of Ephesus, with whom the Companions of the Cave are often identified, was current in the Christian world, and remains so today, where they are identified as Christian martyrs. They are part of the Roman martyrology; there is even an Eastern Orthodox icon depicting them. Other translators, however, either leave those whom Muslims are not to question about the number of the Companions unidentified, or identify them with the Pagans, or never define such a group at all. Following Rodwell's extrapolation, however, we can further conjecture that the number of the Companions was not seven, since any Muslim who asked the Christians their number would likely have been answered "seven", in line with the Seven Sleepers story. And the Qur'an even more explicitly denies that the number is either three or five, since these are defined as mere "guesses."

According to the inner voice I heard, their number is "Nine", with their Dog (presumably) being the Tenth. What evidence might be brought forward in support of this intuition? And (assuming that Nine is the right answer and that I was not subject to deception) what might the Nine Companions and their Dog symbolize in terms of the more arcane levels of meaning enfolded by the Noble Qur'an?

The Book itself tells us to *be clear in your discussions of them* (Rodwell), or *contend not concerning them except with an outward contending* (Pickthall), or *do not argue about them other than by way of an obvious argument* (Muhammad Asad), or *enter not, therefore, into controversies concerning them, except on a matter that is clear* (Yusuf Ali). We are being told, in other words, that the answer to this riddle is something clear and explicit, not a vague ethical sentiment or mystical reverie. And this, if the truth be known, is the way with all good riddles: they carefully avoid abstraction; their answers are always clear and concrete. Likewise, in performing exegesis of sacred scripture, the best practice is always to first clarify the literal meaning as much as possible; only then will the concrete symbols appear that can support a more *batini ta'wil*, a more esoteric hermeneutic.

In quest of such clarity, I did a short internet search, and found a *Wikipedia* article on the legend of the Seven Sleepers, where it was asserted—incorrectly—that the Qur'an explains the 300 + 9 years that the Sleepers occupied their cave as representing the 9 year discrepancy between 300 solar years and the same length of time computed in lunar years, since during their long sleep the calendar had been changed from solar to lunar. The unnamed writer of the article undoubtedly drew upon a second writer, also unnamed, who saw in the number 300 + 9 in the *surah* of *The Cave* the discrepancy between solar and lunar calendars; it is to this second writer that I am *absolutely* indebted for the confirmation of my original intuition. And so, calculating as *clearly, explicitly* and *outwardly* as I can—since I was unwilling to leave an assertion by an unknown source uncorroborated—I can now confidently state, given that a solar year is approx. 365.24 days, and a lunar year, approx. 354.38 days, that over 300 solar years the discrepancy between lunar and solar time amounts to approximately 9 (lunar) years. The Youths in the Cave symbolize these Nine years, with their Dog—the *Tenth*—representing the *remainder* of 0.0077886 years—in the *decimal* system, that is, based on the number ten. (The Dog waiting quietly at the mouth of the Cave over the long centuries, with his two paws outstretched, also immediately suggests the posture of the Sphinx, patroness of riddles—and the Egyptian solar calendar, or the calendar they used to keep a time closest to solar time, with a discrepancy of only 12 minutes per year from true solar time, was calculated based on the rising of Sirius—the Dog Star.)

This, as far as it goes, seems a satisfying solution to the Riddle of the Cave—perhaps further corroborated by the fact that, in the translations of Pickthall, Muhammad Asad and Yusuf Ali, the Companions of the Cave are first mentioned in the *ninth* verse (the number of the *surah* of *The Cave*, 18, also being divisible by 9). But it is now time to ask: what is the *symbolic significance* of the discrepancy between solar and lunar time? At this point I am willing to say only that it has to do with *the union of sun and moon*, since the Companions occupied the Cave for a *single* period of time that amounted to 300 solar, and approximately 309.0077886 lunar years. For now, however, I want to address certain other symbolic aspects of the *surah* of *The Cave*.

According to 18:16–17, in Yusuf Ali's translation, the sun *in its rising, inclined away from the cave on the right, and on its setting, turned aside from them on the left.* This is the basis for his contention that the Cave faced to the north. Accepting the common identification of the Companions of the Cave with the Seven Sleepers of Ephesus, though he does not accept their number as necessarily seven, Yusuf Ali says:

> In the latitude of Ephesus, 38° north, i.e., well above the sun's northern declination, a cave opening to the north would never have the heat of the sun within it, as the sunny side would be the south. If the youths lay on their backs with their faces looking to the north, i.e. toward the entrance of the Cave, the sun would rise on their right side, declining to the south, and set on their left sides leaving them cool and comfortable. [*The Meaning of the Holy* Qur'an, translated by Abdullah Yusuf Ali, eleventh edition, note 2347]

To the view from within a northward-facing cave north of the Tropic of Cancer, the sun itself would not be visible—if the occupants were deep enough within the cave, that is, not directly at its mouth. If the topography allowed for it, however, the light of sunrise would appear at the right and shining towards the left, and the light of sunset at the left and shining toward the right; so there is some justification for Yusuf Ali's picture of the Cave of the Sleepers as opening toward the north (a conclusion shared by Muhammad Asad).

North is considered a sacred direction by many peoples, most notably the Shamans of northern Asia. The *zenith* above us symbolizes the eternal (not temporal) point of origin of all things, the Throne of the Most High God, of Allah according to His Name *al-Ali* ("the Exalted-Above-All"). But when zenith-as-eternal-origin is projected upon the horizontal plane, its point is becomes the *north*. (In the first chapter of Ezekiel, the vision of the Throne of God, which Sufis consider the apex and proximate source of the created order, arrives from the north.) The *axis mundi*, the vertical path connecting God and His creation, is vertical at any point on the earth's surface, as revealed by the fact that one of its central symbolic manifestations is the human spinal column and the erect stature of the human form, in view of the fact that humanity alone is bearer of *the Trust* [Q. 33:72]. But the axis of the earth's rotation, which is the *axis mundi* in planetary terms, points to the north, which may thereby be considered as "the earth's zenith". Therefore, when cyclical symbolism is expressed on the level of the four directions and the four seasons, its special point of origin is north, and its temporal point the winter solstice; this is the place of the beginning and the end of all things. (Among the various mythic expressions of this truth is the legend of Hyperborea, the "Land Behind the North Wind," the original homeland of the human race, a land of eternal Spring. The idea of a land of Eternal Spring in the far north was undoubtedly suggested by early explorers' tales of the Arctic summer, during whose "white nights" the sun never sets; this "never-setting sun" was most probably the origin of the idea of a Hyperborean Apollo, one of whose epithets is *Sol Invictus*, "The Sun Unconquered.")

The Qur'an presents the Companions as taking refuge in the Cave order to separate themselves from a hopelessly profane world. This, as well as the state of suspended animation in which they exist for 300 years, which seems to them to last no longer than part of a day, shows that the Cave symbolizes a higher level of reality than this terrestrial earth.

When the vision of the Immanence of God degenerates—a vision mediated by *tashbih*, the practice of comparing God to created things in order to better understand Him—God becomes progressively identified with the material world, leading first to an idolatry of various natural forms and forces, which are taken as gods beside God, and ultimately to atheistic materialism. Against this degeneration, the Companions of the Cave take refuge in God's pure Incomparability and Transcendence—in *tanzih*, symbolized by the rigor and cold of the north. To face in the direction of the Arctic and its numbing cold suggests the path of apophatic contemplation, the realization of God in His purely Transcendent aspect, which requires a death to this world, an ascetical *metanoia* by which the contemplator turns his inner attention away from God's richly multiple and perilously confusing outer manifestation in the cosmic south, and toward the north as "the still point of the turning world" (in the words of T. S. Eliot from *The Four Quartets*), the quarter of *al-Qutb*, the Pole—the "esoteric *qibla*" where the stars circumambulate (counter-clockwise) the Pole Star, just as earthly pilgrims circumambulate (also counter-clockwise) the Kaaba. The rigor of this Transcendence is symbolized in Ezekiel 8:3 by the "inner gate [of the Temple] that looketh toward the north, where was the seat of the image of jealousy, which provoketh to jealousy". The Transcendent God is a "jealous God", Who "will have no strange gods before Him", Who allows no comparisons to be made regarding Him: *He neither begets nor is begotten, and there is nothing to which He might be compared* [Q. 112:3–4]. (That God's Transcendence is not to be taken as absolute—because if it were, not only would we never be able to know of Him, but we would not even exist to know Him because there would be no universe—is established in another verse of the Qur'an [Rodwell, 16:62]: *God is to be likened to whatever is loftiest.*)

Henry Corbin, in *Spiritual Body and Celestial Earth: From Mazdean Iran to Shi'ite Iran* [Princeton University Press, 1977], says the following about the north as an esoteric *qibla* in Islam, following the exposition of Shaykh Karim Khan Kirmani:

> The spiritual history of humanity since Adam is the cycle of prophesy following the cycle of cosmogony; but though the former follows in the train of the latter, it is in the nature of a

reversion, a return and reascent to the pleroma . . . that is exactly what it means to "see things in Hurqalya [the Eighth Clime, the Imaginal Plane, the *alam al-mithal*]". It means to see man and his world essentially in the vertical direction. The Orient-origin, which orients and magnetizes the return and reascent, is the celestial pole, the cosmic North, the "emerald rock" at the summit of the cosmic mountain of Qaf, the very place where the world of Hurqalya begins. . . . [p.71]

The Earth of Light, the Terra Lucinda of Manichaeism, is also situated in the direction of the cosmic North. In the same way, according to the mystic 'Abd al-Karim Jili, the "Earth of souls" is a region in the far North, the only one not to have been affected by the fall of Adam. It is the abode of the "men of the Invisible," ruled by the mysterious prophet Khizr. A character-istic feature is that its light is that of the "midnight sun," since the evening prayer is unknown there, dawn rising before the sun has set. [p.72]

Insofar as we are justified in identifying the Cave of the Sleepers with al-Jili's Earth of Souls—as well as with other sacred precincts and caverns, such as the Zoroastrian Var of Yima, many of which represent the mid-point between this earth and the celestial para-dises, just as the spiritual Heart in Sufism (*al-Qalb*) is considered to be mid-point between the human body-soul and *al-Ruh*, the Spirit—we can see the Cave as a kind of terrestrial paradise which remains unaffected by the apocalyptic destruction of this material earth, or at least by the total spiritual degeneration of the world. As such it is a reality roughly equivalent to Noah's Ark, where the spiri-tual potential latent in humanity, represented in the *surah* of *The Cave* by the Sleepers, is preserved from the general destruction until it can again find a place in, and act as the subtle seed of, a new aeon of creation. (According to Islamic legend, the Ark carried not only Noah, his family, and the pairs of animals, but also the corpse of Adam—the archetype of Man.)

So much for the symbolism of the Cave of the Sleepers consid-ered as opening toward the north. But is Yusuf Ali really accurate in ascribing this orientation to it? Certainly the fact that the sun neither rises nor sets directly in front of the Cave mouth means that the Cave could be facing neither to the east nor to the west. But the fact remains that the sun is described as being visible from the Cave mouth, which would not be the case if it faced north. And if it faced toward the south the sun itself would be visible, but it would rise to the *left* and set toward the *right*. Furthermore, the sun is not pictured as moving from the east (at the right) to the west (at the left), or vice versa, but as moving *away* from the cave mouth *to the right when rising*, and *to the left when setting*. Rodwell (18:16) has: *And thou mightest have seen the sun when it arose, pass on the right of their cave, and when it set, leave them on the left.* And Pickthall (18:17): *And thou mightest have seen the sun when it rose move away from their cave to the right, and when it set go past them on the left.* And Arberry (18:16): *And thou mightest have seen the sun, as it rose, inclining from their Cave towards the right, and, when it set, passing them by on the left.* And Muhammad Asad (18:17): *And thou might have seen the sun, on its rising, incline away from their cave on the right, and, in its setting, turn aside from them on the left.*

There is no natural motion of the sun which would correspond to this account. Therefore we must conclude that the sun is pictured as *emerging from* the cave, or from the point directly in front of it, and then alternately moving toward the right in order to rise and toward the left in order to set. And since the sun of this world moves in one direction only—except when, at the end of time (which is the dawning of Eternity) it rises in the west—it is clearly an other-worldly sun which is being depicted, or the sun as seen from an other-worldly perspective. For the Companions of the Cave, the sun is already beyond this world, beyond the cycles of time; the Cave is thus the Cave of the Heart, the cave of Eternity, where what is experienced as *a day, or part of a day* [18:19] is projected into the outer world as an entire era of 300 solar or 309 lunar years. (It's interesting to note in this context that the root for "heart", QLB, is the same as that for the verb "to turn" which is applied, in Yusuf Ali 18:18, to the "turning" of the Companions of the Cave in their sleep; their motion is described as *now to the right, now to the left*, like the motion of the sun. In the words of the prophetic *hadith*, "The hearts are between two of the fingers of the All-merciful; He turns it wherever He desires." And this is all the more interesting in view of the fact that the Hindus, as well as certain Sufi and Jewish mystics, picture the Spiritual Heart as a cave—a cave which the sun, in some Hindu yogic practices at least, is called upon to occupy.) The parable of the Companions of the Cave thus demonstrates that it is possible, in the inner world, the realm of the *batin,* to realize eternity in this life, because the inner consciousness of humanity (*sirr*) is already situated beyond the cycles of time.

But what is the inner or esoteric significance of the union of sun and moon? This union is alluded to in the *surah* of *The Cave* in several different ways. For example, the story of the mysterious figure Dhoulkarnain (Dhulkarnain; Dzulkarnain; Zulkarnain; Dhool Karnain), whose name means "the two-horned", and who is often identified (without Quranic authority) with Alexander the Great, appears in Rodwell 18:82–96. Dhoulkarnain travels to the extreme east and the extreme west, like the sun as seen from the mouth of the Cave of the Sleepers—but of course it is the Moon, not the Sun, that can be described as "two-horned".

Verse 17 of the Rodwell translation says of the Sleepers, *Thou wouldst have deemed them awake, though they were sleeping.* In other words, their state of consciousness is one in which wakefulness (the sun) and sleep (the moon) are synthesized; as it says in *The Song of Solomon* (5:2): "I sleep, but my heart waketh". In his book *Primordial Alchemy* [Sophia Perennis, 2008; pp. 240–242], Rodney Blackhirst deals with this theme of the union of sleep and wakefulness as it appears in an Islamic context:

> The deep sleep state is the ground of prophecy... Muhammad ... according to the *hadith* ... would suddenly drop into deep slumber (and even snore) when receiving the Quranic revelation. Deep sleep is analogous to the prophetic state—to the Unlettered purity of Muhammad, in Islam—in its pure passivity. [According to] the axial symbolism of *khalifah* and *abd* ... the waking, conscious mind of man accompanies his uprightness of posture, while he returns to the horizontal plane to sleep, and the waking mind is indicative of his dignity as *khalif* while the opposite to the waking mind, the mind in

deep sleep, is perfectly passive, *abd*. The standing posture of the [Muslim ritual] prayer [*salat*] therefore symbolizes the waking consciousness, the bowing posture the dreaming mind, and *sajda* [prostration] the mind in deep sleep....In *salat, sajda* is the point at which the worshipper seeks to utterly submit to his Lord, to annihilate the false ego, to be perfectly submissive to Allah's every impression, like clay, like a prophet, like the sleeping mind, like an obedient slave to God.

Throughout the holy month of Ramadan the pious pray through the night, [this being] amongst [the] other ways [in which] the fast reverses the normal flow of diurnal and nocturnal life. This is because the so-called "dark sun", the "sun at midnight", is central to Islam's core. By this we mean *the union of waking consciousness with the sleeping mind*, or in other terms, *conscious submission*. This is the very essence of Islam's lunar symbolism. The moon is nothing less than the sun of the night and a symbol of the waking mind united with the complete passivity of the sleeping mind. This again is what is enacted in the *salat*. Time and time again, cycle after cycle, in five sets per day, the believer, standing in *qiyam*, falls to the floor in *sajda*, which movement enacts *carrying the waking state to the sleeping state.*

As is true in most cases of "dualistic" symbolism, the polarity between the two symbols in a pair-of-opposites can be expressed in two different ways. The moon, as ruler of the night, can be taken as symbolizing the Timeless, the Undifferentiated, as expressed in the state of deep sleep, as opposed to the sun, whose greater light brings out the many and varied particulars of our waking experience, thus unveiling contingency. Prof. Blackhirst has dealt with this aspect of the symbolism of sleep and wakefulness above. But an opposite and complementary attribution is also possible, according to which the sun, which does not go through phases like the moon but is the same whenever it appears, symbolizes the Eternal, whereas the "inconstant" moon represents the contingent "sublunary" world ruled by the cycles of time. According to this perspective, the Companions of the Cave would represent the union of sun and moon in terms of the reabsorption of the moon into the sun, time into Eternity; in the words of the *surah The Resurrection* or *The Rising of the Dead*, the Day of Resurrection is the day *when sun and moon are united* [Q. 75:9, Pickthall translation]. This is the same event, or level of reality, symbolized by the "eschatological" miracle attributed to the prophet Muhammad, peace and blessings be upon him, who pointed to the moon in the sky, at which point it split in two. The splitting of the moon in Islam is considered to be a sign of the Hour of Judgment; the prophesy in *Apocalypse* 21:15 that after the coming of the Heavenly Jerusalem there will be no more sea has a similar significance, given that the moon rules the sea. In both cases the symbolism points to the dissolution of the contingent, relative *lunar* world before the direct, unveiled *solar* light of the Absolute. And in terms of the human microcosm, the union of sun and moon symbolizes the perfect conformity of the soul or psyche (the moon) to the Spirit (the sun)—the completion of the spiritual Path. In the Words of William Blake, "when a man rejects error and embraces truth, a Final Judgement passes upon that man."

So the Nine Companions of the Cave symbolize what of the human essence may remain after either the Hour of Judgment or the total degeneration of human spirituality on earth, which must ultimately result in the arrival of that very Hour—the imperishable seed that is capable of initiating the next aeon of humanity on the "next" earth, on the earth resurrected from its latent state by a new revelation from God: *Were such His pleasure He could make you pass away, and cause a new creation to arise* [Rodwell, 14:22]. Such a revelation, however, can certainly not be received by "this world" as we know it; for this cycle of manifestation, Muhammad is the last of the prophets.

Both the arrival of the Hour and the dawning of a new spiritual dispensation are indicated more explicitly in verse 20 [Rodwell translation] of this *surah: . . . as to "the Hour", there is no doubt of its coming. When they disputed among themselves concerning what had befallen them, some said "Build a building over them [the Companions of the Cave], their Lord knoweth best about them". Those who prevailed in the matter said, "Surely we will raise a place of worship over them."* In view of this, are we really justified in limiting the significance of the Companions of the Cave to a simple allegory of the discrepancy between solar and lunar time? I don't believe so. In this world they may be a mere allegory of a mathematical relationship; in their own, higher world, they are entirely real—real enough to meet and speak with, face to face.

And finally, the Companions and their Dog can be understood in terms of Sufi "ontological anthropology." The cave, as we have seen, is the spiritual Heart, the point of intersection between the psycho-physical man, composed of body and soul, and the realm of the Spirit. That the Companions are *deaf* means that they are unaffected by the threats and promises emanating from the profane world outside. The sun, which *thou mightest have seen ... when it arose, pass on the right of their cave, and when it set, leave them on the left*, symbolizes the Spirit, *al-Ruh*, to which the Companions are perfectly obedient, both when it is revealed and when it is hidden; when God says *and We turned them to the right and to the left,* He is presenting them as strictly following the motions of that sun in their waking sleep, like heliotropic flowers. Furthermore, since it is God who turns the Sleepers, we are allowed to imagine the possibility that their motion might actually be the secret *cause* of the motion of the sun—given that the Qur'an presents humanity, not the natural elements, as the bearer of *the Trust.* And the Dog, waiting silently and vigilantly on the Cave's threshold, is a common Sufi symbol of the soul or *nafs*, the lower psychic self—in this case the *nafs al-mutma'inna*, the "self-at-peace", the ego and lower instincts perfectly submissive to God. The Spirit, taken in and of itself, knows only what is spiritual; it has no need of being guarded from the attacks of the passions and the world they define. But the human being, taken as a whole, does need this kind of guardian; though the Spirit can never become a slave of the passions, it can certainly be *veiled* by them when it takes up residence in the human microcosm. This is why the spiritual Heart needs to be guarded against the passional world—and the Dog is that guardian. The *nafs* is the seat of the passions, and this does not cease to be true just because it has become submissive to God; a dog may be well-trained and loyal, but it still remains a dog. And it is this intrinsic relationship to the passions that allows the *nafs*-at-peace to act as a vigilant guardian against them. The Spirit in itself is beyond all purity and impurity; it need not seek to establish purity as a virtue because it is inherently incorruptible. But the *nafs*, having first betrayed purity (as the *nafs al-ammara*, the "commanding self") and then fought against its own impurity (as the *nafs al-lawwama*, the "accusing self"), can now, as the self-at-peace, guard the Cave of the Heart against all that is impure, against passional intruders from the world outside. To train the purified lower psyche to mediate between the spiritual Heart and the world leaves that Heart free to concentrate upon the Spirit; this is one of the things Jesus meant when he said, "let not your right hand know what your left hand is doing."

And insofar as the Dog acts as a *watchdog*, it may also symbolize a certain aspect of the *nafs al-lawwama*, the "accusing self". In Sufi symbolism, the dog most often represents *anger*. In terms of the commanding self, anger is a passion; in terms of the accusing self, it corresponds to the positive aspect of what Platonists call the "incensive faculty" (the Greek *thymikon*, the Arabic *ghadhab*)—the power to firmly repel temptation, to be "angry at anger" (or greed, or pride, or lust). To the degree that our dog is well-trained and submissive to its Owner, it can act as a good watchdog: friendly to friends, wrathful to enemies, and able to tell the difference.

In the story of the Companions of the Cave, God is teaching us how to spiritually separate ourselves from a profane world, a world based (as ours is today) on the worship of the passions, at a time when open combat against that world would be hopeless, when it would only involve us further in worldly corruption. Muslims too have their catacombs; the catacomb of the Muslim is the Cave of the Heart. (And if someone were self-confident enough to believe he had solved the Riddle of the Cave, and then foolish enough to fail to enter that Cave himself, then *God is the best of plotters. . . . God . . . leadeth astray whom He will.*)

SIX GNOMES

THE POWER OF BELIEF

A *belief* is not a fantasy I have chosen to take as true; a *belief* is a firm conviction that something actually *is* true, and would continue to be true even if I didn't believe in it, even if nobody at all believed in it. Therefore: *Beliefs do not create realities*. Rather, true beliefs conform us to realities, while false beliefs separate us from them.

❧

THE PRIMAL METAPHYSICS OF GENDER

God Almighty as Pure Being, Creator of Heaven and Earth, is masculine. Like a King, He holds sway over both nature and society, which are feminine in relation to Him.

Beyond Being is feminine. She is like the Black Virgin, like the *Layla* of the Sufis, whose name means Night. As the divine Essence she has precedence over the Creator as Pure Being, Who, like a son, is masculine in relation to Her. If He creates *ex nihilo*, She is that very *Nihil*.

In the Manifest World, man has precedence over woman; in the Unmanifest, woman has precedence over man.

And in either world, God, Who is beyond gender as well as beyond Being, but Who manifests through both of them—with not the shadow of a distinction between His Essence and the essence of His Manifestation—has precedence over all.

❧

BATIN AND *ZAHIR*: *TANZIH* AND *TASHBIH*

According to Ramana Maharshi, the psycho-physical disposition reflective of *jñana* is the opening of "the heart on the right"—a secret also alluded to in the Qur'anic passage *Whomsoever God desires to guide, He expands his breast for Islam* [Q. 6:125]. The heart on the left, the subtle aspect of the physical heart, is the site of God's Transcendence, *tanzih*. The heart on the right is the site of His Immanence, *tashbih*. In the first, God is intuited as hidden behind the seventy-thousand veils of His creation, in the *batin* (the "inner"), in the *sirr* (the "secret"). In the second, God is revealed in the *zahir* (the "outer") as well. In the words of Fariduddin Attar, "The *zahir* is the shadow of the Rose/ And the rending of the veil"— *shadow*, in that the forms of the cosmos are not in themselves God; *the rending of the veil*, in that God's theophany in the Outer, at the point most distant from the dimensionless point of His Essence, leaves not the shadow of a veil between He and He.

❧

KNOWLEDGE NEEDS IGNORANCE

Every instance of true Knowledge
Is a sign of the Unknowable, the Essence.
The Divine Essence is totally indescribable:
Every entity, or being, or event in the universe
Is merely one more attempt to describe It.

❧

PRAYING FOR THE MOUNTAINS TO FALL AND COVER US

Attraction to unreality
in the face of terror
—especially *unconscious* terror—
is the high road to Antichrist.

❧

LOVE AS INTELLECTIVE REALIZATION

Love is the power to realize existentially, in the totality of the human form, in the marrow of our bones, the Truth that Intellection reveals.

Love alone prevents the fruits of Intellection, which derive from a Reality beyond the thinking mind
From falling to the level of that mind, the level of rational discourse and memory, thus becoming indistinguishable from mere human thought.

Intellection is *crystallized* only by Love. "Love is the highest form of knowledge" (Maimonides said), because Love is *operative* Intellection.

> *And we, who have always thought*
> *of happiness climbing, would feel*
> *an emotion that almost startles*
> *when happiness falls.*

—Rainer Maria Rilke, *The Duino Elegies, X*

A METAPHYSICAL EXEGESIS OF TWO TRADITIONAL BALLADS FROM
AM I BORN TO DIE,
AN APPALACHIAN SONGBOOK

BY MASON BROWN & CHIPPER THOMPSON

for Barry McDonald

ANYONE FAMILIAR with the language of metaphysics, as well as with the particular dialect of that language known as *mythopoeia*, will easily understand (as soon as they turn their eyes in the right direction) that certain traditional folk songs are actually tight, consciously-composed little metaphysical essays. *Scarborough Fair*, for example, is the story of God's quest for the human soul exiled in this lower world, while *The Lady Gay* treats of the lesser mysteries situated within the order of nature, versus the greater mysteries which transcend that order.

Ananda K. Coomaraswamy has this to say about folklore as metaphysics:

> ... by "folklore" we mean that whole and consistent body of culture which has been handed down, not in books but by word of mouth and in practice, from time beyond the reach of historical research, in the form of legends, fairy tales, ballads, games, toys, crafts, medicine, agriculture, and other rites, and forms of organization, especially those we call tribal. This is a cultural complex independent of national and even racial boundaries, and of remarkable similarity throughout the world....

> The content of folklore is metaphysical. Our failure to recognize this is primarily due to our own abysmal ignorance of metaphysics and of its technical terms....

Folklore ideas are the form in which metaphysical doctrines are received by the people and transmitted by them. In its popular form, a given doctrine may not always have been understood, but so long as the formula is faithfully transmitted it remains understandable; "superstitions", for the most part, are no mere delusions, but formulae of which the meaning has been forgotten. . . .

We are dealing with the relics of an ancient *wisdom*, as valid now as it ever was. . . . We shall only be able to understand the astounding uniformity of the folklore motifs all over the world, and the devoted care that has everywhere been taken to ensure their correct transmission, if we approach these *mysteries* (for they are nothing less) in the spirit in which they have been transmitted ("from the Stone Age until now")—with the confidence of little children, indeed, but not the childish self-confidence of those who hold that wisdom was born with themselves. The true folklorist must be not so much a psychologist as a theologian and metaphysician, if he is to "understand his material". . . . Nor can anything be called a *science* of folklore, but only a collection of data, that considers only the formulae and not their doctrine. . . . [*Selected Papers: Traditional Art and Symbolism*, edited by Roger Lipsey, Princeton University Press, 1977]

But if some traditional ballads are actually consciously-constructed metaphysical essays, then who composed them? René Guénon gives us part of the answer:

The very conception of *folklore*, in the generally accepted sense of the term, is based on an idea that is radically false, the idea that there are "popular creations" spontaneously created by the mass of the people. . . . As has been rightly said [by Luc Benoist], "the profound interest of all so-called popular traditions lies in the fact that they are not popular in origin"; and we will add that where, as is almost always the case, there is a question of elements that are traditional in the true sense of the word, however deformed, diminished and fragmentary they may be sometimes, and of things that have a real symbolic value, their origin is not even human, let alone popular. What may be popular is solely the fact of "survival," when these elements belong to vanished traditional forms. . . . The people preserve, without understanding them, the relics of former traditions which go back sometimes to a past too remote to be dated, so that it has to be relegated to the obscure domain of the "prehistoric"; they thereby fulfill the function of a more or less subconscious collective memory, the contents of which have clearly come from elsewhere. What may seem most surprising is that the things so preserved are found to contain, above all, abundant information of an esoteric order, which is, in its essence, precisely what is least popular, and this fact suggests in itself an explanation, which may be summed up as follows: When a traditional form is on the point of becoming extinct, its last representatives may very well deliberately entrust to this aforesaid collective memory the things that otherwise would be lost beyond recall; that is in fact the sole means of saving what can in a certain measure be saved. At the same time, that lack of understanding that is one of the natural characteristics of the masses is a sure enough guarantee that what is esoteric will be nonetheless undivulged, remaining merely as a sort of witness of the past for such as, in later times, shall be capable of understanding it. [*Symbols of the Sacred Science*, Sophia Perennis, 2004]

Here, following these two masters, is my attempt to discern the metaphysical symbolism in two traditional folk songs. They were "collected" in Appalachia, but their pedigree, like that of most Appalachian ballads, undoubtedly goes back to the British Isles. (We don't have *braes*, for example, in the old USA):

1 : *Going to the West*:
THE PILGRIMAGE OF THE SOUL

In this fair land I'll stay no more,
Your labor is in vain.
I'll leave the mountains of my birth
And seek the fertile plane.
I'm going
To the West.

(*Chorus*):

You say you will not go with me,
You turn your eyes away.
You say you will not follow me
No matter what I say.
I'm going
To the West.

Three years have gone since we first met,
Since you became my bride.
Now I must journey far away
Without you by my side.
I'm going
To the West.

(*Repeat chorus*)

I'll leave you here in this land you love
'Mid scenes so bright and fair,
Where fragrant flowers are blooming
And music fills the air.
I'm going
To the West.

(*Repeat chorus*)

This ballad tells the story of the pilgrimage of the soul from "the mountains of my birth", the celestial world, west to "the fertile plane", this earthly world—"west" being the symbolic quarter of matter, the place where the Sun of the Spirit sets. That the bride of the pilgrim refuses to go west with him identifies her (in Zoroastrian terms) as his *fravashi* or *fravarti*—his celestial counterpart who never incarnates, never descends into material manifestation; by this she may be known as the sign and seal of his power to return to that higher world when his pilgrimage is done.

The number symbolism of the ballad confirms this interpretation. To say "Three years are gone/ Since we first met/ Since you became my bride/ Now I must journey far away/ Without you by my side" indicates a shift, at the beginning of the fourth year, from the celestial plane, universally symbolized by the number 3 (the Trinity in Christianity, the *Trimurti* in Hinduism, etc.) to the terrestrial plane, symbolized by the number 4 (the 4 seasons, the 4 directions, etc.).

This is a fall, but also a *felix culpa*, a "fortunate fault"—an exile, but also the inheritance of a kingdom. The incarnational descent from Heaven to Earth is a loss, but a loss in view of a greater gain. The earthly plane is not purely fallen; it is also "fertile", capable of receiving the seed of the Spirit; the pilgrim himself, in one sense, is this very seed: "Except a corn of wheat fall into the ground and die, it abideth alone: but if it die, it bringeth forth much fruit" [John 12:24]. Ultimately, this fruit is the reunion of Heaven and Earth when the cycle of manifestation is complete.

11: *The Verdant Braes of Skreen*:
MAYA AND ITS TRANSCENDENCE

As I went out one morning
By the verdant braes of Skreen;
I leaned against a hawthorn tree
To view the Sun in the forest green.

I spied a neat young fellow
With a girl all on his knee,
And he so smart and handsome was
And she so fair and fine to see.

(*The young man speaks*):

"Come sit you down all on the ground
On the dewy grass so green,
For it's just been nine months my love
Since you and I've together been."

(*The girl replies*):

"I'll not sit down all on the grass
Nor be a love of thine,
For I find you love a Kingston maid;
Your heart no longer will be mine.

"I'll not trust what an old man says,
His days are well-nigh done;
And I'll not trust a young man's word,
He sets his eye on many's the one.

"But I will climb a tall, tall tree
And rob a wild bird's nest,
And I'll bring home what I do find
All to the arms that I love best."

As I went out one morning
By the verdant braes of Skreen;
I leaned against a hawthorn tree
To view the Sun in the forest green.

The first and last verses of this song tell of a man who goes out "one morning" to "view the Sun in the forest green." The "morning" places the action of the song nearer the archetypal realm than the "evening" would have, which (like the "west" in the first song) would symbolize the world of material manifestation. And "To view the Sun in the forest green" means, precisely, "To contemplate the Divine Intellect via its refraction in the imaginal plane"—the place where invisible, intelligible realities appear as symbolic images, as they did to the knight questing through the primeval forest in so many medieval romances.

In this song we are presented with a classic "May" scene of two young lovers in a leafy glade. And according to Robert Graves in *The White Goddess*, the hawthorn is the tree of the month of May,

sacred to the goddess Maia—who is *Maya*. The hawthorn, paradox-
ically, is both orgiastic and symbolic of chastity. It is also inimical to
marriage, as the orgiastic impulse most certainly is; until this
impulse is tempered by chastity, no fertile marriage is possible. The
young man wants to lay with his lover, but do so nine months after
they first came together—precisely when, that is, she is about to give
birth. And so she repudiates him—"exoterically" because she knows
he has been unfaithful, but "esoterically" because she is about to go
into labor. So who, or what, is she about to give birth to? The
answer is, "Wisdom—the power to see through the veils of *Maya*,
the world-illusion." And what does this Wisdom teach her? It
teaches her to trust neither "what an old man's says", which has no
force, nor "a young man's word", which has no center (though the
phrase "many's the one" reminds us that the "many" actually *is* the
"One", as obscured by our dissipation, our scattered and divided
attention). And when she declares that she trusts neither youth nor
age, it means that she no longer trusts *time*—time which, in the
"natural" course of things, is no more than a passage from force
without wisdom to wisdom without force. Instead, she vows to rob
the nest of a "tall, tall tree"—the Tree of Life, where Spirit lays its egg
in a nest on the highest branch—and bring it "home" to the "arms
that she loves best."

What precisely is "home" to the one who, having seen through
the illusions of time, has given birth, after nine months, to her own
higher self—who after the cycle of spiritual gestation is complete
has reaped in Wisdom what was sown in passion? As William Blake
wrote, in "The Mental Traveler":

> I traveled through a Land of Men
> A land of Men & Women too
> And heard & saw such dreadful things
> As cold earth wanderers never knew
>
> For there the Babe is born in joy
> That was begotten in dire woe
> Just as we Reap in joy the fruit
> Which we in bitter tears did sow

That home is Eternity. And whose are the arms that the girl who has brought forth Wisdom now loves best? They are God's. The Spirit is her true husband, not the "neat young fellow" in the forest (who is only one of His many masks, faithless as all masks are until recognized as such)—which is why she brings back to Him, not to the fickle young man, the *hiranyagharba*, the golden "Orphic" egg of total, primal manifestation.

The Glastonbury Thorn, a hawthorn tree, was sacred to the Virgin Mary, as is the holy ground of Glastonbury Abbey a whole. The Thorn had the peculiarity of flowering twice a year instead of once—on old wood in the Spring (as is normal), but also on new growth in the Winter season. "The Verdant Braes of Skreen" maps out the passage from Spring—from May, the Virgin's month and month of the hawthorn, symbolizing natural eros—to Winter, the season of transcendence, of the Northern or Hyperborean Mary, whose epithet "Star of the Sea" denotes the Pole Star, "the still point of the turning world", the gateway that leads from the cycles of cosmic manifestation to the eternity of the Spirit. And if the "tall, tall tree" whose nest the girl robs is in fact the hawthorn, then she has stolen the power of eros from the orgiastic aspect of that tree (the flower of Spring) and returned it to the chaste, spiritual, transcendent aspect (the flower of Winter). The hawthorn in flower is beautiful, but its thorns are clearly visible, like the thorns of the rose, a flower which is also sacred to the Virgin. When the thorn is seen beneath the flower, when the beauty of the bloom is protected by the purity of the snow—as in the old English and German legends and carols about the Christmas Rose—then beguilement is conquered, the regime of *Maya* ended: the true terms of cosmic existence have been revealed. In the union of Mercy and Rigor, of Beauty (the Flower) and Sobriety (the Winter) embodied by the Virgin (who is *Vidya-maya*), the delusive power of ignorance (*Avidya-maya*) is definitively overcome.

[NOTE: For a longer and better-contextualized exegesis of various traditional ballads, see my book *Folk Metaphysics: Mystical Meanings in Traditional Folk Songs and Spirituals*, Sophia Perennis, 2008]

SIN, KARMA, AND FORGIVENESS

ALL ACTION is sin. "All have sinned and come short of the glory of God" because all must act. But, in reality, only God is the Actor—and even if God Himself commands us to act in His name, we are not thereby exonerated. He gives us our free will—a freedom that immediately binds us because we have no choice but to exercise it; in the words of Frithjof Schuon, we are "condemned to freedom."

The only way we can repay Him for His great generosity to us, is to act—and, by acting, sin. This sin is the door to our true freedom because it convicts us not of this or that transgression, but of the sin of our very existence. As Rabi'a once said to a young man who claimed that he had never committed a sin, "Alas, my son, thine existence is a sin wherewith no other sin may be compared."

Bismillah ar-Rahman ar-Rahim means: God gives us the gift of our existence, and then forgives us for taking it; therefore to repent of our existence is the same thing as being grateful for it. It is God Himself who gives us the chance to repent, before Him, of the sin of self-existence; what more could we ask for? From God's first gift of His Being, poured out upon our nothingness, to His ultimate forgiveness of us for identifying with that gift—it's all nothing but Mercy.

THE BLACK VIRGIN

JEAN HANI, in his book *The Black Virgin: A Marian Mystery* [Sophia Perennis, 2007], plumbs certain aspects of the Marian mysteries by tracing the history and meaning of the cult, shrines and statues of the Virgin Mary in her Black aspect, mostly in Western Europe, as well as drawing certain parallels between her and various archaic goddesses. Likewise Frithjof Schuon, whose mandate as a spiritual teacher was conferred upon him directly through visions of the Virgin, and who consequently named his Sufi *tariqa* the Maryamiyya, was also deeply influenced by the Divine Feminine, an influence perhaps most completely expressed in the chapter "The Wisdom of Sayyidatna Maryam" from his book *Dimensions of Islam*. Hani ultimately identifies the Black Virgin with the Immanence of God, whereas to Schuon (as to Meister Eckhart), the Virgin is a personification of the Substantial Pole, the Divine Maternal receptivity that receives the imprint of the Archetypal Forms emanating from the Essential Pole, the masculine aspect of the Divinity, allowing God to be conceived in the human soul and thus functioning as the matrix of that Immanence.

In our times, as should be clear to all by now, the Divine Feminine has powerfully reasserted herself. Her influence stretches all the way from the exalted metaphysics of Frithjof Schuon, through the dogmatic definitions of the Immaculate Conception and the Assumption of the Virgin by the Catholic Church the 19th and 20th centuries, to the goddess-worship of today's Neo-Pagans; this represents nothing less, in metaphysical terms, than a progressive unveiling of the Substantial Pole. Neither Jean Hani nor the Roman Catholics, however, seem to have fully realized what a theophany of the Substantial Pole means in times like these: it is nothing less than an eschatological sign—a sign of the End. (Schuon, since he made it clear that we are on the very threshold of the end of this cycle, may have understood the cyclical significance of this theophany and simply opted not to declare it openly.)

When, in the Magnificat, the Virgin says: "Because He hath regarded the humility of His handmaid. . . . He hath shewed might in His arm: He hath scattered the proud in the conceit of their heart. He hath put down the mighty from their seat", she is speaking in her wrathful mode: her very humility, by God's power, humbles the proud. And this is far more than simply a tract on "social justice". The "proud" and the "mighty" here include every creature—and every aspect of the human psyche—that believes it is self-sufficient and thus has no need for God: this, precisely, is the "conceit" the Virgin speaks of. To the proud, the mighty, the vain, the worldly, there is nothing more terrible than the vision of spiritual *innocence*—the Virgin, so to speak, being "innocence incarnate"— which is why This World rushes to portray innocence, in every conceivable way, as powerless, laughable, insipid, gauche, socially shameful. As the archetype of the soul's perfect submission to God, the Virgin is symbolizes, and embodies, the *Materia Prima*, the pole of Universal Substance; in Schuon's words, it is she who inspires and empowers us to "become pure prayer". Consequently she is diametrically opposed to the titanic Prometheanism upon which the system of This World is based. And the sufferings of the Virgin at the hands of This World, first in witnessing the suffering and death of her Son, and now through enduring the crucifixion and dismemberment of His Church, undoubtedly form a large part of the contents of that "cup of God's wrath" which she, in 1965 at Garabandal (unless this was a false apparition, as some maintain), told us was already overflowing.

Jean Hani in *The Black Virgin* speaks of the terrible aspect of the archaic Great Goddess, and of the Virgin as well, yet the full implications of this seem to have escaped him. (We need to be clear at this point that the Virgin is not a goddess, but rather a human woman with an immortal soul whom God commanded and empowered to manifest a certain aspect of His Nature—which is precisely the function that the archaic goddesses also fulfilled, in mythopoetic rather than human terms. The gods and goddesses of Paganism were not independent hypostases, but Names of the One God; as soon as this truth was forgotten—as soon as spiritual literalism supervened—polytheism was born.) Hani speaks of the apparition of the Virgin in her beneficent aspect at Lourdes, but fails to mention her appearance in more terrible mode at Fatima, where the Third Secret (fraudulently presented by the apostate Novus Ordo Church as already revealed) undoubtedly had to do, according certain to thinly-veiled remarks by Sister Lucia, with the apostasy of that very Church. Likewise, in Schuon's radiant, "trans-erotic" *shakti* paintings, some of which depict the Blessed Virgin (or his image of her), this terrible aspect nowhere appears—though his validation, in *The Eye of the Heart* [World Wisdom Books, 1997, pp. 114–115], of human sacrifice as practiced by the ancient hieratic civilizations, given that a sacred collectivity is higher than, and thus possesses rights over, its individual members, may possibly represent this aspect of her influence, an influence which is dangerous precisely to the degree that it is not consciously recognized as such. But though Schuon may not have iconically represented the dark side of the Divine Feminine, he certainly recognized that in our days, at the tail-end of the *Kali-yuga*, All-Possibility (effectively identical to the Divine Feminine in Schuon's metaphysics) must allow for the manifestation of all the most negative—as well as the most *trivial*—of possibilities.

The Blessed Virgin, in the Magnificat, speaks as the Justice of God. Whoever flees this Justice instead of seeking it will encounter it not as wisely discerning Justice but as blind Fate: as the Wrath of God manifesting through events, or through an unconscious psychic attraction to dark spiritual realities, along with all the events that such attraction inevitably carries in its train. And in our time, these events and attractions clearly include the darker forms—or, rather, the toxic psychic residues—of the archaic Pagan spiritualities, where human sacrifice held a prominent place.

Schuon's willingness to allow that human sacrifice occupied a legitimate place in the ancient hieratic civilizations requires us to deal squarely with this extremely dark subject, and do our best to evaluate it. In line with this, I would assert the following: If human sacrifice is *voluntary*, as it was at one point in the Toltec religion, then it may function—though only under a religious dispensation that allows for it—as a true "sacred act", somewhat in the spirit of the rigors of the Sun Dance. But if it is *involuntary*—as it was for the Aztecs, and for the Toltecs in their degeneracy—then it can never partake of the sacred, for the simple reason that only the "pure victim" is an acceptable sacrifice, and no-one who goes to the altar of sacrifice rebelliously or despairingly (or as *seduced* to the act in a state of lowered consciousness) can be pure in this sense: this is the precise difference between the redemptive self-sacrifice of Christ and the despairing suicide of Judas. In the case of animal sacrifice, that the victim is a perfect physical specimen of its type is sufficient to render it pure, assuming that various other taboos are satisfied. In the case of human sacrifice, the state of the victim's soul is of paramount importance—given that human beings, though they certainly possess an animal aspect, are not animals.

Human sacrifice, like all "external" immolations, is a "literalization" of the sacrifice of the ego; if it truly serves this *telos*, as in rare instances it may have (though certainly never in Judaism, Christianity, Islam or Buddhism), then it is holy; if not, then it is satanic. "Behold, to obey is better than sacrifice, and to hearken than the fat of rams" [1 Samuel 15:22]. And certainly any civilization that limits human sacrifice to criminals or "undesirables" (as, for example, the immolation by the Nazis of mental and physical defectives, as well as the Jews and Gypsies they considered inferior races, not to mention the destruction of "undesirable" human fetuses in our own time) can be sacred in any sense. The Romans attempted to "sacrifice" Christ as a *criminal*, against His will, to the Roman Empire, its gods and its emperor; instead, He voluntarily offered himself to his Father, as a pure victim, both in order to make satisfaction for the sins of the human race, and to represent, and enact, the apophatic annihilation of "the face of God" (and, simultaneously, the human ego) in the transcendent Godhead, as represented by His words "My God, my God, why have you forsaken me?" By this act He ended the regime of human sacrifice in the lands of the Near East and the Mediterranean, as well as (in virtual terms) in all lands to which Christianity was destined to spread, and thereby inaugurated the regime of the "unbloody sacrifice". Likewise the prophet Muhammad, peace and blessing be upon him, ended the practice among the Arabs of killing female infants, which was human sacrifice in all but name, and may well have been the remnant of an established sacrificial rite, possibly in the cult of the Pagan goddesses (or rather,

Triple Goddess) *al-Uzza, al-Lat,* and *Manat.* And it is certain and undeniable that no divine dispensation is in force today by which God will accept even the voluntary sacrifice of one's life, unless as a side effect of heroic action in defense of the good. The *kamikaze* sacrificed their lives with subjective sincerity, but in the name of an objective evil: Japanese militarism. Likewise the "heroic self-sacrifice" of the suicide bombers is in no way sacred, given that suicide is strictly prohibited in Islam (cf. Q. 4:29); there is a great difference between death in battle at the hands of the enemy, where survival, though highly unlikely, is still possible, and death at one's own hand—particularly in the course of intentionally killing one's fellow Muslims. *Martyrdom* may be sought, if God commands it—but martyrdom is not suicide, nor can suicide ever be martyrdom. Martyrdom, either on the battlefield or in the arena, is not an acting out of personal despair on the part of someone to whom life has become a meaningless burden, as is undoubtedly the case with many of the suicide bombers (though God knows best)—an act that deceptively presents itself as spiritual heroism to both the false martyr and his fascinated "audience" (for Satan too has his "martyrs")— but a heroic witnessing to the Truth in the face of This World, which is founded precisely on hatred of that Truth. If the would-be hero is not both subjectively sincere and acting in the name of objective Truth—as no bomber can be who willfully kills innocent non-combatants—then he is a suicidal murderer, not a martyr, and is thus destined for the Fire.

Jean Hani in *The Black Virgin* asserts that human sacrifice was never practiced by the Celts, though Julius Caesar in his *Gallic Wars* reports that it was. Hani apparently wishes to deny its existence because to admit this would make him less comfortable about drawing his various parallels between the Blessed Virgin and certain archaic goddesses, including the Hindu Kali (who is usually represented as black in her paintings and statues). He puts the "tales" of human sacrifice down to a popular misunderstanding of the initiatory death-and-resurrection symbolism often associated with the Great Mother Goddess, ignoring the fact that the "literalization" of initiatory ego-death that human sacrifice represents certainly affected those very archaic cults in their degeneracy, as witness the well-documented practice, by the *Thugs*, of human sacrifice in the cult of Kali, a practice that was only terminated in India by the British *raj*, and is claimed to continue on a clandestine level even today. (By a similar unwillingness to credit the reality of the dark side of things, Hani speaks of the "pranks" of poet François Villon, whose childlike Marian piety was undoubtedly real, but who was also a gangster, thief and murderer, member of that infamous band of professional criminals known as the *Coquillards*. Nor was Villon the only bloodthirsty thug who ever loved his Mother; that character-type used to be well-enough recognized in the English-speaking world to be convincingly portrayed on the screen by Jimmy Cagney.)

According to René Guénon in *The Reign of Quantity and the Signs of the Times*, in these eschatological days, at the very tail end of the *Kali-yuga*, the cycle of manifestation has descended to the point where the Essential Pole (masculine and formal) is becoming veiled, while the Substantial Pole (feminine and maternal/material) is unveiled; it is in this context that the twentieth century apparitions of the Virgin should be situated. And while these apparitions certainly represent a special grace of the latter days, they are also inseparable from what Guénon called "the reign of quantity." God as Essence is the Supraformal manifesting as Eternal Form: stable, intelligible, radiant, and thus fully capable of functioning as the principle of the Golden Age, where the manifest universe and the forms of human life seem to partake of the eternity of the archetypal Ideas. God as Substance, however, is the infra-formal manifesting as the *universal dissolution of forms*. *Materialism* also is a sign of the dawning of the Substantial Pole, and insofar as all things in these materialistic times are progressively being defined in terms not of their intrinsic forms or qualities, but of matter only—a tendency that is truly universal, without the human form itself being immune to it—they must be defined largely in terms of quantity: *materia signata quantitate*. Beneath the dark, chaotic underworld of infra-formal matter (the *materia secunda*), the Virginal purity and receptivity of Divine Substance (the *Materia Prima*) does indeed subsist—just as, in alchemy, the stage of "whitening", represented by the lunar metal Silver, underlies and follows upon the "blackening", the stage of corruption, mortification and dissolution, represented by the metal Lead. But if our world is indeed destined to return to the Virginal receptivity of the Substantial Pole, its path to that Pole can only lie through that very corruption, mortification and dissolution. This world, in *Kali-yuga*, has become, in every particular, an established and militant denial of God; this is the source of its great instability. Therefore, in order for a Virginal receptivity to God to be renewed, this world must be destroyed. This, in fact, is the very meaning of the term "*Kali-yuga*". In this Yuga, eternal Form is relativized, fragmented, submerged, and apparently annihilated; the relative, the contingent and the temporal are absolutized. As W.B. Yeats put it in his poem *The Second Coming*, "Things fall apart; the center cannot hold." All distinctions are dissolved in the name of a universal *equality*: distinctions between races, between nations, between cultures, between religious revelations, between the sexes, between what used to be discrete and viable ecosystems—and even between words, where not only shades of meaning but clearly distinct colors of denotation are becoming indistinguishable—all are destroyed. Qualities themselves—discrete and intelligible forms which draw their stability and radiance from their proximity to the Essential Pole—are becoming unintelligible to us. Number alone remains. And the most terrible thing about this development is that the Absolute Herself is now appearing *as* number, matter, time and chaos (*matter*, of course, being cognate with *mater*). The primal creative polarity, that between the Absolute and the Infinite, is breaking down; the Substantial Pole, the infinite field of manifestation and All-Possibility, is itself appearing *as* the Absolute: and this is Kali. If the macrocosm is to return to its original and Virginal innocence—by virtue of the Substantial Pole ultimately unveiled as the Mirror of the Essential Pole—it can only be through that black and terrible Door.

As for individuals, however—and, just possibly, small groups— it is possible to return, in spiritual terms, to the Essential Pole, before physical death. Such a return only appears to be based on a nostalgic clinging to older forms of the sacred in a world that has doomed them to ever-swifter destruction (though a defense of whatever still remains viable in earlier sacred forms is a natural outcome of this return), whereas in reality it is the full accomplishment of the Apocalypse in personal terms—in other words, the successful completion of the Spiritual Path. As William Blake said, "when a man rejects error and embraces truth, a Final Judgement passes upon that man." The practice, simply, is to feed whatever is worldly in us—our vices, our vanity, our dissipation, our very primal act of self-definition—to the rising hunger of Kali, whose spiritual function is precisely to devour our ego, our *nafs al-ammara*; as She destroys the world, so She also destroys the world *in us*. When we have finished surrendering all we have held ourselves to be, all our self-images, all our cherished beliefs and memories, all our *material*, into that devouring maw, (pardon the entirely appropriate pun!), including our very will to live, then She will turn (only then!) and become that pure Virginal receptivity within us that is capable of being imprinted, anew, by Sacred and Eternal Form emanating from the Essential Pole (both beyond us and within us), thereby inaugurating "a new heaven and the new earth".

The dawning of the Black Virgin is, as Jean Hani suggests, the unveiling of the Divine Immanence—and total Immanence, since it dissolves the polarity between God and creation, destroys the world (and equally the ego, which is the world's microcosmic reflection). Yet what could be more merciful than the full and immediate presence of God, where the rigor and aloofness of Transcendence gives way to the intimacy of Union? The wrath of the Virgin, like the Wrath of God, must ultimately be seen as a servant and extension of God's Mercy. In entertaining the spiritually necessary vision of worldly evil and the Divine Wrath necessarily invoked by it, we must never lose sight of the Mercy of God, and of the fact, expressed in the *hadith qudsi*, that "My Mercy takes precedence over My Wrath". As Frithjof Schuon teaches, God is not somehow half good and half evil; He is all Good—Goodness being inseparable from Reality, just as evil is from the unreal. It is this very Goodness that makes Him appear as wrathful to those who hate and fear the Good; therefore we can say that the contemplation of God as the Sovereign Good, a contemplation which in no way denies or represses the terror of worldly and spiritual evil, but rather *swallows up* that terror, as "death is swallowed up in victory", is perhaps the nearest approach humanity can make to the black and unknowable

Reality of the Divine Essence, to which the Substantial Pole is the "lower door". And the Black Virgin, inseparable (in Christian terms) from Christ—as Form and Substance are inseparable in God—is the most direct path, via pure receptivity and simplicity, to this intimacy and this knowledge.

FOUR ANSWERS ON CHIVALRY

TO QUESTIONS POSED BY SCOTT A. FARRELL

OF CHIVALRY TODAY

(WWW.CHIVALRYTODAY.COM)

1) *Your book* [Shadow of the Rose: The Esoterism of the Romantic Tradition, *Sophia Perennis, 2008*] *examines the exchanges taking place between the Western and Muslim worlds as a source for the beginning of chivalry. Where and how did the exchange of ideas take place in this period that gave rise to the concept of chivalry in Europe?*

It would be hard to trace all the avenues of this exchange of ideas (which include Muslim Spain and the Islamicized court of the Holy Roman Emperor Frederick II in Sicily), but a big one was the Crusades. When the "rude Franks" encountered the highly civilized Saracens, they were often quite impressed—which demonstrates that Medieval Europe (unlike Europe or America today) actually *wanted* to be civilized. Saladin, for example, by his chivalrous treatment of prisoners and conquered populations, became a type of chivalry for many of the Crusaders, and they brought such tales home with them to Europe.

2) *What are the ideals of* Futuwwah *that parallel those of chivalry? Does the "youthful" aspect of both* Futuwwah *and chivalry imply that trying to achieve these ideals is something of a childish or immature goal?*

Both *Futuwwah* and Chivalry are based on the ideal of heroic self-sacrifice, not necessarily in battle. Al-Sulami's *The Way of Sufi Chivalry* [Inner Traditions International, 1991] is full of stories of heroic courtesy and self-abnegation in day-to-day circumstances, and Western Chivalry too is not without its sense that self-abnegation is inseparable from valor, as in Parzival's self-purifying encounters with the shameful consequences of his own foolishness. (See *Parzival*, by Wolfram Von Eschenbach, and *Parsifal*, by Chrétien de Troyes.)

Only a culture like ours where nobody grows up could confuse youthfulness with childishness (though of course Parzival, almost alone, was both youthful in the heroic sense and childish in the shameful one). The concept of "youth" in chivalry, both east and west, simply recognizes the fact that military heroes are, by and large, young. (When Cervantes in *Don Quixote* wanted to satirize chivalry, he presented us with a middle-aged knight trying to act like a young hero.) But in a spiritual sense, youthfulness can symbolize a responsiveness to the needs of the moment, and to God's will as it appears in the moment, an emotional and spiritual "readiness". In this sense, the virtue of "youthfulness" can apply to someone of any age.

3) *You say that the basis of chivalry (in both cultures) is a sense of dignity—and that sort of dignity can be found in both the customs of battle (between warriors) and of romance (between men and women). What is the purpose of this sort of "chivalrous dignity," and why is it important in such seemingly contradictory situations?*

It's unfortunate but not surprising that we see battle and romance as so contradictory nowadays; as is demonstrated by such proverbs as "all's fair in love and war" (a sentiment I do not subscribe to, by the way), our ancestors often saw them as inseparable. This sentiment is perfectly encapsulated by the Andalusian poet Ibn al-Qabturnuh (in Lysander Kemp's translation):

> I remembered Sulayma when the passion
> of battle was as fierce
> as the passion of my body when we parted.
>
> I thought I saw, among the lances, the tall
> perfection of her body,
> and when then bent toward me I embraced them.

But now that war is largely mechanized and impersonal, and with women engaging in combat, the whole basis for this identification between war and romance has gone up in smoke—except in the case of what the Eastern Orthodox Hesychasts have termed the "Unseen Warfare", and the prophet Muhammad, peace and blessing be upon him, the "Greater Jihad". And if we have to ask "What is the purpose of human dignity?", we had better begin by asking "What is the purpose of a human being? Why not just start World War III and annihilate the whole race? What have we got to lose?" Dignity is another name for self-respect, and without self-respect, human life is indeed not worth living. Furthermore, the Powers that Be have realized that if they can destroy the concept of self-respect in the masses, and the virtue of loyalty in human relationships that goes along with it, they can control us with very little effort.

4) *You cite two stories—the "affair of the necklace" from Islamic tradition and "Launcelot, the Knight of the Cart" from European tradition—to point out the difference between "egotistic" chivalry (concern about one's own reputation) and spiritual chivalry (the importance of self-sacrifice). What message do you hope readers will take away from these ancient stories in today's world, where self-sacrifice is often portrayed as naïve or simplistic (and egotism is too often exalted as the road to gratification)?*

Any man who thinks that self-sacrifice is naïve and egotism is exalted is probably beyond help; such a person already has been castrated by what the Christians call "This World"—and then taught to like it. But as for those men who still have their testicles attached—and even more to the point, for "men of heart"—they may still come to an understanding that self-sacrifice, whose basis is the war against the ego, requires infinitely greater courage than the confrontation with any outer enemy. Some people—the suicide bombers, for example—would rather be blown to bits than ever once catch sight of the Inner Dragon they fear.

This World is the collective expression of the ego; consequently anyone who goes to war with his or her own ego will earn the wrath of This World. In a corrupt and deluded world that sees self-sacrifice as naïve and egotism as exalted, the true Knight will encounter the dragon of social shame—and there are plenty of people who would literally rather die than face that particular beast. Only he or she to whom God is both constantly present and infinitely realer than the shadows of This World will be able to defeat that dragon, in the understanding that, in the words of the Noble Qur'an, *all is perishing but His Face.*

Launcelot had to die the death of the social ego; he had to purify his intent to rescue the Queen from any taint of desire to bask in the glory of being her rescuer. If the evil knight who abducted Guinevere is taken as the ego, then it's obvious that to rescue the Queen (i.e., the Soul) from him, and then get the big-head about it, must lead to ultimate defeat. As for the Prophet Muhammad, peace and blessings be upon him, he, the great spiritual and military leader and hero of his people, could not even use his personal power and prestige to defend A'isha, his most beloved wife, from the slander of adultery; he had to wait until God Himself, via a new *surah* of the Qur'an, defended her. What an ordeal, what an abasement, for a warrior and lover such as he!

It is necessary at this point to explain what the stories referred to above, "The Knight of the Cart" and "The Affair of the Necklace", are all about. In the *Launcelot* romance of Chrétien de Troyes, in the episode known as "The Knight of the Cart", Queen Guinevere has been kidnapped by an evil knight, and the knights of Arthur's round table fan out in search of her. On his way Sir Launcelot encounters a dwarf driving a cart, and it is explained to the reader that in those days such carts represented a profound social shame; any man of good reputation who mounted one was eternally disgraced. The dwarf calls out to Sir Launcelot: "Get into my cart and I'll tell you where the Queen is." Launcelot hesitates for a split second, then gets in. After many adventures and battles, which include crossing a moat on a bridge consisting of a keen sword-blade, which cuts deeply into the knight's hands and feet, he finally rescues the Queen—and the first thing she says is: "You *hesitated* before getting into the cart! You have covered yourself with shame!" And Launcelot humbly submits. The split second in which he placed his reputation above the Queen's welfare has seriously compromised his honor, and not even all his subsequent sufferings and exploits, even his successful rescue of her, have paid the debt incurred in that moment.

"The Affair of the Necklace", from the Islamic tradition, was as follows: Once upon a march, when the caravan had stopped for rest, A'isha, the favorite wife of the Prophet Muhammad, peace and blessings be upon him, lost her necklace, and retraced her steps in order to find it. She did find it, but when she returned to where her camel had been resting, she saw that the entire caravan had departed. She decided to wait until they missed her and returned for her, and while waiting fell asleep. While she slept a straggler, Safwan, discovered her. He offered her his own camel's howdah, and led the camel on foot to the next stopping-place, where they caught up with the caravan.

In the following days, this incident led to rumors and speculations that A'isha and Safwan must have had a sexual encounter, and this nearly led to blows between the companions of the Prophet and those who had hatched the rumors. The Prophet defended A'isha in public (without letting her know, however), but this was not enough to silence the rumors; all, including Muhammad, were waiting for a revelation of the Qur'an to settle the question, but this was long delayed. (It should also be noted that, in line with the Arabic misogyny of the time, which was not far different from the misogyny of most other races in other places and times, it was A'isha, not Safwan, who was the main object of the slanderous rumors.)

The Prophet Muhammad, peace and blessings be upon him, was in a real quandary. This classic "love triangle", though it only existed in the minds of the Muslims, was insoluble on its own level, as love triangles usually are. It created great stress in the lives of the Prophet, his wife, her rescuer, and the community at large, stress of the kind that could have torn that community apart.

The Prophet was in an unenviable position. If he accepted the slander as true he would be forced to punish his beloved wife without any real proof, but if he defended her openly he would appear as the cuckold, a man so dominated by an adulterous wife that, to his public shame, he was even forced to become her accomplice. If he ordered punishment of the slander-mongers on his own authority, he would appear to be self-servingly biased in favor of A'isha, but if he refrained, caving in to the slanderers, he would appear as weak before the people. Some of the Prophet's other wives defended A'isha to him, and the response of Ali ibn Abi Talib was: "God has not restricted you, and there are many available women besides her. But question her maidservant and she will tell you the truth". But of course no-one could replace A'isha in the eyes of the Prophet, because he loved her; he could take no solace from Ali's remark that, in effect, "there are plenty of fish in the sea." Following Ali's suggestion, A'isha's maid Burayrah was questioned on her impressions of A'isha's character, and she reported only good.

Finally the Prophet himself questioned her. Her answer was, "I know that if I say I am guilty you will believe me, and if I say I am innocent you will not, but God knows I am guilty of nothing." Then a new revelation of the Qur'an broke upon the Prophet: *Verily they who brought forth the lie are a party amongst you. . . . When ye took it upon your tongues, uttering with your mouths that whereof ye had no knowledge, ye counted it but a trifle. Yet in the sight of God it is enormous. Why said ye not when ye heard it: To speak of this is not for us. Glory be to Thee! This is a monstrous calumny. God biddeth you beware of ever repeating the like thereof, if ye are believers.* [Q.24:15–17]

This event, and the revelation that resolved it, are the archetype and the essence of Muslim chivalry. [For a fuller treatment of chivalry and romance in terms of the spiritual Path, see my *Shadow of the Rose: the Esoterism of the Romantic Tradition*, Sophia Perennis, 2008.]

WHAT IS LEVIATHAN?

LEVIATHAN is, precisely, the whole order of nature falsely conceived of as independent of God; in terms of the human microcosm, it appears as the passions. The passions are in many ways like a great sea beast—invisible, beneath calm seas, until they suddenly breach surface and do their damage. Leviathan, if we let him, will devour all that is spiritual in us, all our higher faculties, and our human form itself; this is what will happen to us if, like Jonah, we flee the divine call to spiritual development, if we attempt to take refuge from God in the unconscious heaviness of matter. If we capitulate to Leviathan, we will become subhuman, sunk in the elemental forces of the natural world—lust, aggression, sloth and all the others. In the *natural course* of things, everything in us that is not consciously dedicated to God will go to feed Leviathan—the lower passional soul, the *nefesh* (strictly equivalent to the Arabic *nafs*).

This natural course of things is symbolized in *Genesis* by red, hairy Esau, or Edom, the natural man; when ruled by our natural inclinations rather than the Spirit of God, we will always sell our birthright for a mess of pottage. And the agent and recipient of the spirit of God in *Genesis* is Jacob, who cunningly steals the birthright from Esau, and so receives the patriarchal blessing. In like manner, all of us must courageously and *cunningly* liberate the cosmic creative impulse from the grip of Esau before it sinks into sub-human dissipation, and place it in service to the spiritual Path, the way of return to the Promised Land, to the Messianic Kingdom, to the presence of God. Esau, then, is a type of the *nefesh*, and Jacob a type of the *neshamah* (equivalent to the Greek *nous* and the Arabic *ruh*). The *nefesh* is the soul we inherit from our ancestors; its course is what the Hindus call the *pitri-yana*, the way of the fathers, the road that leads to the cycles of rebirth. But we receive the *neshamah* directly from God; in Hindu terms, the course of the *neshama* is the *deva-yana*, the path of the gods, the road that leads to final Liberation.

So in this fallen world, we are progressively devoured by Leviathan. But in the world to come, things will be reversed. Instead of Leviathan feeding upon us, we will feast upon Leviathan at the Messianic Banquet, which will be held under a tent or tabernacle made of the monster's skin; the elemental forces of nature will go to nourish the higher spiritual faculties, not devour them; *nefesh* will feed *neshamah*. This hope is expressed at Succoth, the Feast of Tabernacles, in the following prayer: "May it be your will, Lord our God and God of our forefathers, that just as I have fulfilled and dwelled in this sukkah, so may I merit in the coming year to dwell in *the sukkah of the skin of Leviathan,* next year in Jerusalem" [i.e., in the next aeon, in world to come]. Succoth would appear to be the holy day specifically dedicated to the transformation and sublimation of Eros, as evidenced both by its "holiday" atmosphere and its rustic, pastoral beauty, undoubtedly meant to present an image of the terrestrial paradise. Therefore it is also—appropriately enough—the feast that celebrates the reconciliation of Jacob and Esau, the divine and the human, the spiritual man and the natural man. In the words of the *Zohar,* "the Messiah will not come until the tears of Esau are exhausted."

The transmutation and sublimation of the elemental forces of nature, in terms of the human microcosm, is expressed in the Hindu tantric tradition by the arousal of the *kundalini* (a word that means "coiled"), conceived as a serpent situated at the base of the spine, and the raising of this serpent-power to the *sahasrara,* the crown-*chakra* at the apex of the skull. This represents, and actually enacts, the reversal of the cosmogonic process, the resorption of the entire manifest universe into its eternal Principle. The same concept appears in the Kabbalah as the ascension of the Tree of Life by the kabbalistic practitioner, the climbing of the ladder of the *sephiroth* back to the primal sephirah *Kether,* or the Crown—the Jewish equivalent of the *sahasrara.* And the steed he rides is Leviathan himself—whose name, like *kundalini,* also means "coiled." The natural powers within human nature, when "uncoiled", purified and sublimated, are precisely what empower us to rise to the vision of the Eternal God. Such purification, however, is no easy task—a truth made clear in the 41st chapter of the Book of Job:

Canst thou draw out Leviathan with a hook? Or his tongue with a cord which thou lettest down?

Canst thou put a hook into his nose? Or bore his jaw through with a thorn?

Will he make many supplications unto thee? Will he speak soft words to thee?

Will he make a covenant with thee? Wilt thou take him for a servant forever?

Wilt thou play with him as with a bird? Or wilt thou bind him for thy maidens?

Shall the companions make a banquet of him? Shall they part him among the merchants?

Canst thou fill his skull with barbed irons? Or his head with fish spears?

Lay thine hand upon him, remember the battle, do no more.

Behold, the hope of him is in vain: shall not one be cast down, even at the sight of him?

None is so fierce that dare stir *him* up: who then is able to stand before *Me*?

God here is denying, or actually satirizing, the foolish and arrogant idea that the instinctual powers of the psyche are ours to use however we will, that we can control them with ease because they are "who we really are." To "play with him as with a bird" is to believe that we can control our own thoughts simply by deciding to, while to "bind him for thy maidens" to "make a banquet of him" and to "part him among the merchants" refer to the equally foolish belief that lust, gluttony and greed can be controlled in the same way. "None is so fierce that dare stir *him* up: who then is able to stand before *Me*?" means that God alone has the power to subdue Leviathan. Our sole duty in the war between God and the great sea-beast is to "lay thine hand upon him"—that is, not to repress or deny the *nefesh,* but simply to stay "in touch" with it, while in every other sense *getting out of the way* so that God Himself can subdue it. To "remember the battle" is to remember that only God fights this battle and only He can win it; it is also and equally to understand that the remembrance of God *is* the battle, and that constancy in this remembrance is entirely our own responsibility. The power to subdue and pacify the *nefesh* is God's alone; our part is simply to *be the channel* by which the power of God can come to grips with it. Thus the ultimate weapon in the battle against Leviathan is, precisely, the act of spiritual attention. As it says in Psalm 110:1: "The Lord said unto my Lord, sit thou at my right hand, until I make thine enemies thy footstool." In this passage God counsels the spiritual warrior not to fight against the passions (the "enemies") blow for blow, on the level of the will, but rather to place himself in God's hands, on the level of the *neshamah*, the spark of God within him, the Uncreated Intellect who is "*my* Lord", and allow Him to subdue them by His own power. If we want to haul that great sea beast up on shore, butcher and roast it, and feast upon it at the Messianic Banquet in the world to come, there is really no other way.

WHY

THERE ARE SOME who can accept any fate as long as they can understand its meaning, as God in His mercy gives them to understand it—and such understanding is indeed a great mercy. But people like this often begin to struggle and rebel as soon as they encounter events or situations that seem impenetrable to the light of knowledge, things they simply cannot understand. When they don't know "what to think" or even "what to feel" about a certain situation, it looms before them as an opaque, cruel, meaningless enigma.

This attitude arises from a weakness of faith. Speaking in Sufi terms, submission to God's Acts in the light of knowledge and insight indicates annihilation of the ego on the (higher) level of God's Names and Attributes. But submission to God's Acts without such light is something else again. To those who have never been granted the capacity to witness those Names—and what flows from them in terms of both events and unveilings—such submission is rudimentary, though it is the necessary foundation of all that is to come. To those who have already been given this capacity, however, submission to God's Acts in the darkness of the understanding is another thing entirely: a direct participation in God's Essence, which is Pure Darkness to every human faculty.

"Who are you to ask *Why*?" He says. "What could I tell you, so that you might understand it, about *Why*? The truth is, I AM Why—and that is the end of the discussion. Everything you call knowledge is actually recollection. Later on, in recollection, in memory, you might indeed understand something—something chosen and lifted out of the world of reverberations, of echoes. I do not begrudge you that; that, too, is a part of My generosity. But the true Reality of *anything* is a thunder too loud to hear, a flash of lightning too brilliant to see. *Why* and *What* come late in My manifestation; they appear in the afternoon of my day, the autumn of my year; the widening rings on the face of the pool partly ask and partly answer them, but they are not the Stone I dropped, and continue to drop, now, in this moment, before all possibility of veiling or unveiling. There is no *Why* in Me because I do not debate with Myself; I keep My own counsel. There is no *What* in Me because I am not included in the catalogue of things that must be this or that in order to claim their separate existence. I Am That I Am."

We must never forget, however, that the despairing resignation often expressed as "You can't really know, so don't ask, don't try" is a universe apart from the great Unknowing that is the mother of all knowledge, eternally unaffected by whatever might or might not be known. THAT is the goal of faith; THAT is the mark of submission; THAT is the Reality that lies beyond the answer—and the question— of *Why*.

HOMER, POET OF MAYA

[A slightly shorter version of this essay appeared in my book *Knowings, in the Arts of Metaphysics, Cosmology and the Spiritual Path*, Sophia Perennis, 2008; the present version appeared in the fourth issue of *Eye of the Heart, A Journal of Traditional Wisdom*]

IN HIS GREAT EPICS the *Iliad* and the *Odyssey*, Homer expresses a complete doctrine of *Maya*, and of the cycle of Divine manifestation as unfolded and dissolved by *Maya*. Taken together, the two poems constitute a mythopoetic *cycle* in the strict sense of that term: the story of the creation and destruction of the universe (a word that means "one turn")—which, in sober fact, is the only story there is.

According to the Hindus, Maya is the Great Mother of manifest existence; She is the creative illusion or magical apparition of Brahman, the Formless Absolute, in terms of the finite field of forms. Maya is not strictly unreal or non-existent; it's simply that She is not what She seems; to use the traditional Hindu simile, She is like "a rope mistaken for a snake." Maya appears in two forms: *avidya-maya* or "ignorance-apparition", and *vidya-maya* or "wisdom-apparition." Since Maya is not what She seems, She seduces us to try and make sense of Her, a task which is both inescapable and ultimately impossible. As *avidya-maya* She lures us into a false identification of Absolute Reality with the relative world, and in so doing creates that world; as *vidya-maya*, She lures us (as in Plato's *Symposium*) toward identification with ever higher and more comprehensive images of Absolute Reality, each of which is progressively discarded in favor of a greater conception, until all images and conceptions are finally transcended and Absolute Reality realized.

The *Iliad* is the epic of *avidya-maya*, the *Odyssey* the epic of *vidya-maya*. Helen, the cause for an expansive, imperialistic war, the "face that launched a thousand ships", is *avidya-maya*, the power that lures men into worldly identification, conflict and dissipation. Penelope, the wife of Odysseus "the cunning", the image of retreat, of withdrawal from the world, of home, is *vidya-maya*. She is the power of recollection, of return to the "center in the midst of conditions"; she is Holy Wisdom. In the epics of Homer, Troy is the City of This World, and Ithaca is the City of God. And Athena, the weaver-goddess who transcends the action of the epics but whose power is immanent everywhere within them, is *Mahamaya* herself.

The end of the expansive and dissipative attempt to "conquer the world", to control material conditions, to possess and dominate the "ten-thousand things" is, precisely, *apocalypse*—the end of the world—the burning of Troy. And Odysseus knew this. Like any wise and cunning man, he knew that the war to conquer the world would end in destruction and nothing else, that Troy would burn, that the victorious Agamemnon would be murdered—and that Helen, once "rescued," would simply become irrelevant. And so, of course, he tried to avoid the conflict; he flinched at the call to be born into this relative and conditioned world. He, like many "draft dodgers" in the Vietnam War, feigned madness to avoid service; he tried to plough his field with his plough harnessed to an ox and an ass, expressing the inevitable divergence of intent and division of the will that this world is made of, due to the fragmentation of the original human character (as the giant Ymir in Norse myth, and the Hindu Purusha, were dismembered to create the universe). But when his son was placed in front of the plough, he turned it aside—proving that he was not mad enough to destroy his own spiritual center and destiny. And so he had to go to war. He was wise enough to foresee the inevitable tragedy of the fall into this world of division, conflict and destruction—but Maya, the deceiver, was wiser than he. Only She knew the darkest secret of existence: that the descent into this world is really a *felix culpa*, a "fortunate sin"; that in the depth of the Great Mystery, the loss of God—felt and fought against and suffered through and finally redeemed—is in fact the deepest realization of God, that after "My God, my God, why hast Thou forsaken me?" comes "Into Thy hands I commend my spirit; it is finished."

Helen, in the *Iliad*, is shown sitting in Priam's palace in Troy, weaving a "double purple cloak" upon which appear the scenes of the great war between the Trojans and the Achaeans that she herself precipitated; by this she is revealed precisely as *avidya-maya*, who

weaves the pattern of manifest existence. But Penelope, Odysseus'
wife, is also a weaver. She has told her many suitors that she will wed
one of them when the shroud she is weaving, the shroud of her
father-in-law Laertes, is finished—but every night, in order to put
them off, she unweaves what she had woven during the day. Laertes,
father of Odysseus, is his Principle and Origin, the aspect of God
that pertains most directly to him, his archetype *in divinis*. And this
world, to the wise, is not a cloak of the living, a purple garment fit
for kings, depicting glorious and heroic struggles, but, precisely, the
shroud of God, the veil that covers Him in death. This world unfolds
in all its convincing multiplicity only when God is dead to us; only
then, under the influence of *avidya-maya*, do we mistake this perishing world for Reality itself. Helen weaves the cloak of the world-illusion, but only Penelope shows it for what it is. Only *vidya-maya* can
reveal to us the secret of Maya per se, that the pattern of existence
woven on the Day of Brahman is unwoven again in the Night of
Brahman, that the world created by Maya is not a stable reality, but a
coming and going, a wheel of birth and death, an outbreathing and
inbreathing of the Great Sleeper who dreams the universe.

The course of *vidya-maya* embraces the many journeys and battles and awakenings and realizations that are the spiritual Path; the
Odyssey, the epic that depicts the struggles of Odysseus to be
reunited with Penelope, with Holy Wisdom (under the guidance of
the goddess Athena, the providential manifestation of that Wisdom,
and Hermes her emissary), is the story of that Path. The stations of
Odysseus' spiritual journey, symbolized by his long return from
Troy to Ithaca, are as follows:

1) The raid carried out by Odysseus and his men on the Cicones
of Ismarus, in which they are defeated. This symbolizes the defeat of
worldly ambitions, the proof that this world no longer holds anything of value for those who have embarked upon the spiritual Path.

2) The land of the Lotus Eaters. This station, under the metaphor
of drug addiction (possibly to opium) symbolizes the overcoming of
the World Trance, the nearly universal addiction of the human race
to the sort of worldly experience that denies any possibility of spiritual experience—either that, or the habit of unconsciously translat-
ing the dawn of true spiritual experience back into a different kind

of worldly experience, notably the intoxicating complacency represented by the Buddhists as *Deva-Loka*, the realm of the long-lived
gods where "ignorance is bliss." In terms of the spiritual Path,
Vajrayana practitioners are warned not to fall into "the beautiful
Hinayana peace", into the complacent illusion that Enlightenment
has already been achieved; by this they are challenged to overcome
the curse of the lotus-eaters.

3) The Island of the shepherd Polyphemus, the one-eyed Cyclops,
who devours several of Odysseus' men. Jesus said, "if thine eye
become single, thy whole body will be filled with light"; Polyphemus represents the dawning of this truth, the truth of the Absolute
One, on too low a level, resulting in the "absolutizing of the relative", the precise error that creates religious fanatics, and then
devours them. The premature identification with the Transcendent
One at the expense of Its multiple manifestation results only in
destruction; the rigor of Transcendence can be safely encountered
only after the soul has been unified in submission to God's will.
Before that time, the Eye of the One—like the "third eye" of Shiva,
the opening of which destroys the world illusion—must be blinded,
veiled; otherwise it will burn up all the traveler's spiritual potential
instead of putting it to effective use. Furthermore, to contemplate
Unity at the level of the *head* can never be complete; Unity can be
realized in a stable way only at the level of the *heart*. However, what
appears to be only a disaster is in fact the secret beginning of that
necessary unification of soul. Throughout the *Odyssey*, Odysseus'
followers are gradually killed off, until only he remains alive; this
symbolizes the process of *recollection*, the mortification of the various divergent impulses of the soul, in terms of the affections, the
will and the thinking mind, until all that remains is unity of character and one-pointedness of spiritual attention and intent. As it says
in the *Tao Te Ching*, "Knowledge is gained by daily increment; the
Way is gained by daily loss—loss upon loss, until at last comes rest."

The name "Polyphemus" means "many-voiced"; what might be
the symbolic meaning of a figure with many voices but only one
eye? In terms of the contemplative act—one of whose sites, in
Hindu *kundalini-* or *raja-yoga*, is the "third eye", the *ajña-chakra* in
the center of the forehead—the Eye of God is One; according to

Meister Eckhart, "the Eye through which I see God and the Eye through which He sees me are the same Eye"—which is to say that, in contemplation, the knower is one with the thing known. However, the *reflection* of this contemplative Unity on the mental level (whose yogic site is the *visshudha-chakra* situated at the throat) is multiple, like the image of the Sun reflected in the waves of the sea. We may be granted—or we may *steal*—a glimpse of spiritual Unity, but if we have not paid the price required for the full and stable realization of that Unity, this incandescent glimpse will immediately fall to the level of discursive thought with its many voices; consequently the mental substance will become over-energized, driving us to the obsessive and futile attempt—all-too-clearly evident in today's world—to *think every possible thought*. This is what it means to be "devoured by Polyphemus".

4) Aeolus, the god of the winds, gives Odysseus a bag containing all the winds of the world, so that he will always have a fair wind in his voyage back to Ithaca. But his followers, out of curiosity, open the bag while Odysseus is asleep, let the winds loose, and all their ships are blown off course, back to their starting-point. This represents a wrong relationship to Divine Providence, based on lack of trust in God. If we dig up the seed every day to see if it is growing, the plant will never mature; if we arrogate to ourselves the right to see into the mind and Spirit of God, so as to better understand all the ramifications of our spiritual destiny—as if we could be better guardians and administrators of that destiny than God Himself— then we will be blown far off course. While Wisdom sleeps, curiosity wakes up and starts looking around; in the words of Frithjof Schuon, "mental passion pursuing intellectual intuition is like a wind that blows out the light of a candle."

5) Landing on the Island of the Laestrygones, who are cannibals, Odysseus' men encounter a young girl, daughter of the king of the island, who invites them to her father's court, where many are devoured. The princess symbolizes *avidya-maya*, who lures men to eat themselves up in worldly pursuits; spiritual curiosity ultimately results in a regression into worldliness. Nonetheless, the great purification continues. Cannibals are "self-eaters"; under the hidden influence of the Spirit, the divergent tendencies of the soul begin to

destroy themselves by their own folly. As William Blake said, "If the fool would persist in his folly he would become wise."

6) Next Odysseus and his men land on the island ruled by the witch Circe, who—weaving at an enormous loom—is Maya incarnate. She transforms half of Odysseus' men into pigs, symbolizing their total defeat at the hands of the lower passions, but also the dawning of *discernment*, the power to distinguish between the impulses of the lower self and those aspects of the psyche that may properly be called human. But Odysseus, the center of the spiritual Heart, is not overcome. Hermes provides him with a "sobriety drug", an "anti-illusionogenic" called *moly* (Ethiopian coffee, perhaps?) which is the exact opposite of the drug taken by the Lotus Eaters. Moly is the power of spiritual vigilance; it is this that allows him to overcome Circe's spells and turn his pigs back into men. And precisely *because* Odysseus resists her charms, Circe falls in love with him; when the contemplative "Center in the midst of conditions" is established and maintained, the manifest, conditional world turns to serve that Center. This is the great enantiodromia, where *avidya-maya* is changed into *vidya-maya*; Circe is here transformed from the *maya* that deludes Odysseus into the *shakti* that empowers and serves him. From now on she is not an enchantress, but a guide.

7) Circe now sends Odysseus to the western edge of the world, the limit of manifestation beyond which nothing remains but the One, where he invokes the shade of the seer Tiresias.

Tiresias had been transformed into a woman by the goddess Hera for a period of years, for the crime of striking a pair of copulating snakes with a staff. Later she strikes him blind as well, but gives him in return the gift of foresight. The striking of the snakes with the staff invokes the caduceus of Hermes, who also has an hermaphroditic aspect. The caduceus represents the power to unite opposites, as the *ida* and the *pingala*, the masculine and feminine psychic currents (the two snakes), are united by being woven around the central *sushumna*, the *axis mundi*, in the practice of *kundalini-yoga*. Tiresias, having been changed from a man into a woman and back again, is beyond the pairs-of-opposites which are the warp and the weft of the world illusion. He is blind (like Homer was) to the multiplicity of this world, but his gift of foresight shows him the final end of the spiritual Path. He advises Odysseus on how to travel that Path to reach the final goal.

After Tiresias, Odysseus speaks with the shade of his mother, who reveals to him the plight of his wife Penelope, beset by unwanted suitors in Ithaca, and also encounters the shade of Agamemnon, who tells him of his own murder at the hands of his wife Clytemnestra. Here the necessity of completing the spiritual Path is revealed, along with the final destiny of all who fail to complete it: division and death, in a world woven on nothing but division and death—the world of the double cloak.

Odysseus and his men return to Circe's island where she advises them further on the journey ahead, and they set sail again.

8) Odysseus and his men encounter the Sirens, symbols of the delusive and destructive side of spiritual Beauty—*al-Jamal, al-Malakut*—whose beautiful songs lure sailors to death on the rocks. His men put wax in their ears so they will not hear the Sirens' songs, but Odysseus asks to be tied to his ship's mast—the *axis mundi* again—so as to be able to hear the songs, while being restrained from following them. The lesson here is that only those who have fully attained the centrality of the human form can witness the Beauty of God and the esoteric secrets of the spiritual Path without being led to destruction. The Beauty and Mystery of the Divine are gifts that come in their own time; to run after them and try to grasp them—like the lustful brave, in Lakota myth, who wanted to rape the beautiful emissary of Wakan Tanka, White Buffalo Cow Woman—is to be destroyed by the Majesty of God.

9) Next the voyagers encounter Scylla, a many-headed sea-monster, and Charybdis, a whirlpool. The whirlpool is *samsara* (often compared to a whirlpool by the Buddhists), the engulfing and obliterating power of the world of relativity and formal manifestation; the sea-monster is the division of the soul—mind, affections and will—between many worldly concerns, each of which takes a piece of us. Odysseus chooses to brave Scylla instead of falling into Charybdis, losing only six men (perhaps corresponding to the Six Lokas of samrasic existence in the Buddhist Kalachakra, or the six directions of space withdrawn into the Center) instead of the entire

ship, and thereby demonstrating that even though the struggle with worldly necessity wounds us, to ignore it is fatal, and that passing beyond the pairs-of-opposites is not accomplished by failing to distinguish between them, but by choosing always "the lesser of two evils". One does not transcend good and evil by treating them as if they were the same thing, but by always choosing the good, at whatever cost, until the Sovereign Good is won—that Good which lies beyond the opposition of good and evil because, being all good, it has no opposite.

10) The voyagers now land on the Island of Trinacis, where—contrary to the advice of both Circe and Tiresias—Odysseus' men hunt and slaughter the Cattle of the Sun. In punishment, all are drowned in a shipwreck except Odysseus, who is washed up half dead on the island of the goddess Calypso, where he must remain as her lover for seven years. The Cattle of the Sun represent a glimpse into the Divine Intellect and the Majesty of God—*al Jalal, al-Jabarut*—producing a spiritual exaltation that the ego attempts to appropriate, ultimately resulting in a titanic inflation and fall. Odysseus is back in the clutches of this world—the nymph Calypso. Nonetheless, though he seems to have been defeated, the merit he gained through his earlier spiritual victories is still working in secret.

11) Hermes now appears, and convinces Calypso to let Odysseus go; where spiritual *works* (necessary but not sufficient) must fail, the power of *grace* intervenes. So he builds a raft and sails to the island of Scherie. He is washed up on the beach exhausted, and there encounters the princess Nausicaa, symbol of *vidya-maya*. She introduces him to her parents, the rulers of the island (who are a foreshadowing of his reunion with Penelope), and when he tells them the story of his journey they decide to help him. With their aid he returns to Ithaca, disguised as a *swineherd*—as one who has gained the power to control the impulses of his lower self.

12) Odysseus, in Ithaca, is recognized by his old housekeeper due to a scar on his thigh he received in his youth from a wild boar.

[NOTE: A friend of mine (a poet) once showed me, as a more-or-less magical object, a stone taken from the barrow-tomb known as The Grave of Queen Maeve, in Ireland. That night I dreamt I was a sacred swineherd; a boar came and slashed the outside of my right

thigh, two or three inches above the knee—a wound I later identified as the wound of Odysseus. This dream took place on the night
of the first full moon after the winter solstice—the one night of the
year, according to Robert Graves in *The White Goddess*, when the
ancient Egyptians ritually consumed swine-flesh.]

Odysseus enters his palace, still in disguise. The next day Athena
prompts Penelope to issue a challenge to the suitors: to string Odysseus' bow and shoot through the holes of twelve axes placed in a
row (These holes are sometimes called "helve-holes," as if they were
holes in the hafts of the axes by which they could be hung on a wall,
but I see them rather as the semi-circular spaces between the two
upward-curving corners of the Cretan double-axe.) None of the
suitors can even string the bow, but Odysseus can; he shoots an
arrow through the holes of the twelve axes and wins the contest. He
kills all the suitors, as well as the twelve maids who slept with them.
He reveals himself to Penelope, who is uncertain of his identity
until he describes the bed he built for her when they were first mar-
ried. They are reunited.

The axes through which Odysseus shoots are double-headed axes
with crescent blades, representing the waxing and waning phases of
the Moon, the waning phases symbolizing the fall into the darkness
of this world, under the power of *avidya-maya*, and the waxing
phases the stations of the spiritual Path, under the power of *vidya-
maya*. According to the *Bhagavad-Gita*, darkened souls destined for
rebirth enter the waning Moon after death, while sanctified souls
destined for Liberation enter the waxing Moon, and from there pass
on through the Door of the Sun. And in Sufi symbolism, the double
axe represents the cutting off of attachment both to this world and
the next, leading to the realization of God not after death, but in
this very life.

The twelve axes, which are twelve moons or months, are a *zodiac*,
an entire cycle of manifestation, like the twelve gates of the Heavenly Jerusalem and the twelve stations of the *Odyssey* itself. That the
twelve maids who slept with the suitors are killed symbolizes a passing beyond the sphere of the Moon, the cycles of nature and rebirth,
and a realization of full Enlightenment. The number of Penelope's
suitors is 108, a sacred number in Hindu and Buddhist lore. The

suitors symbolize the level where worldly multiplicity is always seeking the blessing of spiritual Unity, perpetually struggling to possess the One without first *becoming* the One—an impossible task. When this level is killed, only Unity remains. The pre-eternal Unity, symbolized by the marriage-bed of Odysseus and Penelope, that held sway before Principle and Manifestation were polarized, is re-established; the spiritual Path is complete.

This is secret Orpheus knew.

[NOTE: Buddhist mathematician Koenraad Elst explains that the number 108, considered purely in mathematical (not necessarily mythological) terms, is the principle of ontological hierarchy, of total possibility, and of repeating pattern. It might be called the number of *kosmos*; in the *Odyssey* it would seem to represent *kosmos* considered as *samsara*, as the round of births and deaths (the round of the circling spheres, the generation of repeating patterns in astronomical and human and biological life—i.e., *reincarnation*) that the philosophical character or spiritual hero seeks to be liberated from. He says:

> [Given the division of the circle into 360 degrees], the angle of 108 has a unique property: the ratio between the straight line uniting two points at 108 degrees from each other on a circle's circumference (in effect, one of the sides of a 10-pointed star) and the radius of that circle equals the Golden Section. Likewise, the inside of every angle of a pentagon measures 108 degrees, and the pentagon is a veritable embodiment of the Golden Section, e.g. the ratio between a side of the 5-pointed star and a side of the pentagon is the Golden Section.... The Golden Section means a proportion between two magnitudes, the major and the minor, such that the minor is to the major as the major is to the whole, i.e. to the sum of minor and major. In living nature, there are plenty of sequences where every member stands to the preceding member in a Golden Proportion or its derivatives (square root etc.), e.g. the distances between or the sizes of the successive twigs growing on a branch, the layers of petals on a flower, the rings of a conch,

the generations of a multiplying rabbit population, etc. What this symbolizes is the law of invariance: in every stage of a development, the same pattern repeats itself. The son is to the father as the father was to the grandfather. Wheels within wheels: every whole consisting of parts is itself likewise part of a larger whole. And the principle of order: the underling obeys the orders of his master to the same extent that the master obeys the requirements of the whole ... 9 is the Hindu number of planets, and 12 is the Zodiac, so 108 is the total number of planet-in-Zodiacal-sign combinations. This makes it into the total set of all possible planetary influences taken separately, or in a more generalized symbolism, the matrix containing all possibilities. [http://koenraadelst.bharatvani.org/articles/misc/why108.html]

ON PLATONIC REALISM
AND THE NAME OF GOD

A CHRISTMAS DREAM

ON THE NIGHT of Christmas Eve, 2007, I had the following dream:

An extremely tall, blond man came to my door, along with two other men and a woman. They were Protestant ministers. They had come to talk with me, but they began by continuing a conversation that had been having among themselves—and when they started to talk to me directly, they ended up preaching to me, not really conversing. I began to reply to them, talking to the woman in particular, but I could no more get through to her than she could to me. "We're just talking past each other," I said.

The point I was making was that in order to practice the Invocation of the Name of God, one needed to be a Platonic Realist, not a Nominalist. "You can't really get a sense of the Transcendent without Plato", I said; "a Nominalist can't do the Jesus Prayer."

What might I have meant? I probably meant that Platonic Realism, which recognizes the existence of universals transcending sense experience, is also the basis of the notion that things have *real names*, not simply more-or-less arbitrary verbal conventions by which we refer to them. Realism gives eternal and universal Ideas precedence over their names, and is thus able to understand the name of an Idea as a necessary reflection and intrinsic aspect of that Idea. If a thing is real it can have a real name; to *call* something by its name is to call that thing to be present, to *invoke* it. (To invoke something in this sense is not, however, to magically command its presence, but rather to recognize that presence as already established; it is not a command, but an unveiling.)

Nominalism essentially gives names precedence over the "ideas" they refer to, as if those names in some sense had the power to *create* the corresponding ideas by defining them. But from the Realist

perspective, the Idea, as it were, eternally radiates its own significance, eternally speaks its own Name—just as God the Father
speaks His Own Name in Eternity, Who is His only-begotten Son
(the Holy Spirit being the Breath, the Voice, the Energy of that
Divine speech, as the Son is the formed and "incarnate" Word of it).
The traditional doctrine that "God and His Name are One", which is
theological justification for the Invocation of the Name of God—
and which is inseparable from the declaration of Jesus Christ, "I
and the Father are One"—is thus affirmed by Realism but denied by
Nominalism. Therefore no Nominalist, since he cannot posit the
existence of Jesus Christ apart from and prior to our linguistic concept of Him, can say the Jesus Prayer; only a Platonic Realist is capable of praying that prayer in Spirit and in Truth.

> I saw three ships a-sailing in
> *On Christmas Day, on Christmas Day*
> I saw three ships a-sailing in
> *On Christmas Day in the morning*

THE *JÑANIC* GOAL
OF *KUNDALINI-YOGA*

THE PROCESS of *kundalini-yoga* involves the awakening and raising of a force known as the "serpent power", conceived of as coiled up like a snake at the base of the spine, in the *muladhara* or root-*chakra* (*kundalini* means "coiled"), by means of various psycho-physical practices—*mantras*, visualizations, *asanas* (physical postures), and most notably *pranayama* (breath-control), and directing it up the spinal column—or rather the subtle analogue of the spinal column, the *sushumha-nadi*—until it unites with the *sahasrara* or "thousand-petalled lotus" in the brain center, whose mid-point is the crown of the skull. When this is accomplished, the phenomenal world dissolves, as it were, into an undifferentiated field of incandescent white light.

The *kundalini* is one aspect of what the Hindus call *shakti* (somewhat similar to the Eastern Orthodox/Palamite notion of *energeia*), the Self-manifesting Power of the Absolute. When the creative Spirit of God or *mahashakti* ("great power") unfolds universal manifestation, ontological hierarchy—the Great Chain of Being—is established, and appears as the cosmic order. And in terms of the human microcosm, the Great Chain of Being manifests as the ladder of the six *chakras* (plus the seventh center, the *sahasrara*), placed along the erect spinal column of the human form. This form, as the bearer of what the Qur'an calls "the Trust", is the "medial" reality that both separates the manifest world from, and simultaneously unites it with, its invisible Source, thereby maintaining this world in existence. The creative power of *mahashakti*—equivalent in Islamic terms to Allah as *al-Rahman*, the Merciful, the One Who has mercy upon all the possibilities locked inside the prison of non-entity in the Night of the Unseen, thereby releasing them into existence— creates the universe by a process of "involution", of *turning in* upon itself so as to produce form and limitation. The final limit of this involution is reached at the level of the material plane, where *mahashakti* is entirely "wound up" or *involved* so as to become the lowest or root aspect of what the Aristotelian/Thomistic tradition calls *potentia*, the subtle power latent in matter itself—in other words, the *kundalini*. As we have already seen, the goal of the initial course of *kundalini-yoga* is to awaken this *shakti*, this latent *potentia* or stored power, and cause it to rise up the ladder of the *chakras*, the microcosmic aspect of the Great Chain of Being, until it unites with the crown-center or *sahasrara*. When this process is complete, potency has been fully *actualized*, unveiling the presence (as St. Thomas Aquinas would say it) of God as Pure Act. The ascent of the *kundalini* takes place by a process of "evolution" in the original meaning of the word: an "unwinding", a *turning out*. As the creative *mahashakti* winds itself up to produce the forms of the created universe, so now the reintegrating and liberating *shakti*—in microcosmic terms, the rising *kundalini*—unwinds itself, and in so doing progressively unmakes all created forms, thus reversing the cosmogonic process; this is why *kundalini-yoga* is sometimes called *laya-yoga*, the "yoga of dissolution". This reversal of the flow of creation is strictly equivalent to Allah in His name *al-Rahim*, by virtue of which He has compassion on the suffering of all the sentient beings who make up the universe, and responds by establishing the Spiritual Way—*sirat al-mostaqim*, the "straight path"—by which all things may return to Him.

Many practitioners of *kundalini-yoga* believe that the final goal of it is precisely the "supreme experience" of the union of the *kundalini* with the *sahasrara*, which they identify with *moksha* or Liberation. However, since this state of consciousness can still be differentiated from other states and thus exists relative to them; since it is still identifiable (at least in memory) with a particular subject experiencing it; and given that it has a beginning and an end, it cannot represent final Liberation. The union of the *kundalini* with the *sahasrara* remains an *experience*, one that both requires and posits an experiencer, while *moksha* is, precisely, the total transcendence of both experiencer and experience. The goal of *kundalini-yoga*, then, is not the attainment of some supreme mystical experience, but the complete transcendence of all experience. But if experience is to be transcended, it cannot remain latent; all the levels of possible experience must be entirely deployed; potential must be totally actualized; *potency* must become *Act*.

As the *kundalini* rises, it passes through the *chakras* (literally "wheels") of the human psycho-physical or subtle nervous system. (Strictly speaking, there are only six *chakras*; the *sahasrara*, while sometimes called the "crown-*chakra*", is not really one of them, but rather the proximate source from which they are projected and into which they are resolved.) And every *chakra* is in itself an entire universe or plane of potential human experience. The hierarchy of these planes of experience, which are equally levels of being, comprises those related to *security; pleasure; power; empathy; acquired knowledge; immediate knowledge;* and *mystical Union*. It is impossible, of course, for the human microcosm to entertain every experience held in potential in all the universes of the *chakras*, or even one of them—seeing that man is not God. As we all know, or should know, our various quests for security, or pleasure, or power, or acquired knowledge are effectively endless. And if we foolishly attempt to exhaust all the possibilities latent in any one of these levels, we will never rise to higher ones, but dissipate ourselves instead in a *quantitative* craving for a particular *quality*—a contradiction in terms. What is required is simply for the yogi to taste the essential quality of the universe of experience proper to each *chakra*, and then move on.

The first chakra, the root *chakra* or *muladhara*, is the universe of the most primal survival instincts, as represented by eating, digestion and excretion; it is dominated by the quest for security. In terms of sensual/affective experience it is the *anal* realm. On the level of consciousness represented by the root *chakra*, the "other" is simply food.

The second *chakra*, the *svadhisthana*, centered in the genital area or directly above it, is the universe of sexuality, in all its conceivable manifestations, physical, sensational, affective and imaginal, including any sensual (i.e., not yet fully human) relationship to the natural world, to one's family or social group, or to society as a whole; in larger terms, it represents the quest for pleasure of any kind. Here the "other" is an object one desires to possess. (To the degree that sexuality is used as a drug to anesthetize against fear, it also serves first-*chakra* interests.)

The third chakra, the *manipura*, centered in the navel or the solar-plexus, is the world of power, aggression, competition, mastery, and self-will. Here the "other" is a rival one desires to eliminate or subjugate. ("Pure" self-will wants only to eliminate the other; to the degree that the operative desire is to subjugate the other, it will begin to exhibit certain second-*chakra* traits.)

The fourth chakra, the *anahata*, centered in the middle of the chest, is the world of empathy, of human love, and all the virtues that make love and empathy possible, including humility, compassion, respect, receptivity, and courageous ("heartful") defense of the good; it also embraces protective love for lower forms of life and devoted love for higher spiritual beings. Here the "other" ceases to be merely an object, but is recognized as a subject in its own right. We do not only see the other, but are seen *by* the other; our will is not merely to act upon the other, but to allow ourselves to be acted upon as well.

The fifth *chakra*, the *vishuddha*, centered in the throat, is the world of the Platonic *dianoia*, the *ratio* of the Scholastic Philosophers, of thought and logic, of the mental reflections of intellectual Truth; as such it is also the world of language, and of mental images as mediated by language. Here the "other" is an object of the discursive or dialectical knowledge of the thinker. Insofar as it is an object of that thinker's *individual* understanding, a subtle possessiveness remains; however, to the degree that this discursive or dialectical knowing is motivated by the desire for objective Truth alone, and consequently remains faithful to the necessary operations and conclusions of logic—logic being the mental reflection of Transcendence, of Necessary Being—the possessiveness of the thinker over his "own" ideas is progressively sacrificed in the name of that higher Truth.

The sixth *chakra*, the *ajña*, centered in middle of the forehead, is the world of the Scholastic *Intellectus*, the Platonic *Nous* (or its first intimation), the world of contemplative witnessing, where the "other" is no longer *other* than the knower, but one with him in Knowledge; here the witnessed is a perfect mirror-reflection of the one witnessing, and vice versa. This is the world of Intellection, where the knower sees Truth directly, just as the eye sees light. This Intellection, however, exists as it were in "a world of its own", a higher, subtler world which is not yet the center of the human microcosm; consequently it cannot be called *pure* Intellection in the spiritual sense, where Knowing and Being are one. Everything seen from the point of view of the Sixth Chakra becomes a *mandala*, with the *ajña* or "third eye" as the center of it.

The *sahasrara*, the "thousand-petalled lotus", is the world where subject and object are united and annihilated in a unitary field of Pure Being, in which Being is not other than Knowing. It is beyond even the world of "seeing Truth directly, face-to-face." In it, both the witness and the thing witnessed are obliterated; this is the state known as *nirvikalpa-samadhi*.

To some yogis, the opening of the *sahasrara* by the rising *kundalini*, and the union of the *kundalini* with the *sahasrara*, is the ultimate goal of spiritual development. But this is not really the case. *Nirvikalpa-samadhi* is temporary, either naturally coming to an end or ending in death. And when it does come to an end, the yogi is either thrown back, psycho-physically imbalanced and exhausted, into a barren world, pathetically narrow and constricted as compared with the wonders he has seen, or else he succeeds in consciously directing the incandescent energy of the *sahasrara* back to the lower *chakras*, one by one. As the rising *kundalini* opened these *chakras*, unfolding the successively wider universes of experience hidden within each of them, so the descending overflow of energy from the *sahasrara* (called *amrita*) now crystallizes them—not as experiences, but as intrinsic aspects of the eternal Human Form, objective to the Indwelling Divine Witness. (*Amrita*, usually translated as "nectar", literally means "deathless", and is thus precisely synonymous with the Greek word *ambrosia*, the food of the gods.) The true end of the spiritual Path, then, is not to transcend the human faculties—though this is a necessary stage—but, without destroying them, to break their bondage to the ego, and submit them to the will of God, until they are known as direct manifestations of Him in, and as, the Human Form. Even security, pleasure and power, the qualities of the three lower chakras, can be sanctified

and placed in relation to the Divine—as servants, not as masters—
once the hold of the ego is broken. These things are necessary to
human life; God did not create us half good and half evil, nor ask us
to return to Him by making ourselves half human.

Among the Eastern Orthodox Fathers, Diadochos of Photiki
describes Hesychast contemplation, based on the invocation of the
Name of God—what the Sufis call *dhikr* and the Hindus, *japa-
yoga*—as effecting "the descent of the *Nous* (the Spiritual Intellect)
into the Heart", so that it becomes what both the Hesychasts and the
Sufis call "the Eye of the Heart." (Likewise Ramana Maharshi speaks
of "the descent of the mind into the Heart".) The *Nous* is the Scholastic *Intellectus*, which we've already defined as the faculty that perceives Truth directly as the eye perceives light. As long as it remains
seated at the sixth *chakra*, however, its knowledge, while true in the
abstract, remains unrelated to the *existential* condition of the
human soul; it may produce flashes of insight into eternal Truth,
but these flashes will not necessarily alchemize the soul, nor act to
conform all the human faculties—the rational mind, the will, the
imagination, the affections and the memory—to the Truth this
Intellect perceives. Consequently, this level of rarefied and sublimated Intellection will become progressively subject to spiritual
delusion, to what the Russian Orthodox Hesychasts call *prelest*.
Only if the Intellect descends into the Heart so as to become the Eye
of it, thus uniting the Intellective and the Existential poles, will the
Hesychast, the Yogi, or the Sufi truly Be what he Knows.

When the *sahasrara* opens, it begins to resonate harmonically
with a deeper level of the Heart than that represented by the *anahata-chakra*, which was opened up during the phase when the *kundalini* was still rising. This is the level that the Hindus call the
Hridayam, the "Cave of the Heart"—the same one that, in Vajrayana
Buddhism, is posited by the mantra *Om Mani Padme Hum*, "Hail to
the Jewel (the *Nous*) in the Lotus (the Heart)", or by the Hesychast
invocation *Jesu-Mariam*, where—as in the Orthodox icon "The Virgin of the Sign"—*Jesu* stands (on one level) for the *Nous*, and *Mar-
iam* for the Heart. The *anahata-chakra* is simply one degree of
psycho-physical unfolding, whereas the *Hridayam* is the center and
epitome of the whole psycho-physical system, and also the door

that leads beyond that system entirely, beyond all self-referential subjectivity. When this station is reached, the Heart is the Witness of all experiences; when the *Intellectus*, the *Nous*, the *Ruh* (a Sufi term meaning "Spirit") is seated and/or recognized in the Heart, so as to become the Eye in the center of it, then the entire Human Form is enlightened; *every* faculty becomes, as it were, an organ of Intellection, in which Knowing and Being are one. This is what Jesus meant when He said, "If your eye become single, your whole body will be filled with light." And, on its deepest level, the Eye of the Heart is the portal of the *atman*, the Indwelling Divine Witness, the One Self at the center of all. The final goal of *kundalini-yoga*, then, is not merely to allow us to experience higher levels of being, but to make all levels of being, "high" or "low", objective to the Indwelling Divine Witness. The total annihilation of sense experience, mental images and concepts is *nirvikalpa-samadhi*, and is related to the *sahasrara*; this is the full realization of the Divine Transcendence. The still deeper station where sense experience, mental images and concepts are witnessed without being in any way identified with is *sahaja-samadhi*, and is related to the *Hridayam*; this is the flowering of the Divine Immanence. Here the relative has lost all power to veil the Absolute, but is fully revealed as Its manifestation, Its *shakti*, Its creative power.

As long as we identify with this or that experience, we cannot fully experience it because we cannot completely witness it; the part of it we identify with—that is, the part of it we wrongly identify with the Indwelling Divine Witness—becomes opaque to us, and thus can no longer either witness or be witnessed. But when the Absolute Witness is unveiled—when the identification of It with this or that experience or level of experience is broken—then experience becomes, as it were, *complete* for the first time. But since "experience" is precisely a subjective and therefore intrinsically *incomplete* perception of something, the end of our *identification* with experience—which is the very thing that produces such partiality in the first place—is the also end of experience itself. All that remains is the Absolute Witness, Who witnesses only Itself, and witnesses all the infinite number of limited fields of reality or experience that are available to It only as aspects of Itself—as a unitary field of Reality in which experience, experiencer, and object of experience are One. This is *moksha*, Liberation.

Namarupa, name-and-form, is a limitation which must be transcended. But after it is transcended (that is, after the *sahasrara* opens), it is transformed—when the Heart is plumbed and the level of the *Hridayam* reached—from a veil that hides Reality into the radiant manifestation of Reality; this, precisely, is the meaning of *tantra*, and of the Mahayana Buddhist doctrine that "*samsara* is *Nirvana*", epitomized in the *Heart Sutra* by the phrase "Form is Emptiness; Emptiness is Form". In all true renditions of the spiritual Path, the first course is to detach from the manifest world and seek the Transcendent God, while the second course is to return to the manifest world by virtue of the realization of the Immanent God, and know that world as nothing in itself—nothing other than the Self-manifesting radiance of the Absolute.

[NOTE: In the case of either *bhakti-yoga* or *jñana-yoga*, the psycho-physical practice of directly awakening the power of *shakti*, resulting in a grand pilgrimage through all the universes of the *chakras*—a pilgrimage fraught with dangers, especially if undertaken without the ongoing *technical* guidance of a competent *guru*—is not really necessary. Both Love and Knowledge, insofar as they are manifestations of the Grace of God, will eventually awaken the *kundalini* on their own, but they will do so in a balanced way, and in God's own time. The perspective of *kundalini-yoga* does, however, have the virtue of presenting the most complete picture we possess of the true nature and scope—and end—of *experience.*]

THE SUPREME STATION

Sri Shankaracharya teaches that the primal sense that "I am myself", possessed to one degree or another by every sentient being, is not only the first stirring of the ego that veils the Self, the *Atman*, the Absolute Witness within us, but also the sign of the presence of that very Self. Likewise Ramana Maharshi recommends that we return to this primal I-sense as the ever-present and eternally reliable touchstone of the Self, but also defines the Self as that which *witnesses the arising and passing away* of the I-sense. The Self does not define Itself or reflect upon Itself or express Itself or declare Its own existence; such definitions, reflections, expressions and declarations are ultimately only the province of the I-sense, which the Self merely witnesses. And to witness the I-sense without identifying with it is to annihilate it—or rather, it is to rest in the knowledge that the I-sense has never truly existed, and never will. (We might define the I-sense as the consciousness "I am *me*", whoever that me may be, and the Self as the pure consciousness "I Am".)

The I-sense is all *Maya*; it possesses only a virtual reality. The ego is no more than a vague suspicion that something like an ego might exist. According to Ramana Maharshi, when the question "Who am I?" is asked—persistently, and on the deepest possible level—this suspicion is dispelled.

The Maharshi also said, "Whoever practices *japam* gets realization". *Japam* or *japa-yoga* is the Hindu equivalent of the Christian Hesychast *mnimi Theou* and the Islamic Sufi *dhikr Allah*, both of which mean "remembrance of God". The practice is simply to repeat a traditional Name of God, either vocally (usually in a group context), or continuously and silently, with each breath.

The Invocation of the Name of God usually begins as a simple recognition of God's reality on the part of the devotee, combined with the ongoing work of dispelling the habitual distractions that veil this recognition, and consequently interrupt the Invocation. It may also take the form of a petition directed to God, a prayer that

He unveil His presence, that He grant his devotee the Beatific Vision.

This level of Invocation is based on the perception of God as *He* and the devotee as *I*; it is built upon the common assumption that ego is real, and that this ego—humbled, purified, fervent, but still assumed to exist—can witness God, at least partially and intermittently.

Whatever "God" the ego sees, however, is inseparable from the ego. It is a projection of that ego, but it is also the beginning of the realization that there is Something more real than the ego, Something that does not depend upon the I-sense or exist in relation to it, Something that continues to be real whether or not the I-sense appears or disappears. This is why worship of God with form is usually an indispensable prelude to the realization of God beyond form: "None come to the Father but through Me."

From the standpoint of the Self, however, the devotee is not *I* but *he*; the Self is the Witness and the human form the thing witnessed; the psycho-physical individuality is objectified before the face of the Absolute Witness, the *Atman*. According to Ibn al-Arabi, the recipient of this station

> sees nothing other than his own form in the mirror of the Reality. He does not see the Reality Itself, which is not possible, although he knows that he may see only his form in it.... If you have experienced this you have experienced as much as is possible for created being, so do not seek to weary yourself in any attempts to proceed higher than this, for there is nothing higher, nor is there beyond the point you have reached aught except the pure, undetermined, unmanifested [Absolute]. [Ralph Austin, *Ibn al'Arabi: The Bezels of Wisdom*: Paulist Press, 1980; p. 65]

And as Frithjof Schuon puts it, in *Language of the Self* [Madras: Ganesh & Co., 1959]:

> for the "volitional" or "affective" man (the *bhakta*) God is "He" and the *ego* is "I", whereas for the "gnostic" or "intellective" man (the *jñani*), God is "I"—or "Self"—and the *ego* is "he" or "other" [p. 230].

In terms of the Invocation of the Name, the same inversion of subject and object applies. From the *jñanic* standpoint, I am no longer striving to remain aware of God's presence or petitioning Him to unveil that presence. I am not invoking God; rather, the Self is witnessing the Invocation itself *as* God, this being the true meaning of the traditional formula "God and His Name are One"; the individual human form is nowhere to be seen. When my sense of individuality is translated to the *jñanic* level, it is transformed from "I" into "he"—but when the Invocation of God's Name is translated to the *jñanic* level, that objective "He" is no longer my human individuality, but God Himself. But if this is the case, then Who or What is the Subject, the "I"? Who or What could conceivably be the Witness of God? The Subject is the Self, the Absolute Witness—and what that Self witnesses is no longer even my own psycho-physical form, but Pure Being, the personal God—the highest Source and Archetype of all human individuality. The Self as Beyond Being witnesses Being; Brahman (the Godhead) witnesses Ishvara (the personal God); Nirguna Brahman (God without attributes) witnesses Saguna Brahman (God with attributes). As Ramana Maharshi teaches, Ishvara is indeed the Creator and Ruler of the Universe, infinitely greater than my human individuality—nonetheless, from the absolute standpoint of the Self, Ishvara is simply the last thought.

When the Self is veiled by the I-sense, God is witnessed only in part; this is what Ibn al-'Arabi calls "the God created in belief." When the Self is unveiled, then God is witnessed in His Wholeness, since only the Divine Self can know Itself as God; the I-sense cannot. Therefore, to witness God in His Wholeness, beyond the I-sense, is to unveil the *Atman*, the Self, Which alone can function as that Witness; this is the *jñanic* aspect of the Invocation of God's Name.

In practical terms, the Invocation acts to prevent "me" from identifying with the I-sense as it arises by positing the I-sense as God. Pure Being, the personal God, is indeed the Creator of all things, the first primordial stirring of *I Am That I Am*, the Divine original I-sense that will later become the Universe, refracted into all the myriad self-concepts (each paired with a corresponding world-concept) of the sentient beings that compose it. If the I-sense is identified as "me", it becomes opaque, obscuring the face of the Witness. But if it is recognized as God, it leaves no room for this "me". Revealed as the primal Radiance or primordial Expression of the Self—the Self that, in Its own Essence, never radiates Itself or expresses Itself or departs from Itself, except by virtue of Its *Maya*—God immediately plunges back, as it were, into the ocean of that Self. My ego is *ego* per se, opaque and grasping and terrified because it will not surrender to the Self and be annihilated in It. God is Divine precisely because He *does* surrender to that Self and has always surrendered to It; God as Pure Being knows that, in Essence, He is Beyond Being; that's what makes Him God. On the *jñanic* level of the Invocation, God occupies the place "vacated" by my ego, and the Absolute Self witnesses Him.

The *jñanic* quality of the Invocation is expressed in one of the Sufi forms of the *dhikr Allah, ALLAH HU.* ALLAH ("the Deity", the synthesis of all the Divine Attributes) is the arising of the Divine primordial I-sense as God; HU ("He", a name of the Absolute Essence, the *Dhat*) is the plunging back of all the Divine Attributes derived from the primordial I-sense into the Formless Absolute, the Essence, the Self. That ALLAH is invoked while inhaling indicates that the human form, empty of ego, is now filled with the Spirit or Breath of God, and is thereby transformed into *al-Insan al-Kamil,* the Perfect Man, the primordial Self-Reflection within God that is the eternal archetype of the human form. That HU is invoked while exhaling—or *expiring*—indicates the extinction of the human form and the I-sense that produced it, the annihilation of the entire illusion of other-than-Self. Thus the natural rhythm of the breath, inhaling and exhaling, posits:

GOD, *GODHEAD;*
ISHVARA, *BRAHMAN;*
SAGUNA BRAHMAN, *NIRGUNA BRAHMAN;*
ALLAH, *HU.*

The Invocation of the Name of God recollects the mind so that it becomes able to ask the question recommended by Ramana Maharshi: "Who am I?" The answer to this question is not any of the imaginable replies, not even "I am the Self"—since to affirm "I am the Self" is simply to produce one more idea, one more refinement or modulation of the I-sense. The only true answer to "Who am I?" is: *I am the One presently asking this question.* The Invocation of the Name divinizes the I-sense and renders it transparent—until the Self reasserts Itself definitively, at which point the I-sense dissolves.

This is the Supreme Station.

THE REMNANT

[A longer version of this essay, with sections interpolated from 'The Black Virgin' above, appeared in *Sacred Web 24*]

THE GENERATION of the Traditionalist School centered around Frithjof Schuon have—for the most part—presented the revealed religions in their celestial essences, *sub specie aeternitatis*. That was their duty and their function, and we may thank God that they fulfilled it so brilliantly. But though they carried on René Guénon's critique of the modern world, they had much less to say than Guénon did about the degeneration of the religious revelations themselves in the face of that world (the most notable exception to this lack being Rama Coomaraswamy). We, however, must face this degeneration, and determine as best we can—with God's help—how to deal with it.

As the spiritual pillars of the world crash and fall, one by one—you can hear them going down, in the distance, in the rainy dark, after midnight—Roman Catholicism beheaded by Vatican II; Eastern Orthodoxy Protestantized and shot through with heresy, at least in North America, right in line with Vatican II; much of Sufism politicized, increasingly divided since 9/11 between Islamicist militancy and the "harmless, universalist", hardly Islamic Sufism sponsored by the West, as exemplified by the exponential growth of the "Rumi industry"; Hinduism descending into ethnic separatism; American Buddhism neatly dovetailing with postmodern nihilism to become the ideal religion for materialists—what can one do?

The Book of Revelations, Chapter 12, speaks of the "woman clothed with the sun, and the moon under her feet, and upon her head a crown of twelve stars"—clearly the Virgin Mary—and "the Remnant of her seed" upon whom the Dragon—Satan—makes war. Likewise according to the *hadith* of Muhammad, peace and blessings be upon him, "Islam began in exile and will end in exile—blessed are those who are in exile!" Insofar as this seed of the Remnant may still sprout and scatter seeds of its own this late in the cycle, much of that seed will necessarily fall upon barren ground—hardness of heart—or be eaten up by the birds of the air, by (in the words of Frithjof Schuon) "mental passion pursuing intellectual intuition". This, of course, is true of all epiphanies, all revelations—the world being what it is. And so, how can we—or can we at all?—find, or be, the kind of Remnant that doesn't decay into worldly sterility, if it is not in fact co-opted by the developing regime of Antichrist?

To begin to answer this question I must ask another: as the religions fall, as their forms are shattered, their *material* is released. What is the nature of this material? (I am not talking about whatever material we may unearth that pertains to *dead* religions, like that of the Egyptians; I am referring to living religions that are on their last legs, but that will—God willing—be with us "all days, even to the consummation of the age".)

This material is composed, let us say, of scriptures, doctrines, the writings of sages, spiritual practices, relics, ritual objects, sacred buildings and/or sites, and the personal teaching and influence of whatever true exemplars of the religion in question may remain—none of which will be spiritually efficacious in the absence of the particular *grace* proper to the revelation in question, a grace that is conferred, precisely, by initiation, taken in the widest sense of that word to include both "esoteric" initiations, such as those conferred by the representatives of intact Sufi *silsilahs*; "exo-esoteric" ones like the Christian sacraments, notably Baptism; exoteric ones, such as the Islamic *shahadha*; and those that could be classed as "exo-eso-teric" except for the fact that, in the tradition in question, no such polarization between the esoteric and exoteric domains in fact occurred; I am thinking specifically of the Buddhist initiation whereby one "takes refuge" in the Buddha, the *dharma*, and the *sangha*. Whoever has received such an initiation *is* his or her chosen tradition, at least virtually; even if he or she were the last Muslim Sufi, or Christian, or exoteric Muslim, or Buddhist in existence, nonetheless—while he or she is still living—it would not be possible to say that *tasawwuf*, or Christianity, or exoteric Islam, or Buddhism has finally departed from the earth.

And if one is true to his or her initiation, then the material of the declining but not yet dead religion that has conferred that initiation may actually *seek one out*. On the level of conscious intent it will be the duty of certain initiates to go in quest of whatever scriptures, doctrines, writings, spiritual practices, relics, ritual objects, sacred buildings and/or sites—or the residual grace that may adhere to such sites—and fully-informed human teachers may still be available. But on a more esoteric level, these things will also be questing for the initiate, whether or not he or she is conscious of being the object of such a quest. Finding themselves refugees, strangers in a strange land, they will undertake the most rigorous and grueling pilgrimages in order to seek out anyone of the Remnant of their tradition who may still speak and understand their language.

Consequently the initiate, whether or not God wills that he or she be conscious of it, may find him- or herself the site of the arrival and dawning of *lore*. But lore is ambiguous. It is not pure intellection; it is not sanctity; it is *material*. It will therefore be largely psychic rather than spiritual in nature—which means that it will either be the empowering *shakti* invoked by intellection, or an example of those dangerous "psychic residues" adhering to dead religions that René Guénon seriously warned us to avoid. In other words, not only will the homeless elements of dying but not yet dead religions seek us out; the dead themselves will also present themselves—and so we had better learn to tell the difference. In Christian terms, this "interregnum" between the fall of the earthly forms of the divine revelations and the dawning of the "age to come" is under the sign of Christ's harrowing of hell, which symbolized (and *enacted*) the invocation and *threshing* of all the psychic residues of this cycle of manifestation—a process that appears, in the Book of Revelations, as the resurrection of the dead, and which is one of the inescapable dimensions and keynotes of the *Kali-yuga*. That's why, in these latter days, we are laboring mightily to call up all the ghosts that geology and paleontology and archaeology and textual criticism can unearth, till we finally decide, a-la *Jurassic Park*, to clone back the dinosaurs. (And let's not forget astronomy, since by looking farther and farther into deep space we are peering into the past as well, all the way back to the Big Bang.) As we enter Apocalypse, the entire hoard of human and non-human psychic residues, a whole *Mahayuga's*-worth, is turned loose—and it has nowhere to go—nowhere to travel—but to, and through, ourselves. We alone are the stewards of creation; we alone are bearers of the Trust.

So what is the effect upon the human soul of this inundation of psychic material? The answer to this question depends entirely upon whether or not we know how to *thresh* it, to separate the living kernel from the dead husk. The flail that separates the wheat from the chaff is *intellection*, *discernment*; the living kernel, released from the dying but not yet dead divine revelations destined for this cycle, adorns the soul capable of pure intellection—as well as the one capable only of the *virtual intellection* known as faith—and nourishes it. As *shakti* to intellection—virtual or actual—it gives that soul the power to live, grow, and (if God so orders) express itself in this radiant and dying world.

If intellection is veiled, however, discernment will fail. And without discernment, the soul will lose the capacity to separate the elements of true and living revelation, that are still under Grace, from the chaff of dead religions, and the husks of ancestral human experience, that are only under Memory—the regime that Blake was referring to when he said, "Memory is Eternal Death." Consequently it will become glutted and polluted with toxic psychic residues. Closed to the light of the Spirit by all this detritus, it will become elvish, ultrapsychic, without stable boundaries, *pixilated*, jinn-possessed; this is the state the Noble Qur'an refers to, in the *surah The Calamity*, when it says that in the last days people will *become like scattered moths* ("moth" = *psyche*).

If, however, the faculty of intellection, and thus of discernment, is awake in a particular soul—either actually, through pure intellection, or virtually, through faith—it will then be possible for that soul to distinguish between the living psychic elements of Tradition (living because still connected, via Grace, to the Spirit) and the toxic psychic residues of traditions and universes of experience that are effectively deceased. Consequently that soul will be able, via a process of psychic "digestion", to assimilate the living, nourishing elements and eliminate the dead residues. As the dead awake, as the ancestors rise up through our souls on their pilgrimage of resurrection, they will, in the process of unburdening themselves of their baggage so that they may ascent unencumbered to the higher worlds, and ultimately to God—a process known as *purgation*—leave this baggage behind for us to deal with. This is when the discerning soul, on its end, must learn how to release those souls back to their Creator, while retaining whatever of their discarded baggage it can truly put to use. And it must also learn how to release into the divine fires of annihilation whatever psychic chaff is no longer of any use to either the living or the dead. Thus from one point of view we may say, speaking in Eastern Orthodox terms, that the intellective soul is itself the site of the posthumous "aerial toll-houses", or at least participates in their function. And this is precisely what it means, speaking again in intellective terms and using the language of the Western Church, for the living to "pray for the good souls in Purgatory."

Among those Traditionalists/Perennialists who were willing to strictly adhere to, and defend, a single revealed religion, while continuing to assert that God has sent more than one revelation, established more than one path by which we may return to Him—one who did not only realize the transcendent unity of religions intellectively but practiced it existentially—was the traditionalist physician, psychiatrist and traditional Catholic priest, Rama P. Coomaraswamy. I learned from him the following three principles, which between them define, in my opinion, much of what it is to be a Traditionalist: 1) You must adhere to a divinely-revealed—i.e., orthodox—religious tradition; 2) You should expect little from this world, which is a vale of tears; 3) You should prepare yourself to be alone. (You won't necessarily find yourself totally alone, but still, you'd better get ready for it.)

These three principles lead us to ask, "what exactly does it mean to adhere to an orthodox tradition and at the same time be alone"? We often speak of "being in the world but not of it", but is it also possible—and sometimes necessary—to be in one's religion but not of it, and even in one's "esoteric" group (presuming one has sought and found such a group) but not of it? Isn't spiritual community, *sangha*, the "communion of the saints" just as important as this thing of *being alone*? I intend to answer this question as fully as I can, but before I do, I want to push *being alone* to its final limit, because from one point of view—that of Sri Ramana Maharshi and Meister Eckhart—it is also necessary to be in one's body but not of it, in one's psyche but not of it, even in one's mind but not of it. And the only "One" who is in the world, the group, the body, the psyche, the mind, but not of it, is the Absolute Reality itself, the *atman*, the Divine Witness; in the words of Meister Eckhart, "my truest 'I' is God." Here we can see how the preparation of a Remnant takes place by a sort of homeopathic concentration; the weaker the solution is in quantitative terms, the more powerful it is in terms of quality. This process is indicated in the Gospels by the falling away of the apostles from Jesus in the Garden of Gethsemane—and ultimately by "my God, my God, why have you forsaken Me?"

But short of this Absolute Aloneness, which can only be the immanent transcendence of God within us, what does it mean to be both integrated into a sacred and orthodox spiritual tradition and community, and at the same time be totally alone? ("I am a stranger in Your country and lonely among Your worshippers" said the Sufi saint Rabi'a; "this is the substance of my complaint".)

To begin with, it means that the purpose of a true spiritual community is that the members support each other in the inner work of being alone with God. To be in a group or congregation where people are not always looking "sideways" at each other, but where each is striving to put his or her attention fully on God, is a powerful support for the realization of one's intrinsic aloneness; and it is only through this aloneness with God that one comes to be a member of the communion of saints. In a profane group, on the other hand— and there are certainly plenty of religious groups that are, in effect, entirely profane—the act of holding together with the other members *replaces* the act of holding one's attention upon God. So instead of being alone, and then finding that one is actually alone with many others, one obsessively strives to hold together with others, only to find oneself becoming more and more alienated and lonely, alienated from both true solitude and true communion. In a sacred community the group act of renouncing ego and concentrating on God supports the same act in its individual members, while the individual act of renunciation equally supports and deepens the group act; this is one of the central purposes of all collective ritual, the other being the theurgical invocation of the presence of God. But in a pro-fane group, the growth of the group ego only stimulates the growth of private egotism in each of its members, thus alienating them from the group and binding them to it at the same time; just as those pri-vate egos are "chartered" by the group ego, so they are "taxed" to fur-ther build up the ego of the group, in a vicious cycle.

So in terms of a profane community—and a profane world—the Remnant are those who opt out of the group ego (that is, the World) by the act of renouncing the individual ego—which, initially, is a very lonely thing to do; only after this loneliness is endured and lived through and offered to God as a sacrifice of self will it give way to true solitude, just as the group-identification that once fed it simul-taneously gives way to the communion of saints.

Since to be a member of the Remnant is clearly a grave responsi-bility, we tend to say, "If the true and comprehensive understanding of my tradition, as it certainly seems, has come down to me alone—though there must be others somewhere, even if I never meet them in this life—then *why me*? I'm not a saint or a holy sage; I'm not a hero; I'm not even a *genius*. Why has this heavy responsibility been placed on the shoulders of a weakling such as myself?" (For a won-derful fictional treatment of this encounter with one's destiny as a member of the Remnant, I refer the reader to C. S. Lewis' novel *Per-elandra*.) At this point a particular analogy is useful: When our entire unit has been wiped out and we are the only survivor, do we then ask: "Why has this great honor been granted to one so insignif-icant as myself? I'm not at all sure I'm worthy to accept it." No: We pick up our gun, collect our ammunition, and continue the fight. We don't hurl ourselves alone against the enemy lines; our main task will be to find other units of our army that may still be intact. But if we do happen to get a good shot at the enemy, from decent cover, and with a path of retreat open to us, then—like good guerrillas—we certainly don't hesitate to take that shot. (I hasten to add that the only enemy here is *error*, not the body or soul of the individual human being who may accidentally be the bearer of it.)

And we certainly don't waste a great deal of time and energy try-ing to "convert" the fellow members of our tradition who don't seem to really understand it, or—if we are disappointed in this effort—in bitterly looking down upon them from our supposed superior position. When Luke 12:28 says, "(from him) to whom much is given, much will be required", one meaning is that while humility is required of the simple believers, nothing short of annihilation is required of the elect. (This, incidentally, is one of the many meanings of Groucho Marx's brilliant line satirizing snobbery, which undoubtedly originated among the Hasidim and is entirely in the spirit of the inimitable Mulla Nasruddin: "I would *never* join a group that would have *me* as a member!" Let all those who may feel called to be part of the Remnant take this as their *koan.*) Insofar as our fellow worshippers are truly of the pious faithful, their presence will support us in spirit, no matter how far apart our conscious understandings may be. And insofar as they are worshippers of the profane group ego, they will alert us to our own egotism as nothing else ever could. They will irritate us, depress us, and thereby demonstrate exactly how our depression and irritation are nothing but our own failure to submit to the Will of God. As Rama Coomaraswamy often said, "Your responsibility (with God's help) is to save yourself; saving the Church is God's business."

In view of the fact that we are living in the last days of this cycle of manifestation, two tasks present themselves, which should be pursued concurrently: To *search for* the Remnant, and to *be* the Remnant.

If we only search for the Remnant, we may find a group that identifies itself as "Remnant", one that certainly seems traditional enough in its piety and its faithfulness to its particular sacred form. Such a group, however, may eventually become morally corrupt through the very pride of considering itself the chosen few, and then gradually—or suddenly—turn apostate before our very eyes. But if we have not also worked at *being* the Remnant, we may be blind to this development, either through lack of insight or lack of courage—and we should never underestimate how often lack of insight is based upon lack of courage. We ourselves may in fact have contributed to this corruption and apostasy by our own unwillingness, or incapacity, to *be* in our own essence what we have sought from others. If we join the army hoping only for its protection, unwilling to carry our share of the fight, then we are not good comrades-in-arms; if we come to the table bringing only our hunger, we have not contributed to the feast, but stolen food from the mouths of our companions.

If, however, we only strive to *be* the Remnant, we may find ourselves sealed apart in lonely pride (like the poet Robinson Jeffers was, at least in certain respects), and consequently fail, through personal egotism, through lack of the kind of "reality check" that other people can provide (even if we don't *agree* with them), through simple lack of love, to embody the *fitrah*, the primordial human nature, which any Remnant worth its name exists only to defend, preserve, and deepen. We may forget that the *atman*, the *imago dei* is not our personal property, but exists—either veiled or openly—in every human heart, as well as every star, *ev'ry Bird that cuts the airy way*, every *spear of summer grass*, every stone beneath our feet, from which God always retains His power to *raise up children unto Abraham*. The misanthropic recluse is alone with nothing but his passions; the true hermit, in his ability to be alone with God, is thereby alone with all things.

MARYAM

"My path is a path of rigor"

I am the Darkness that allows God to be born.
I am Theotokos;
In Islam, I am Layla.

I am infinitely less than He,
And nothing in myself—
It is by this I bear Him to you
With a human form and face,
To meet your own form, your own face.

But when I am Black
I am before all faces;
I am the Sign of the Essence.
I am the listening darkness within Muhammad
That heard the word "Recite!"

And when I am White
I am the Guarded Tablet
Virgin and immaculate before the Pen,
Ready to bear the words of all things—
Of which you
Are only one
Among many.

I am the sister of your annihilation:
Prostrate beside me, not to me.
I am your elder sister
In the Night you seek.

APPENDIX

THE THREE PILLARS OF CLASSICAL
TRADITIONALISM / PERENNIALISM

I: THE TRANSCENDENT UNITY OF RELIGIONS

GOD HAS SENT more than one revelation to humanity. Some are extinct (the Egyptian and Chaldean religions, for example, as well as Platonism considered as an operative spiritual path); several others are presently in force.

These revelations may be considered to be branches of a single Primordial Tradition, but this Tradition is not presently in force as a religious dispensation; it is not a religion that can be practiced. The only viable spiritual paths exist as, or within, the presently-living revelations: Hinduism, Zoroastrianism, Buddhism, Judaism, Christianity and Islam. Various "primal" religions—as, for example, certain Native American ritual forms—may also contain viable paths, at least for the ethnic groups to which they pertain, but this is certainly not true of any of the "Neo-Pagan" revivals of the postmodern age. And it is uncertain as to whether Taoism still exists in any complete and viable form.

One must choose and remain faithful to one of the revealed religions and never try to mix them; the differences between the religions are as providential and necessary as their similarities. Though the doctrines of the different revelations may illuminate each other in certain respects, each contains all that is necessary for salvation/illumination/liberation. Some embrace discrete "estates" dedicated respectively to the exoteric and esoteric dimensions (Islam); some are more or less explicit "esoterisms" (Buddhism); some are esoterisms that have so to speak become "exoterized" (Christianity).

The esoteric centers of the revealed religions are much closer to unanimity than their exoteric expressions, but they are never identical, at least on the plane of form; their final *unity* is truly *transcendent*.

These facts precisely demonstrate the real, objective existence of God and the metaphysical order, as well as God's total transcendence of form when considered in terms of His Essence, as *Ungrund*, Godhead, *Dharma-kaya*, *Nirguna Brahman*, *al-Dhat*, the Formless Absolute.

Thus we can say that while there is a *sophia perennis*, a unanimous and perennial metaphysical wisdom of the human race, in our time there can be no *religio perennis*, no way to practice the Transcendent Unity of Religion in a discrete and concrete form, given that "transcendent" means precisely "transcending all form".

II: COMMITMENT TO ORTHODOXY

THE DEEP AND COMPLETE understanding of the revealed religions requires (but cannot be limited to) an understanding of metaphysics, both in terms, first, of the universal principles whereby the nature of Absolute Reality, its relationship with its own outer manifestation, and the parameters of the spiritual Path can be discerned; and secondly, in terms of the relationship of metaphysics to the orthodox theological dogmas of the faiths. Metaphysics may illuminate these dogmas but it can never contradict them, since the dogmas in question are essentially concretizations and providential limitations of metaphysical principles, in order to render them efficacious for salvation in terms of the various religious collectives.

"Perennialism" must never be used as an excuse to play fast and loose with orthodox theological doctrines; the duty of the Traditionalist/Perennialist, if conditions and personal destiny allow, is to defend the orthodox revealed religions against both external attacks—including worldly skepticism (an aspect of René Guénon's "anti-tradition"), as well as infiltration by agents of what Guénon called the "counter-tradition", for the conscious purpose of spreading subversive doctrines and ultimately destroying the tradition in question—and also against internal subversion: both heresy, either overt or implicit, and the erosion, destruction or inversion of traditional ritual and sacramental forms.

In view of this commitment to orthodoxy, the Perennialist will be extremely wary (though not absolutely dismissive) of the Interfaith Movement, which so often asks us to sacrifice or erode or soft-pedal orthodoxy in the name of a *worldly* (not transcendent) unity of religions, and which is presently being widely funded and promoted by the global power elites, whose religious wing increasingly resembles what Guénon, in *The Reign of Quantity*, called the "counter-tradition" and the "counter-initiation", forces which have as their goal the establishment of the "inverted hierarchy" of the latter days, otherwise known as the regime of Antichrist.

III : AN UNDERSTANDING OF
UNIVERSAL ESCHATOLOGY AND ITS IMPLICATIONS

THE "Classical Perennialists"—Ananda and Rama Coomaraswamy, René Guénon, Marco Pallis, Titus Burckhardt, Martin Lings, Alvin Moore, Frithjof Schuon—understood that we are living in the extreme latter days of the *Kali-yuga*. They based this conclusion on the traditional doctrine, found in one form or another in Hinduism, Zoroastrianism, Judaism, Christianity, Islam, even Buddhism—as well as in the Greco-Roman tradition and many of the primal religions—that history is not essentially progressive but rather entropic, that terrestrial existence is a cycle which moves with ever-increasing rapidity from an initial condition of elevation, stability and mass openness to Divine Reality, to a terminal state of materialism, chaos and blindness to the Spirit, ultimately ending in the apocalyptic dissolution of the "present world".

Consequently we must expect, and prepare ourselves for, both the rapid degeneration of the revealed religions and their infiltration, if not their not always visible replacement, by various satanic counterfeits.[1] In line with this worldview, the classical Traditionalists/

---

1. A case in point is the present "Novus Ordo" Catholic Church, most especially in light of the encyclical *Caritas in Veritate* by Benedict XVI, published in June of 2009, in which Ratzinger all but offers his church to the globalist elites as a candidate for the role of Chaplaincy of the New World Order; the Tony Blair Faith Foundation, strongly supported by the Vatican, may represent a "feeler" in this direction. (After Tony Blair—the Rex Mottram of the 21st century—converted to Novus Ordo

Perennialists—after Guénon abandoned his hope for a renewal of Tradition in the West through the influence of Eastern doctrines (as expressed in *The Crisis of the Modern World* and *East and West*), and replaced it, in *The Reign of Quantity*, with his version of universal eschatology, and *certainly* after Vatican II—held out little hope that Traditionalism/Perennialism could have any real influence on worldly collectives, "religious" or otherwise, as presently constituted; consequently their teachings were, in effect, directed largely to individuals. Nonetheless, their writings showed little evidence of a barren nostalgia for "better days", but were most effective insofar as they helped us understand how to make the most of the unique spiritual opportunities afforded by the apocalyptic milieu of our own times. And by virtue of their ultimate realization that the collective "degeneration of the cosmic environment" cannot be reversed, though temporary and limited "redresses" may still be possible, they provided us with the principles—specifically, Guénon's doctrine of the "counter-tradition", the "counter-initiation" and the "inverted hierarchy"—that allow us at least to question whether *any* adoption of Traditionalist/Perennialist doctrines by any

Catholicism, he traveled to the Yucatán to participate in a Mayan ritual, demonstrating just how "catholic" a constituency he wishes to appeal to.)

The New World Order is *Now Hiring* religions and religious networks, especially those with global reach, to function as the religious wing (for which read the propaganda and psy ops wing) of the coming global regime, and Benedict XVI, in the name of his apostate church, is applying for the job; *Caritas in Veritate* is his resumé. Like an advertising agency executive trolling for clients, Ratzinger gives every impression of wishing to act as a kind of False Prophet to an Antichrist, yet to appear, whom he is eager to herald. My prediction is that he will find him (or it).

In *The Reign of Quantity and the Signs of the Times*, René Guénon speculates that the regime of Antichrist might take the form of a re-established "Holy Empire" characterized by an "inverted hierarchy". In the case of the Holy Roman Empire, it was the Pope who crowned the Emperor; at least in the doctrinal and ritual domains, the imperial order was chartered by the sacerdotal order. But today we see a false pope seeking a charter of legitimacy for his church from a nascent Global Imperium: the inverted hierarchy, precisely. (Various conservative conspiracy-theorists expect the rise of an evil empire based upon a rehabilitated Hapsburg dynasty, but their simplistic historical mythology—like the eschatological scenarios of many Evangelical Christians—largely blinds them to the actual scenarios unfolding before their very eyes.)

contemporary collective, whether or not it considers itself an "elite", would not in fact represent their co-optation for the precise purposes of that counter-tradition, counter-initiation and inverted hierarchy.

❧

Up to a point these three "pillars" represent my own synthesis of doctrines taken from Schuon and Guénon, which not all Perennialists/Traditionalists may subscribe to in every detail. Nonetheless, an adherence to these principles, at least in their broad outlines, constitutes the minimum requirement for anyone who wishes to call him- or herself a "Classical Perennialist/Traditionalist" (again, only according to my own definition), and one who is also aware of what is now going on in the surrounding world, particularly in the realm of religion. Who among my readers identifies with these principles? Who disagrees with them? Who largely accepts them, but with reservations? Please respond, if you feel moved to do so:

Charles Upton
706 Pasadena Drive
Lexington, KY 40503
cupton@qx.net
859-278-3444

www.ingramcontent.com/pod-product-compliance
Lightning Source LLC
Chambersburg PA
CBHW031558110426
42742CB00036B/240